Sister Mary

*The Everyday
Living Approach to
Teaching Elementary Science*

John M. Scott, S. J.

The Everyday Living Approach to Teaching Elementary Science

Parker Publishing Company, Inc.
West Nyack, N.Y.

© 1970, BY

PARKER PUBLISHING COMPANY, INC.
WEST NYACK, N.Y.

ALL RIGHTS RESERVED. NO PART OF THIS
BOOK MAY BE REPRODUCED IN ANY FORM
OR BY ANY MEANS, WITHOUT PERMISSION
IN WRITING FROM THE PUBLISHER.

LIBRARY OF CONGRESS
CATALOG CARD NUMBER: 70-113758

PRINTED IN THE UNITED STATES OF AMERICA
0-13-293514-7 B & P

Previous books by the author:

WONDERLAND—*Loyola Press, Chicago*
ADVENTURES IN SCIENCE—*Loyola Press, Chicago*
RAIN, MAN'S GREATEST GIFT—*Culligan Press, San Bernardino, California*
OUR ROMANCE WITH SUN AND RAIN—*Culligan Press, San Bernardino, California*
ADVENTURE AWAITS YOU—*Culligan Press, San Bernardino, California*

DEDICATED TO
MY MOTHER AND FATHER
WHO INTRODUCED ME TO
THE WONDERS OF OUR
FASCINATING UNIVERSE

* * * * * * * * * *

Special thanks to Mrs. Geraldine Hood for gracing these pages with her artistic skill in the many attractive illustrations that give life and action to the printed text.

The Scope and Purpose of This Book

Teaching techniques that are practical and down to earth offer the greatest stimulus to learning, and this book contains the material I use each year in teaching General Science classes. It covers the techniques I find most useful in making science appealing to young minds, and concentrates on three principal factors:

1. DEMONSTRATIONS

    - All the demonstrations listed in these pages have been tested in the classroom.

2. EXPERIMENTS

    - There are many experiments for young people to do personally. Young people love doing experiments—and learn so much.

3. APPLICATIONS

    - Students understand science better when they can see it at work each hour of every day of their lives. In addition to the applications given, I continually ask students to offer applications of their own.

Our motto should not be "listen and learn" but rather "join us in learning more." Instead of telling students what to think, help them to think; help them, above all, to feel intensely about science in our lives—and indeed, there is evidence all around us as to the effect of science on our lives. Above all, strive for student cooperation. Encourage them to suggest applications, and under your direction, develop experiments of their own for the benefit of the class.

During the past few summers I've journeyed to Creighton University in

Omaha, Nebraska, to conduct a science program for elementary school personnel. These summer school institutes afforded me the priceless privilege of meeting many elementary school teachers, principals, and supervisors. I became acquainted with their problems, their hopes, and their ideals, and it is obvious thousands of teachers are searching for better ways to bring science to young minds that are unfolding to the mysteries and wonders of our world.

How can we turn the classroom into a launching pad of exciting new ideas to boost the minds of young people into orbits of knowledge and inspiration?

If Confucius had taken time out to observe a demonstration in science, he would, no doubt, have added, "One demonstration is worth more than a thousand pictures." The unique feature of this book is that it offers many classroom demonstrations in science which can be done with simple equipment, and with ordinary household items. No expensive outlay is required for complex demonstration equipment. There are no time-consuming pieces of apparatus to build, and each experiment directly relates to the world around us. The busy teacher, who has to make the most of what is easily available, will, I sincerely hope, find in this book a wealth of information on how to make use of ordinary, everyday objects in presenting demonstrations in science.

We will concentrate on experiments your students will take delight in doing. In particular, the many applications of science to daily life will help turn the big, wide world around us into a lab to carry on experiments. Even though all your students may not be junior-grade Einsteins, it does not matter. This book presents science so that everyone may enjoy it, thrill to its discoveries, and come to realize that science is part of the fabric of life. You will acquire an entire set of activities, including presentations, discussions, experiments, and demonstrations.

As we advance further into the world of science, it seems fitting to recall the words of Dr. Wernher von Braun, one of America's foremost rocket experts: "We have just opened the door into the limitless reaches of the universe. We can see just far enough ahead to know that man is at the threshold of a momentous area. Here is opportunity, challenge, adventure so tremendous as to exceed anything that has gone before. Here is the tomorrow youth wants to embrace."

JOHN M. SCOTT, S.J.

Table of Contents

Chapter 1—Establishing the Importance of Gravity 15
How to introduce students to the invisible world of unseen forces . . . Evaluating the influence of gravity on our lives . . . Key factors in determining the attraction of gravity . . . How to determine your weight! . . . Guidelines on applying this chapter to everyday life.

Chapter 2—How to Go into Orbit 29
Acquiring an appreciation for Newton's First Law of Motion. . . Key factors in showing why 5 miles per second is the "magic speed" for astronauts walking around planet earth . . . Safety hints from Newton's First Law . . . How to demonstrate centrifugal force.

Chapter 3—How to Travel in Space 42
Three keys for understanding how to travel in space . . . How to demonstrate a jet engine . . . How to estimate the pounds of thrust required for a rocket . . . Analysis of the principle that puts a "kick" in a gun, and "pushes" a rocket into space . . . Evaluating the role of retro-rockets.

Chapter 4— Our Canopy of Air 56
Key factors in realizing how many ways the air protects us . . . How to demonstrate the "toughness" of our air shield . . . Suggestions on how to present Boyle's Law in dynamic demonstrations . . . Analysis of how we breathe.

Chapter 5—How to Weigh Air 69
Guidelines for methods to "weigh" air . . . Analysis of barometer and altimeter . . . How to measure student's

lung power . . . Evaluating the importance of the "lifting power" of air.

Chapter 6—Increasing Our Knowledge of Weather **84**

Comparison between relative and absolute humidity . . . . . . How to make it "rain" in the classroom . . . How to use maps to show correlation between geography and rainfall . . . How to use ping-pong balls to show why it rains . . . How to use a mechanical "drinking duck" to explain the the evaporation process.

Chapter 7—Establishing the Importance of Oceanography and Its Potential Value to Your Students **95**

Key factors in explaining Pascal's Law and Archimedes' Principle . . . Guidelines to illustrate what a pop bottle with its cap just removed has in common with a sea diver with the bends . . . Key factors in determining the "squeeze" . . . How to calculate buoyancy . . . Analysis to show why the ocean is so dangerous to man.

Chapter 8—Investigating the World of Matter **115**

Evaluating the importance of one thing in the lives of your students with which they are always in contact . . . Guidelines for exploring Brownian movement . . . Practical tips on demonstrations with a "dry" liquid . . . Analysis of surface tension . . . How to make buckshot . . . How to demonstrate that molecules are of different sizes.

Chapter 9—Developing a Practical Appreciation for Acceleration Due to Gravity **133**

How to analyze acceleration with the help of a short plank and a toy automobile, or with an ice pick and a block of wood . . . Key factors in demonstrating positive and negative acceleration . . . How to take the "pulsebeat" of planet earth . . . Case history of the Army rifle that "shoots at itself with round-trip bullets."

Chapter 10—Establishing the Importance of the Bernoulli Principle .. **144**

Key factors in helping students realize the importance of Bernoulli's Principle in keeping our Boeing 747's in the sky . . . Evaluating the importance of design in airplane wings . . . Practical hints on using a table fan to demonstrate how an airplane gets its lift . . . Analysis of baseball curves . . . Key factors in winning an auto race by the hair-raising technique of drafting.

CONTENTS 11

Chapter 11—Increasing Students' Awareness of the Importance of Energy **151**

Guidelines for showing why this is the "energy transfer" generation . . . Analysis of potential and kinetic energy . . . Suggestions for demonstrations to show how to convert one type of energy into another . . . Key factor to understanding why we still use the term "horsepower" in our machine age . . . How to capture energy from the sun.

Chapter 12—Establishing the Importance of Heat **161**

Analysis of heat . . . Key factors in determining expansion . . . Guidelines for study of conduction, convection, and radiation . . . How to put the "life saving" trait of metals to work . . . How to use a thermos bottle to summarize methods of heat transfer.

Chapter 13—Investigating the Importance of Friction **187**

Key factors in determining coefficient of friction . . . Practical hints on demonstrations both in class and outside class . . . How to make friction work for you . . . Evaluating statement that "Friction is the menace of the space age."

Chapter 14—Developing an Awareness of Our Magnetic World **194**

Acquiring an appreciation for what magnetic fields do for us . . . How to learn about something we can't see . . . Practical tips on how to make magnets and detect magnetic fields . . . Discuss theory that changing magnetic fields are responsible for evolution . . . Guidelines for discovering earth's changing magnetic fields.

Chapter 15—Understanding Static Electricity **206**

Key factors and suggestions for introducing static electricity . . . Most important safety lessons to be learned in this chapter . . . How to demonstrate principles behind broadcasting . . . How to detect the presence of static electricity . . . What to do in a lightning storm.

Chapter 16—Exploring the Mystery of Electricity from Chemical Changes **218**

Evaluating the importance of electricity in your body . . . Acquiring a contemporary approach to electrochemical reactions . . . Investigating the electrical output of the human brain . . . A look into the future of bioelectronics . . . Guidelines for demonstrations on electrochemical effects.

Chapter 17—Developing an Understanding for Electromagnetic Forces   228

Key factors in applying the discoveries of Oersted, and Faraday . . . How to demonstrate electromagnetic forces . . . Guidelines for study of electromagnetic forces in everyday life . . . Analysis of motors and generators . . . How to construct simple transformers.

Chapter 18—Increasing Our Knowledge of Light 254

Evaluating the peculiar behavior of light . . . Key factors in discussing refraction and reflection . . . Suggestions on how to bend light and bounce it . . . Guidelines for study of optical illusions . . . Analysis of U.F.O. reports.

The Everyday Living Approach to Teaching Elementary Science

This chapter will enable you to capture the interest of the "Go-Go" generation, and make them "Come Alive" to one of the most fascinating and mysterious forces that controls each second of our lives.

You can introduce your students to the fact that science is often like a master detective story. We

1

Establishing the Importance of Gravity

Photo courtesy of NASA

Photo 1. *Cape Kennedy is a monument to our fight against gravity.*

don't come "face to face" with the "character" we are "tracking down." All we know about "him" is his M.O. (Method of Operation). The evasive "character" of this chapter is *gravity*.

In presenting this chapter, you have a magnificent opportunity to break open to young minds the startling truth that we live in "two worlds" —a world of matter we can touch and see, such as cabbages and kings, and gingersnaps and tacks—and a world of force whose existence we know only through its effects.

Gravity is both universal and unique. As far as is known, no substance, no physical state, no fields of any kind of energy will shield or attenuate a gravitational field. In this respect, it is completely unique.

Light, for example, which is an electromagnetic wave, can be absorbed by opaque objects, deflected by prisms, and reflected by mirrors. Electric and magnetic signals can be transmitted along certain pathways. Gravitation, however, is something we cannot increase, diminish, or bend. It pervades and permeates everything.

You will realize the importance of this chapter when you consider that it is gravity that keeps us "anchored" to planet earth, and keeps planet earth "anchored" to the sun. Not only does gravity cascade water from a drinking glass into your mouth, but also its holds distant stars in their appointed orbits.

Since we are all astronauts aboard our spaceship, planet Earth, this chapter is fundamental. It deals with one of the most dynamic aspects of our "Space Odyssey."

Throughout the many years I've been teaching science to young teachers at Creighton University during the summer sessions, I was frequently asked to: "Write a book that will show how you present science to your classes; use the same style you do in teaching your General Science students; and include the demonstrations and examples you find most useful."

The opportunity to capture my experiences in teaching in book form and share them with you came to me with great delight. In these pages I will share with you the various demonstrations, experiments, and applications I have built up and accumulated in almost a quarter of a century of teaching science.

And there will be an extra "bonus" and "payoff" for you! These pages will provide you with a convenient "lesson plan" and, at the same time, enable you to provide interesting information and captivating demonstrations.

If you wish, you may do what I do, and begin the first class with the following:

"T minus 90 seconds and counting," rumble the bullhorns across the palmetto scrub of "Spaceport No. 1," Cape Kennedy, Florida. As the count goes to zero, a mighty Saturn rocket spouts orange streams of fire, like molten steel, out the flame bucket. Thunder shakes the earth as the "Big Bird" leaps for the sky.

In reality, our "conquest of space" is really a "conquest over gravity."

Cape Kennedy is a throbbing, dynamic monument to our fight against gravity. Hundreds of scientists at "Spaceport No. 1" spend untold man-hours and millions of tax dollars to overcome gravity—to send big birds (ICBM's) bootstrapping up at T-time from ivory towers (vertical stands).

If there were no gravity, you could become an astronaut by simply giving a little jump straight up. With nothing to anchor you to planet earth, you could cruise delightfully out through space, somewhat like Wynken, Blynken, and Nod, who sailed off towards the moon in a wooden shoe on a river of crystal light with no thought of high-energy, boron-based fuels, or Saturn vehicles.

If there were no gravity, in fact, you would "fall" off planet earth. Mother Earth couldn't hold on to you!

Gravity is truly a "Secret Agent"! We never meet "him" face to face. All we know of him is his M.O. (Method of Operation). We can't see him directly, we see only his effects.

In his excellent article in *Science World,* Simon Dresner points out: "No one is really sure what gravity is. In the latter part of his life, Einstein tried to show that gravity, electricity, and magnetism were all parts of one universal law, but he did not complete his work."

In a fascinating article on gravity in *Space Digest,* Hal Hellman says, "We not only haven't been able to put gravity to work, but still don't know what it is. Newton, himself, never claimed to have explained its nature, only its behavior. Why have the secrets of gravitation remained so stubbornly locked up?"

No wonder Dr. Wernher von Braun, America's greatest rocket expert, made the following comment during a commencement address he delivered at St. Louis University, "Nature around us still harbors many thousand times more unsolved than solved mysteries."

According to Newton's Law of Universal Gravitation: *Any two bodies in the universe attract each other with a force that is directly proportional to the product of their masses, and inversely proportional to the square of the distance between their centers of gravity.*

The *center of gravity* is that point at which all the gravitational attraction or weight of an object may be considered to be concentrated.

The amazing thing is that the center of gravity need not actually be a part of the body itself. Thus, the center of gravity of a hoop or tire is not a portion of the hoop or tire itself, but is at the center of the hoop or tire, even though that center is an empty hole!

Mass refers to the quantity of material in a body. It is a measure of its inertia. The mass of a body does not change with location.

There is tantalizing mystery in the fact that every mass attracts every other mass. It is as though matter, seemingly so inert, sluggish, and unresponding, has a certain mystic, awe-inspiring quality that can trigger an avalanche, or reach out into space to throttle a rocket leaping for the moon.

Newton's law means that each piece of matter—a bolt, a board, an orange, an apple—attracts other pieces of matter. The greater the mass, the greater the attraction. The greatest mountain on the face of the earth, the "Goddess Mother of the Snows"—as the Nepalese call Mt. Everest—is so massive, it exerts a sidewise pull on a plumb line such as those used by carpenters.

For us earth-bound people, we might even define gravity as the personality trait of a very jealous lady!

Mother Earth is such a dominating, possessive person, she wants to hang on tightly to everything within reach. If you try to wander away, be it on a pogo stick or rocket, she will pull on you with guy ropes—invisible, but strong as steel.

Mother Earth loves every little ounce of you so much she claims you as personal property. You can't ignore her claim check.

The attraction between your mass and the mass of planet earth is called your *weight*. Your weight is a measure of the force with which the earth attracts you.

Your weight is a measure of how much "g" appeal you have! (Earth's gravity is often written g.) If you are a misty wisp of a Miss, light as a feather, and size only 7, g has only a lighthearted interest in you.

If you are a cracker-barrel character, and remind your friends of Jumbo, the elephant, or Marmaduke, the whale, g has a real pull with you. If you are a Two-Ton Tony, you are quite an attractive fellow. But a steam roller is even more attractive—to Mother Earth, that is.

No matter where you wander, o'er land, o'er sea, o'er foam, you will always find Mother Earth singing this song, "Oh, Body, come back to me!"

Even if you go to the South Pacific, you won't be able to "wash g out of your hair." Gravity will leap up and pull your curls down over your eyes until you decide to make a visit to the barber, or be content to saunter around like a Montana sheep dog.

A diet has been defined as the penalty for exceeding the feed limit. Yet it is possible to cut down your weight without cutting down on the calories.

Without benefit of Uncle John's reducing pills or vibrating machines, you can change your weight by going to the moon. The smaller mass of the moon exerts a gravity pull of only 1/6 that of the earth.

Since weight is merely a function of the gravitational pull on mass, your weight would be only 1/6 what it is at present. But your mass would stay the same!

If you tip the scales at 100 pounds on planet earth, you would weigh approximately 16 pounds on the moon. Since Mars has a gravity pull of only 0.38 that of the earth, you would weigh only 38 pounds on that planet.

Mighty Jupiter, on the other hand, has a gravity pull 2.64 times that of the earth. You would weigh 264 pounds on Jupiter. And on the sun you would weigh 2789 pounds.

ESTABLISHING THE IMPORTANCE OF GRAVITY

So far we have considered mainly the first part of Newton's Law of Universal Gravitation which informs us that the force of gravitational attraction between two objects is "directly proportional to the product of their masses."

Now examine the second part of the law which says that the force of gravity is "inversely proportional to the square of the distance between their centers of gravity."

If you were to stroll to the top of the world's tallest mountain, Mt. Everest, you would weigh some 6 ounces less than you do at present.

If you were to move from the equator to the North Pole, you would weigh about a pound more! The North Pole is some 13.6 miles closer to the center of the earth; hence, the attraction between you and the center of the earth is greater.

To do a thorough job of "losing weight" simply ride away in a space-bound rocket. When you are 20,000 miles distant from the center of the earth, your weight will fall to $1/5^2$ or $1/25$ of what it is now.

If you continued to travel far enough in space, you would come to a spot where you could leap out of your spaceship and weigh nothing. The gravity pull of the earth one way would be counteracted by the gravity pull of the moon in the opposite direction.

DEMONSTRATIONS

Tiptoe student

Have a boy stand tiptoe on one foot. He can be pushed over easily. Since a slight tipping tends to lower his center of gravity, he is said to be in unstable equilibrium. Other demonstrations of unstable equilibrium are:

A book standing on one edge.

1:1

A drinking glass resting on its edge.

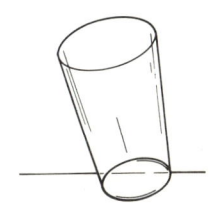

1:2

A funnel standing on its spout.

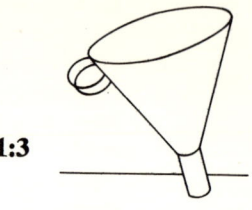

1:3

A camera tripod with its three legs close together under it.

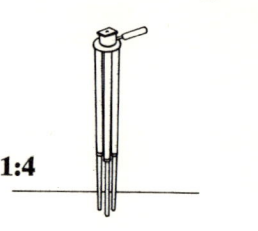

1:4

A meter stick standing upright on its narrow end.

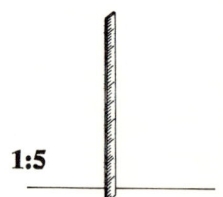

1:5

Power play

Request a boy to crouch over like a football player does before a line plunge or a power play through center. He spreads his feet apart, and lowers his center of gravity as much as possible so as to be in stable equilibrium.

Other examples of stable equilibrium are:

A book resting on its wide side.

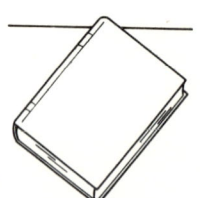

1:6

A drinking glass standing upright.

1:7

ESTABLISHING THE IMPORTANCE OF GRAVITY 21

A funnel sitting on its rim.

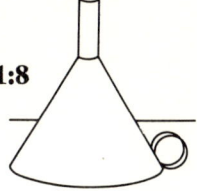
1:8

A camera tripod with its legs outstretched.

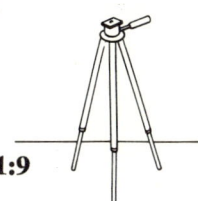
1:9

A meter stick flat on its back.

1:10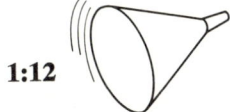

Neutral equilibrium

Roll a ball across the table. Since a slight tipping neither raises nor lowers the center of gravity, it is said to be in neutral equilibrium.

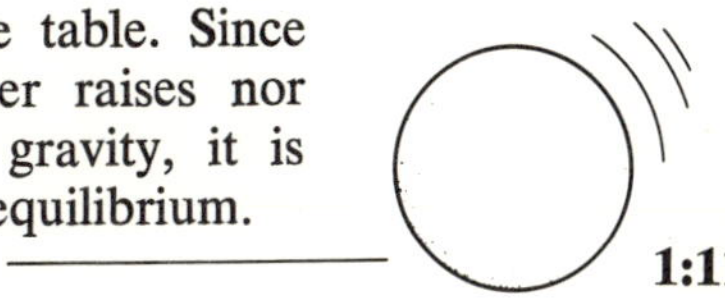

1:11

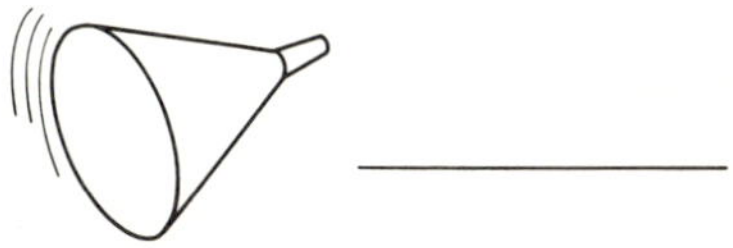

1:12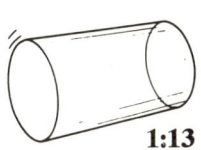

Do likewise with a funnel on its side and a drinking glass on its side. They, too, are in neutral equilibrium. The rolling neither raises nor lowers their centers of gravity.

1:13

Leaning tower

Saw the ends off a rectangular block of wood so that it will lean like the Leaning Tower of Pisa. As long as a plumb line, drawn from its center of gravity, falls within the base, the tower is stable. Now try adding "another story" to the Leaning Tower by placing a block of wood on top of the wooden structure. Keep adding more blocks, and eventually, if the center of gravity is raised too much, a plumb line dropped from the new center of gravity may fall outside the base. If it does, the Tower will topple.

CENTER OF GRAVITY

1:14

Students delight in constructing these "Leaning Towers" for themselves.

How stable are you?

Close both eyes, and stand on one foot. See how long you can keep one foot lifted and maintain your position without swaying, opening your eyes, or clutching for support. As a variation of the above, keep both eyes closed and stand with feet as close together as possible—heels together and toes together. See how long you can maintain this position without swaying.

Can you bend over?

Stand with your back against the wall, heels against the mopboard. Have someone place a book on the floor in front of your toes. Now, reach down *with both arms together* and try to pick up the book without bending your knees! That center of gravity gets into the act, as you will see!

1:15

Stable students

Many of the students in your class may be in such a state of stable equilibrium that they will be unable to get out of their chairs—unless they become unstable. This they will do by leaning the body forward, and/or sliding their feet backward and pushing.

To demonstrate how stable a student may be when sitting in a chair, have him fold his arms over his chest, and *keep both feet in front of him, knees together.* Now, without leaning his body forward, and without pushing against the back of the chair, he is to attempt to stand up!

1:16

Seeing is almost *not* believing

Tie a string in a small circle and slip it over the end of a stout wooden ruler. Now slip the handle of a hammer through the string so that the end of the hammer makes contact with the ruler, as

ESTABLISHING THE IMPORTANCE OF GRAVITY

shown in the sketch. Now rest the other end of the ruler on your finger (see drawing), or, better yet, on a steel rod held in place by a support stand. Move the ruler back and forth gently until it balances. The hammer is then in stable equilibrium, since a slight tipping tends to raise the center of gravity, which, in this case, is in the heavy head of the hammer.

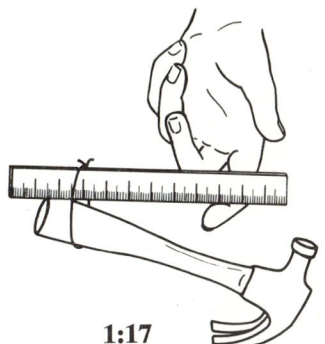
1:17

Roll uphill

Tape a ball bearing or any heavy piece of metal to the inside rim of a tin container, such as one used for candy, fruit cake, etc.

Now place the circular container edgewise on the wedge, or slight incline, as shown. The can will roll uphill, since by so doing, it will be lowering its center of gravity.

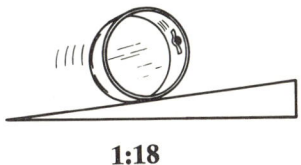
1:18

Rockabye

For variety, simply place the container on the table, on its edge, with the weight near the top. It will rock back and forth until finally its center of gravity comes to rest in the lowest position possible.

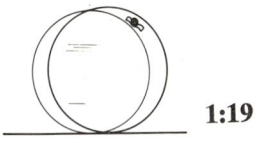
1:19

Marble in balloon

Insert a marble or steel ball bearing into a toy balloon. Blow up the balloon, tie it shut, then give it a shove so that it will begin to move across the top of the table. The bewildering antics of the balloon result from the center of gravity of the unit being centered in the marble or ball.

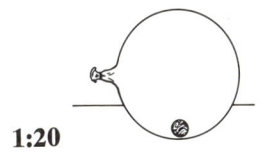
1:20

Sand in vase

Here is a demonstration the girls will appreciate. Long-stem flowers in a tall vase tend to become top-heavy. Pour sand into the bottom of the vase and you will increase its stability.

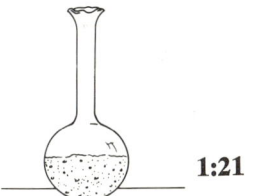
1:21

Roly-poly

A dime-store roly-poly weighted on the bottom has long been a clever demonstration of stable equilibrium. Now, thanks to the Doughboy Co. of New Richmond, Wisconsin, we have a "giant-size" roly-poly named "Bobo." The boy-size balloon blows up into the shape of a clown. His "feet" are filled with sand. No matter what hits Bobo, he bounces back—to show that a "well-balanced" personality has a low center of gravity!!

Tipping flask

In case you don't have Bobo handy, you can try this substitute. Pour sand into a round-bottom flask. Stand the flask upright, as shown. Tip the flask gently, and notice how it recovers its former position, thanks to its low center of gravity.

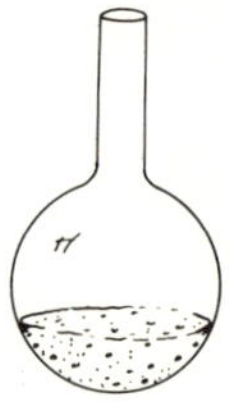

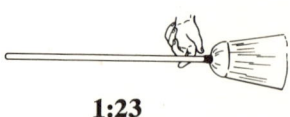

1:22

Find the center of gravity of a broom

Extend the forefinger of your left hand. Place a broom on it and slide the handle of the broom across your finger, until you find a place where the broom balances.

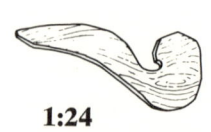

1:23

Belt holder

Have a student carve a life-size wooden duplicate of the drawing sketched here.
A piece of plywood about ¼ inch thick will do nicely.
Now rest a man's belt edgewise in the notched end. The buckle is to be at the bottom, as shown in the subsequent sketch (1:27). Hold the thin edge of the device on the tip of your finger. It makes a breath-taking demonstration of stable equilibrium. It is stable because a slight tipping tends to raise the center of gravity, which is in the buckle.

1:24

1:25

Find pencil's center of gravity

To find the center of gravity of a pencil, tie a string around it, then move the pencil backward (or forward) until it balances. The string will then be at the pencil's center of gravity.

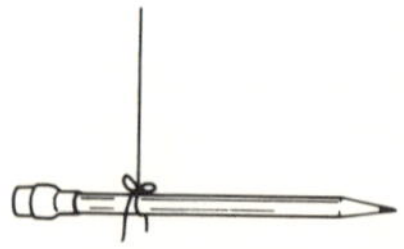

1:26

Hammer home a lesson

A hammer affords some interesting observations. Rest the head of the hammer in your outstretched hand,

ESTABLISHING THE IMPORTANCE OF GRAVITY

with the handle sticking up in the air. With the head of the hammer "nestling" in the palm of your hand, it is "content" to stay in this position of rest, since its center of gravity is as close as it can get to the center of the earth.

Now turn the hammer around (second position), so that the end of the handle is pushing against your palm. With the head of the hammer in the air, note how hard it is to keep the hammer in this new position.

Balance a sharp pencil on your finger!

Can you place the tip of a sharp pencil point down on the end of your outstretched finger, and have the pencil stay there when you release it?

Yes, if first you open the blades on two jackknives and stick them into the pencil as shown.

1:27

Conclusion

We are being followed!

The "Secret Agent" following us is the nearest thing to the invisible man outside the pages of H. G. Wells. He operates in silence and mystery like a modern day Scarlet Pimpernel, and vanishes from view like a Cheshire cat.

Who is this baffling character who follows us each moment of our lives?

To make acquaintance with this baffling character, simply roll out of bed in the middle of a nightmare, or stumble on the top step as you go down the cellar, or simply fall off a ladder. The crushing embrace you will receive will inform you that you have fallen into the hands of gravity.

We can say of gravity what the song writer says of love, "Who can explain it? Who can tell you why?"

Although we can't tell you "why", we can at least mention some of the things it does.

FOLLOW-UP EXERCISES

1. Write a composition on "What Gravity Does for Me."

    Hints: *Did you ever think how gravity comes to your aid* *when you wish to take a drink of water? As you bend your elbow to the sky, gravity pulls the precious cargo of H_2O from the glass and sends it cascading into your open mouth.*

Without gravity you could turn the glass upside down, but the water would remain nestled in the glass. Drinking would be a ticklish problem.

2. Continue the above theme, only accent, "What Gravity Does to Keep Me Healthy."

Hints: *One of gravity's big jobs is to keep you on your toes, both mentally and physically. Without gravity, your muscles would become like putty, your bones like old bananas. Your mind would become a desert with nightmare mustangs trying to outrace their shadows over the shifting sands.*

These ideas are not taken from the confessions of an opium eater, or from descriptions of bad dreams detailed by gentlemen of distinction after swallowing too many wild geronimos, yellow jackets, or blue-heaven thrill-pills.

After 27 years of behaving like a normal earthman, Captain Duane E. Graveline, a well-knit Air Force medic, spent an entire week, clad in a skin diver's rubber suit, afloat on his back in 400 gallons of tepid water at the Air Force School of Aviation Medicine, San Antonio, Texas.

Technically, he was in a state of near weightlessness—the buoyancy of his body and a supporting couch making all muscular and body movement effortless. His muscles and bones were in a state of zero gravity.

After a week of zero gravity, and doing nothing, Captain Graveline attempted to leave his coffin-size tub of water. Things began to happen fast. Graveline's heart pounded wildly, his blood pressure dropped, his handsome face turned blue. He couldn't stand straight or form coherent sentences.

Graveline went through intensive medical tests. The results were surprising. "The body was literally disposing of unneeded muscle and bone," explained Graveline. "My muscles were like dough and my bones were becoming softer. . ."

Fortunately, Captain Graveline was back to normal in four days.

His experiment showed that if forces are not applied to bone tissue, the bloodstream takes away the minerals which make them hard. If muscles are not exercised, they become limp and flabby. Even the walls of blood vessels become dangerously weakened if not exposed to forces.

One of the most important forces that keeps our bones, muscles, and blood vessels strong is gravity. As has been proven by our Gemini astronauts, however, the weakening effects of zero gravity may be offset by exercises.

3. Tell how the most spectacular scenery in the world was given to us by gravity.

Hint: *The Grand Canyon is the world's most spectacular example of erosion—gravity at work with water for a chisel.*

4. If the force of gravity exists between any two objects, why am I not aware of it? If I walk past a big building, why doesn't it pull me to one side?

The answer lies in the almost unbelievable weakness of gravity. Gravitational force is so small that it is not observable in day-to-day affairs unless it concerns objects of really enormous mass—planets, stars, moon, etc. This is why we tend to think of gravity as a property peculiar to the earth, rather than one possessed by all objects.

Put two books on the opposite sides of a table. The books won't be so attracted to each other that they will "fly" together, like long-separated lovers. But, take the table away, and the books will "fall" or be attracted to planet earth. Thus the much greater gravitational attraction between the books and the earth becomes evident.

It is interesting to note that although Newton gave us the Law of Universal Gravitation, he lacked instruments delicate enough to measure this force of attraction between two objects on the surface of the earth.

Suppose, for example, you park two Volkswagons so their centers of gravity are 10 feet apart. They will attract each other with a force of less than $\frac{1}{10,000}$ of an ounce.

Two giant aircraft carriers 100 yards apart would exert a gravitational pull on each other of approximately 5 pounds.

5. How do we know which way is "up" and "down"?

A built-in sense of "up" and "down" is produced by the semicircular canals in the ear. These are filled with a fluid that is free to react to changes in position, movement, and gravity. Damage to the delicate, gravity-sensing mechanism of the ear can produce dizziness, nausea, and an inability to move about freely. Those of you who recall seeing the motion picture, "Vertigo," will remember what a world of terrifying, tumbling verticals and unbalance was portrayed. The man who cannot climb a ladder or stand on the edge of a cliff without becoming stiff with fear and losing his sense of balance, experiences a mild form of vertigo.

6. **How does a three-stage rocket demonstrate a superb application of Newton's Law of Universal Gravitation?**

In order to achieve the escape velocity of 25,000 miles per hour (or 6.95 miles per second) needed to break free from the gravity pull of the earth, several rockets are stacked on top of each other, and fired in succession. The velocity increases with each firing, because each section before firing is traveling with the velocity of the preceding stage. And since *gravity pull falls off inversely with the square of the distance, each pound of thrust applied to the rocket 50 miles above the earth will give it more speed than it would when it was closer.*

Lack of air drag at high altitudes is also a distinct advantage. And since gravity pull also decreases with less mass, the rocket reduces its mass at each new firing by dispensing with empty fuel tanks. Energy thus saved from lifting useless mass is used to give further thrust.

Summary

In this chapter, the teacher introduced his students to that "Secret Character"—gravity. All we know about gravity is his M.O. (Method of Operation). As Simon Dresner pointed out, "No one is really sure what gravity is."

Although the teacher cannot arrange a "face-to-face" meeting with gravity, he can show the effects of this mysterious force that pervades and permeates everything. It pulls water down the kitchen sink, and sends mountain streams leaping to meet the far-distant seas.

Thus you are able to break open a chrysalis of truth and expose students to the fact that we live in two worlds—the world of matter we can see, touch, and grasp with our hands and the world of force we do not see, but whose existence is made known through its effects.

The examples and demonstrations helped to illustrate Newton's Law of Universal Gravitation: Any two bodies in the universe attract each other with a force that is directly proportional to the product of their masses, and inversely proportional to the square of the distance between their centers of gravity.

In our first chapter, you were given methods with which to introduce your students to gravity. Now, like an Apollo pilot executing a docking maneuver, you link up gravity with Newton's First Law of Motion so that students may orbit in new-found knowledge of the laws that govern our space-age achievements.

You will find the present chap-

2

How to Go into Orbit

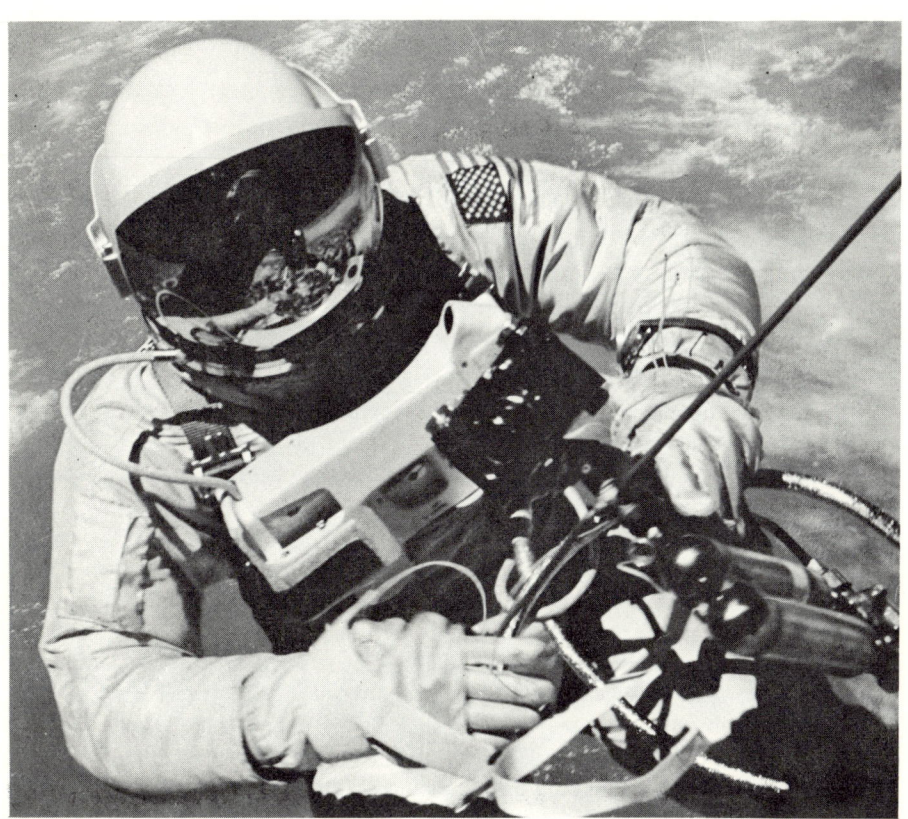

Photo courtesy of NASA

Photo 2. *Newton's First Law of Motion combines with gravity to help an astronaut "walk" around planet earth.*

ter most important in understanding our space age, and providing answers to such questions as: "Why is 5 miles per second the 'magic speed' needed for an astronaut to orbit planet earth?" "Is it true the moon is falling down?"

Even more important than understanding the physics behind the "Space Odyssey" in which we all take part, there is the terrifying vital information needed by all young people captivated by the idea that in a few short years they will be driving the family car.

In this chapter, you have an opportunity to illustrate a fact that many students never think of; namely, the same law that helps keep an astronaut in orbit around planet earth, or around the moon, also accounts for most automobile accidents.

You can turn this chapter into one on "Driver Education" and bring home the fact that no driver can "get away" or "flee from" nature's "universal traffic laws." The lives of people in years to come will depend on how well students understand and obey Newton's First Law of Motion.

"The life you save may be your own." This, indeed, could well be the main theme of this chapter.

In this chapter, the teacher can show how physics controls our daily lives, and how an understanding of the fundamental laws formulated by Newton many years ago is important to us.

You may wish to begin the first class on "How to Go into Orbit" with the following:

> Astronaut Eugene Cernan has the unique distinction of being the first man in history to "walk" completely around planet earth.
>
> If ever you imitate Eugene Cernan and go "globe-trotting" in space, do you realize what will make your trip around the earth possible?
>
> It is gravity.
>
> "Wait a minute," you object. "Gravity pulls me towards the center of the earth. I want to walk in space, not come crashing headfirst into Lower California."
>
> Strange as it may seem, gravity will help you keep in orbit, and thus make your walk in space around the earth possible.
>
> No doubt you have seen a man on a flying trapeze sail through the air with the greatest of ease. He didn't sail very long, however, before he reached out to grab a life-hold on some object. In his type of work, if there would be no net beneath him, he would make only one miss.
>
> How come gravity doesn't grab hold of an astronaut like it does the man who missed his return trip on the flying trapeze?
>
> The answer—it does!
>
> How come, then, we don't pick up the astronaut in a fish net, or watch him plunge into the earth like a homing meteor?

We hope to illustrate the principles of physics which explain why Cernan stayed in orbit, why the moon is forever "falling down," and why we don't plop into the sun.

Roll a baseball across the kitchen floor. Notice that the baseball does not go 6 inches forward, then suddenly make a right-angle turn, move 4 inches to the right, then back up 10 inches, and, finally, turn left.

The baseball continues to move forward in a straight line. Only some external force, like the wall or the kitchen stove, will make the baseball change its straight-line path.

For your second demonstration, run down the sidewalk in front of your house as fast as you can. While still running at top speed, make a sudden, right-angle turn into the driveway!

The famous Sir Isaac Newton most likely never rolled baseballs across the kitchen floor, nor ran down the street to make a quick turn into the driveway. However, he sized up the results of our investigations quite nicely when he devised his First Law of Motion: *Every body continues in its state of rest or uniform motion in a straight line, unless compelled by an external force to change.*

A Navy pilot who forgot Newton's First Law of Motion shot himself down. This fantastic accident, the first of its type in aviation history, occurred while test pilot, Tom Attridge, put his Grumman F11F-1 into an 888 miles per hour dive and fired two quick bursts over the Atlantic Ocean near Long Island.

The Navy gave this probable explanation of the accident. "When a stream of cannon shells spewed from the four guns at the rate of 1000 rounds per minute, or better than 64 rounds for each four-second burst, they were traveling more than 1500 feet faster than the airplane. The shells were traveling forward, but were also falling towards the earth. They were following a curved course toward the ocean. The jet meanwhile went into a steeper dive and increased its speed.

"About 2 to 3 miles from the point where the firing began, the plane and shells collided. One shell shattered the bulletproof glass in the jet's windshield. A second shell pierced the engine, which died, causing the jet to crash land in a woods. The 33-year-old pilot was hospitalized with a fractured leg, and three broken vertebrae."

If you happen to be driving your car through the mountains, you may find Newton's First Law of Motion staring you in the face at the next curve in the road.

It will be disguised in brief words, "Sharp curve; 15 miles per hour."

Put into plain language, the sign says, "If you drive more than 15 miles per hour, the friction between your tires and the road will not be enough to keep your car from obeying Newton's First Law of Motion. Your car will keep on moving in a straight line—over the edge of the cliff, and out into the wide, blue yonder!"

Did you ever stop to ponder over the fact that any object traveling around a curve, or in a circle, is trying to travel in a straight line!

The only reason the object does not travel in a straight line is that some "external force" is compelling it to change.

Consider your family car. The only "external force" that enables dad's car to make a turn in the road is friction between the tires and the roadbed. When the road is covered with ice, there is less friction. The chance of making the turn is decreased.

In fact, we may say, "Most cars that make wrecks of themselves going around curves do so because the cars obey Newton's First Law of Motion, rather than the sudden whims of their drivers."

In the Bible we read that David dispatched the Philistine giant by one application of Newton's First Law. He whirled a rock around in a sling, then let it go. The most famous missile of Biblical days continued its motion in a straight line—until compelled by the giant's brow to stop.

Every second that David was twirling the rock around in the sling, the skull-cracking boulder was trying to move in a straight line. To keep it from so doing, David had to pull on the strings holding it in orbit.

If the rock had been too heavy, or the string too weak, the brain-creasing rock would have gone sailing off in a straight line tangential to its path, before being beamed on target.

Since a body in motion wants to travel in a straight line tangent to its circular path, a force must be exerted on it at right angles to make it travel in a circle. The inward force necessary to keep an object moving in a circular path is called *centripetal force*. (Centripetal is a Latin word meaning "to seek the center.")

Centripetal force seeks to pull an object traveling in a circular path to the center of the circle. David exerted an inward force on the whirling rock by pulling on the strings of the sling, thus causing the stone to turn away from its straight-line path, and travel in a circle until the moment of release. Now consider what happens on a spinning sphere.

The spinning motion of the earth causes its equator to bulge out like an October pumpkin or a juicy tomato. The equator is 13.6 miles farther away from the center of the earth than the North or South Poles.

The result is that the Mississippi River in going from Minnesota to the Gulf of Mexico does not flow downhill. It is "thrown uphill" towards the equator.

If our trusty spaceship, planet earth, were to spin 17 times faster than it does at present, you would never dare take an ocean trip to Panama. The dizzy whirl at the equator would be so tremendous, you would be thrown out into space.

Why doesn't an astronaut, or satellite, moving at high speeds, keep on going out into space as shown by the straight line AB, and thus leave the earth, never to return?

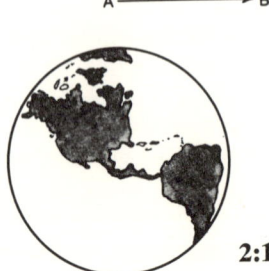

2:1

Gravity comes to the rescue. Like an invisible string gravity holds on to the astronaut, and supplies a "center-seeking" force that causes him to "fall" or "seek the center of the earth."

If left to himself, an astronaut would continue to travel in a straight line, soaring out into the vast, trackless oceans of space, leaving planet earth far behind.

Consider for a moment what gravity does to rocks and bullets here on the surface of planet earth.

Suppose you place a .22 rifle in a horizontal position with the muzzle pointing out over the edge of a cliff 16 feet high. At the same time you pull the trigger, your pal drops a rock from the edge of the cliff.

Which will hit the ground first, the rock or the bullet?

Strange as it may seem, *both* bullet and rock will hit the ground *at the same time!*

Why?

Because both will be pulled down by gravity at the same rate. Though both objects hit the ground at the same time, the bullet will be farther from the foot of the cliff. *Reason*—the forward, horizontal flight of the bullet is independent of the downward pull. The forward velocity of the bullet, and its pull downward, operate independently of each other.

During the first second of free fall, all objects (neglecting air resistance) will drop 16 feet. But while the rock has been merely falling in a vertical position, the bullet, in addition to falling "downward" like the rock, has also been moving forward.

If the forward velocity of the bullet is 1000 feet per second, it will land 1000 feet from the base of the cliff, and at the same time the rock lands.

The resultant of the bullet's forward motion and downward motion is a curved path called a parabola.

All the above information is mighty important to you if you wish to shoot a moose!

If you are 6 feet tall, and hold your rifle at shoulder level in a perfect horizontal position lined up with a distant moose, you will never hit him!

Remember that during the first second of its flight, any object will drop 16 feet. If the forward speed of your bullet is 1000 feet per second, and the moose is 1000 feet away, he may continue to chew peacefully on lily pads, content in the confidence that your bullet will never reach him, as long as the rifle barrel is pointing directly at him.

To hit the moose, you have to tilt the barrel of your rifle to the place where the moose is not—*in the sky!*

The greater the distance to the moose, the greater the angle of elevation of your rifle.

Fortunately for the hunter, the only thing he has to do is to adjust the sights on the rifle for the proper range, and the mathematics of flight are taken care of. Since the barrel of the rifle is now pointing upwards, the bullet in flight travels up an "invisible hill" then "coasts down" or is "pulled down" by gravity to make contact with the target. The path of the bullet is a parabola.

Now you know why the pitcher's mound is made higher than home plate. No matter how hard a pitcher tries, he cannot throw a baseball in a straight line. The minute it leaves his hand, gravity begins to pull it towards the center of the earth. The path of the baseball is a curve; hence, the advantage of having a high "starting point."

Here, now, is a most important bit of information. The earth curves so that if you travel 5 miles in a horizontal direction, from A to B, by the

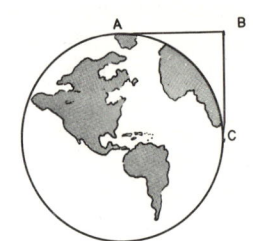

2:2

time you get to B you will be 16 feet "below" where you started. (Illustration is *not* drawn to scale.)

In other words, for each 5 miles of horizontal distance, the earth curves or "falls" 16 feet. This means that instead of being at B, you would be at C.

Now see how all this applies to astronaut Eugene Cernan when he was in orbit. There is no air in space. A breeze is impossible. Since the astronaut is traveling in a near-vacuum, there is nothing to blow him backwards or slow him down.

According to Newton's First Law of Motion, "A body in motion tends to stay in motion in a straight line, unless compelled by an external force to change."

This means that Eugene Cernan continued to travel forward with the same speed as the capsule, approximately 18,000 miles per hour.

Left to himself, Cernan's forward speed of 18,000 miles per hour would carry him 5 miles straight forward, from A to B in one second.

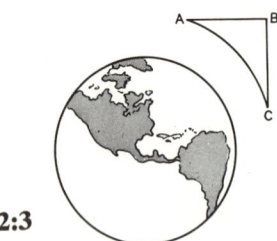

2:3

During the same time, however, gravity pulled both Cernan and his capsule 16 feet toward the center of the earth, as shown by the line BC (*not* drawn to scale).

The resultant of these two forces is that the capsule and Cernan traveled in the path AC. Note that at C the astronaut and capsule are no closer to the earth than they were at A.

Astronaut and capsule repeat this procedure every second. Gravity

HOW TO GO INTO ORBIT

continually pulls him towards the earth, yet he always remains the same distance away. He is always "falling" or being pulled down by gravity, but never landing.

Why has 5 miles per second been the "Magic Speed" for our astronauts and man-made satellites?

Because at this speed, while the satellite is going 5 miles in a forward direction, it is being "pulled down" 16 feet by gravity. This means that its path "matches" or runs parallel to the curvature of the earth. It is continually "falling" over the horizon.

No doubt you have figured out what would happen if the speed of the satellite is less than 5 miles per second.

Instead of "falling over the horizon" and following the curvature of the earth, it would plop down toward our rooftops, since the pull of gravity would be greater than its forward speed.

And if the forward speed were greater than the pull of gravity, the satellite would continue to move out into space, leaving planet earth far behind. The velocity which a satellite must have to remain in orbit around the earth is 5 miles per second, or approximately 18,000 miles per hour.

As we get farther and farther away from the center of the earth, the acceleration of gravity becomes less and less. At comparatively large distances from the earth, a satellite will not fall as far toward the earth as it passes over each mile of the earth's surface. So its orbital velocity need not be as great.

An object as far away as the moon (240,000 miles in round numbers) needs an orbital velocity of about 2000 miles per hour.

When you look up at the moon, it appears to be a "stationary" satellite of planet earth. Actually, the moon is speeding along about three times the speed of sound, as it is "falling down"!

Each second the moon moves forward through space about 3350 feet, and "falls" or is deflected from its straight-line path by about 1/19 inch towards the earth. This "falling" of 1/19 inch each second is just enough to keep the moon in orbit around the earth. If it didn't "fall" it would keep on going in a straight line out into space, and we would have no harvest moon to pour its burnished gold across our cornfields.

We earth-people actually live on a giant-size perpetual motion machine, the planet earth. And we depend upon "falling" to keep us in place!

Each second your watch ticks, planet earth "falls" towards the sun. If it were not for the gravity pull of the sun, our planet would go sailing off into space in a straight line.

Fortunately, the earth's forward speed of some 65,000 miles per hour is "balanced" by the inward pull of gravity exerted by the sun some 93 million miles distant. Our life truly "hangs on a balance"—a delicate, celestial "balance" between the gravity pull of the sun and our forward speed. To replace the force of gravity the sun exerts on us would take a steel cable 5000 miles in diameter to anchor us to our nearest star, the sun.

Our sun is the ringmaster and traffic manager of the solar system.

It is the sun that holds the vast multitude of some 30,000 asteroids or minor planets, plus their larger brothers, whirling in resplendent arcs.

With his power of might, the sun bends over each planet and with vibrant fingers guides it along the uncharted regions of space. The tremendous scheme of the solar system is so complex, yet so orderly, that scientists have marveled at its harmony. As though to give wings to their thoughts, the Adler Planetarium of Chicago has inscribed on one of its beautiful marble walls a pictorial representation of the solar system. Around the resplendent sun circle the planets that swing around it in space. The inscription itself informs us that the purpose of the planetarium is "to further the progress of science, to guide to an understanding of the majesty of the heavens, to emphasize that under the great celestial firmament there is order, interdependence, and unity."

DEMONSTRATIONS

Rolling marbles — Put a couple of marbles in the "back" of an open cigar box. Pull the box rapidly in the direction of A. Stop the box suddenly, and the marbles will obey Newton's First Law and continue to move forward.

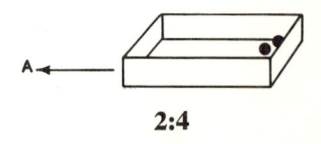

2:4

Eggbeater — Dip an eggbeater into a glass of water, then remove it, and spin it. The spinning motion will fling off drops of water to demonstrate centrifugal force, as the drops of water "flee" from the center of the rapidly rotating beater.

Ping-pong slingshot — Here is a "slingshot" that is safe and won't cause any damage. Get a strong thread or string about 2 feet long. Use a darning needle to run it through a ping-pong ball. After you tie the string to the ball, pick it up and whirl it.

The ball tries to travel in a straight line. It tries "to flee the center." To counteract this centrifugal force, the string must exert an inward, centripetal force.

Now, let the string go. The ping-pong ball becomes a body in motion in a straight line.

Turntable — An old 78 r.p.m. record player with adjustable speed control is an ex-

HOW TO GO INTO ORBIT

cellent unit to demonstrate how centrifugal force depends on weight, radius, and velocity.

Place various weights on the rim of the spinning turntable. The heavier they are, the greater the centrifugal force tending to hurl them off the rim.

Place weights at various distances from the center. The greater the radius, the greater the centrifugal force.

Vary the speed. The faster the table spins, the greater the tendency of the weight to keep traveling in a straight line.

Marble in glass bowl

Put a marble in a big, glass bowl to which you impart a rotary motion. Notice how centrifugal force flings the marble to the side of the bowl.

2:5

Marble in balloon

Insert a big glass marble into a toy balloon. Blow up the balloon. Tie it shut, and then impart a rotary motion to the balloon. Notice how centrifugal force flings the marble to the outside of the balloon. If the balloon is made of a translucent material, students will enjoy watching the marble "climb" the wall of the balloon and go "into orbit."

Pipe and bolt

Run a string through a small pipe about 6 inches long. Tie a washer or cork on the top end of the string, and a much heavier bolt or nail on the other end.

When there is no motion, the heavier bolt will draw the washer to the top of the rim of the pipe, when held in upright position, as shown.

Now rotate the washer. As it spins it will "flee the center" and pull up on the bolt to bring it in contact with the lower rim of the pipe.

2:6

Yo-yo

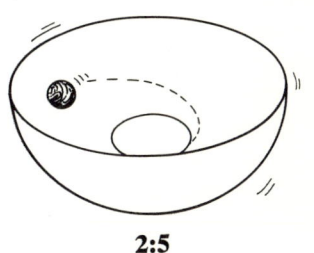

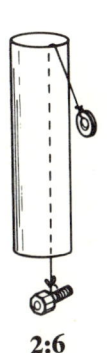

A toy Yo-yo demonstrates that a body in motion tends to keep in motion in a straight line, unless compelled by an external force to change its direction. The Yo-yo falls downward until it comes to the end of the string. It is then forced to reverse direction, and rolls back up the string. This demonstration is much more dramatic if you use a giant-size Yo-yo about 1 foot in diameter.

Block in jar

Fill a wide-mouth gallon jar about ¾ full of water. Place a small wooden block in the water.
Now take hold of the gallon jar with both hands, lift the jar off the table, and turn the jar half a turn clockwise. Even though you turn the jar, the water and block tend to remain at rest, in accordance with Newton's First Law of Motion.
Now remove the block of wood. Put a wooden ruler edge down into the jar and stir the water. When the water is racing around the walls of the jar at maximum speed, remove the ruler and drop the wooden block back in.
This time, note how the rapidly moving water tends to keep in motion, and whirls the wooden block around with it.

2:7

Bike wheel gyro

Mount an old bike wheel on an axle, so that you can grasp it with both hands. Give the wheel a spin, and then try to turn it from a horizontal to a vertical plane. Students delight in trying this experiment personally. And they are fascinated when they do the next demonstration.
If you have a piano stool, or rotating lab stool, the following demonstration with the bike wheel is captivating. Have a student sit on the stool so that his feet do not touch the floor. Have the student

2:8

HOW TO GO INTO ORBIT

extend both his hands, so that he may hold the wheel in a vertical position.

Give the wheel a spin, then ask the student to turn the wheel from a vertical into a horizontal position. Then, ask the student to turn the wheel 180 degrees—from horizontal back to vertical, then on to horizontal. Watch what happens to the piano stool!

Coffee can clothes dryer

Punch holes in the side of an old coffee can. Now make three holes near the top rim, equal distances apart. Tie a string through each of these holes. Tie the free ends of the strings to a screw eye fastened in the chuck of a drill. Place a wet rag inside the coffee can and spin the chuck to see how efficiently your clothes dryer demonstrates Newton's First Law of Motion.

2:9

Lasso

If you spin a lasso, you can give a beautiful demonstration of objects moving in circular paths. The spinning lasso takes a circular form because each portion of the spinning rope tries to escape from the center and go flying off on a tangent. The attraction between the molecules of the rope (cohesion) supplies the centripetal force which keeps the rope moving in a circle.

Squashed world

Here is a demonstration to show how rotation affects the shape of the earth.

Cut two strips of heavy paper or light cardboard about 1 inch wide and 18 inches long. Now bend the strips into circles, using Scotch tape to secure the two ends. Punch a hole in one end of your paper circle and slip it over a long pencil. Attach the upper end of the paper circle to the pencil with a thumbtack. Do likewise with your other paper circle. (Only one such cir-

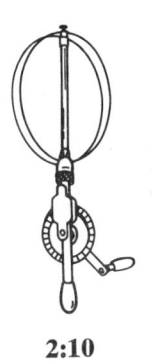

2:10

Mailing tube on bike wheel

cle shown in diagram.) Now clamp the free end of the pencil in the chuck of a hand drill, and spin. Note what happens.

Slit a mailing tube down one side, cut off a section about 4 inches long, and place it around one of the spokes of a bike wheel.

Spin the wheel, and notice how the spinning motion of the wheel throws the mailing tube to the rim.

Hold the bike wheel vertical, and see whether the spinning motion is enough to make the mailing tube stick against the rim throughout the revolution. Vary the speed, and see what happens. A key ring may be used instead of the mailing tube.

2:11

Conclusion

The reason planet earth stays in orbit around the sun is that the centrifugal force of the earth is just balanced by the inward pull of gravity of the sun.

At its distance of 93 million miles from the sun, the speed at which the earth must travel to avoid being pulled into the flaming surface of the sun is 65,000 miles per hour.

If the earth were only half as far from the sun as it now is, the force of gravity would be four times as great. The earth would then have to travel at a much greater speed so that centrifugal force would counterbalance gravity.

FOLLOW-UP EXERCISES

1. Explain this statement: "The boy, David, of Biblical times is no longer with us, but on many lawns across America are modern, mechanized 'Davids' which make use of Newton's First Law of Motion to injure more than 80,000 people every year."

   Hint: The 24-inch blade of a common rotary lawn mower can pick up a rock or chunk of metal and hurl it at speeds up to 240 miles per hour. A piece of wire traveling at this speed can penetrate a shoe, and be driven almost completely through the foot, damaging both bone and flesh. Physicians consider rotary mowers one of the most dangerous pieces of machinery their patients use.

2. Use a camera to show the results of the earth's rotation. Take a time exposure of the night sky on a clear evening when there is no moon. Place your camera on a tripod, or some secure stand, and set it on "time."

Make a number of exposures, from a few minutes up to an hour or more. If you face your camera toward the pole star, you will secure a circling pattern of stars that is most fascinating.

3. Explain how the deceleration problem met by a spacecraft on its re-entry into the atmosphere illustrates Newton's First Law of Motion.

To understand what happens in sudden deceleration, tie an empty shoe box to a skate board. Seat a small doll at the back end of the box. Then give the skate board a swift push so that it rolls swiftly across the top of the table to collide with a heavy rock or brick. Explain what happens to the doll.

2:12

Major Robert White, pilot of the X-15 rocket plane tells us of the problem of re-entry and deceleration, "As you come back into the atmosphere with the speed brakes open," White explained, "the deceleration force tends to throw you against the instrument panel. Some of the tiny blood vessels in my right arm burst at this point, and caused a red rash. The rash cleared up in a day or two."

Summary

In this chapter, the teacher has executed a "docking maneuver" and linked Newton's First Law of Motion to gravity to explain some of the most fundamental laws governing space flight.

The teacher has answered such questions as: "Why is 5 miles per second the 'magic speed' needed for an astronaut to orbit planet earth?" "Is it true that the moon is 'falling down?'"

Even more important, the teacher has brought home to his students the fact that their lives and the lives of their passengers in years to come, when they drive a car, will depend upon their understanding and abiding Newton's First Law of Motion. Remember, "A body in motion, tends to stay in motion in a straight line, unless compelled by some external force to change."

If you are moving at high speed, and try to make a sharp turn, Newton's First Law will keep you moving in the direction you *don't* want to go!

In the previous chapter, you "linked up" Newton's First Law of Motion with gravity to explain why a satellite stays in orbit.

In this chapter, you can help your students find answers to such questions as: "How do satellites get into space?", "How did the Apollo astronauts journey to the moon?"

The answer is tied up with Newton's Third Law of Motion, and the fact that a rocket is really a "gun that shoots a continual stream of bullets!"

3

How to Travel in Space

Photo courtesy of McDonnell Douglas Corporation

Photo 3. *Newton's Third Law of Motion at work in the skies over St. Louis. Hot gases rushing out the tailpipe cause a reaction that thrusts the jet through the sky.*

42

HOW TO TRAVEL IN SPACE

Now for an exciting "turnabout." In the previous chapter, you explained that Newton's First Law of Motion not only helps keep a satellite in orbit, but also is responsible for many automobile accidents here on planet earth.

In this chapter, you can show how the drastic effect of Newton's First Law of Motion may often be averted by applying his Second Law of Motion. Here is a golden opportunity to work the formula that shows why seat belts make for safety, and why the new, experimental "Air-Stop" cushions are better yet.

This same "magic formula" is applied by the man on the flying trapeze and by Olympic skiers—by boxers and divers. The Grand Prix driver, Dan Gurney, uses this formula to corner his car better.

In this chapter, you can show your students that our adventures in space are controlled and governed by Newton's Laws of Motion. Remind students that the next time they look up to watch a Boeing 747 streak across the sky, they are watching Newton's Laws in action over their heads. At Cape Kennedy, we team up Newton's Second Law and Third Law to boost giant Saturn rockets leaping for the moon.

For your first class, you may begin with the following:

What does a .45 Colt six-gun and a throw rug have in common with a rocket bound for the moon?

What do you have in common with a Saturn rocket each morning around 6:20 AM?

The answers to the above questions will show how Newton's Laws of Motion are tied up with our conquest of space.

Why is it that some people prefer to relax in the shade of a palm tree and drink papaya juice, rather than be "up and at them"?

One answer is Newton's First Law of Motion which informs us: *Every body continues in its state of rest or of uniform motion in a straight line, unless compelled by an external force to change.*

This tendency of a body to remain at rest or in motion we call *inertia*. (Inertia is the Latin word for laziness!)

You give a solid example of Newton's First Law of Motion every morning when dawn emerges from night's black wrapping paper to deposit a fresh day on your window ledge. Even though our friend, Brother Sun, is flooding the landscape with dancing sunbeams, you continue in your state of rest.

An ICBM or Saturn rocket sitting on its launching pad is also at rest. To get yourself out of bed, and the rockets off their pads, you will have to make use of Newton's Second Law of Motion: *The force required to accelerate an object is proportional to its mass and the acceleration produced.* $F = Ma$ *(Force equals Mass $\times$ Acceleration)*.

Since a rocket has a lot more mass than you, and will be traveling faster, it needs a lot more force. The force required to lift a spacecraft off its launching pad is measured in pounds of thrust.

Newton's Second Law is the basis for all computations dealing with forces needed to propel spacecraft. A *given force* acting for a *certain time* is required to move a *given mass at a certain speed.*

The amount of *force* produced is equal to the *mass* of the *gas* rushing out the exhaust multiplied by its *velocity* relative to the spacecraft.

To give some idea of the tremendous force required to leap towards the stars, consider the hypersonic plane, the X-15. When Major Robert White catapulted his needle-nosed X-15 from the underside of a Boeing B-52 at 45,000 feet, he pushed full throttle, and the rocket plane X-15 blasted forward with 57,000 pounds of thrust. As the dartlike X-15 flashed upward, it burned half its 15-ton starting weight in one 75-second blast of terrifying force.

When the 36-story Saturn rocket leaped for the moon on December 21, 1968, the 6.5 million-pound vehicle rose out of the flames, thrust upward by a power equal to that of 180 million horses (or 450 diesel locomotives, or 85 Hoover Dams). Cheers followed as the rocket, burning up more than 14 tons of fuel a second, streaked skyward.

The scheduled blastoff came at 7:51 AM Eastern Standard Time. Just two and one-half minutes later, the 7.5 million-pound thrust of the Saturn V first stage ran out of fuel.

In boosting the mighty rocket-spacecraft combination through the atmosphere, 48 tank cars of fuel (kerosene and liquid hydrogen) were burned up. At a height of 57 miles, the huge empty first stage dropped away.

The reaction from the action of the escaping gases thrusts the vehicle upwards. This is according to Newton's Third Law of Motion which says: *To every action there is an equal and opposite reaction.*

Action and reaction are twins. You can't have one without the other. But remember, these two forces of action and reaction act on different bodies. In the application of Newton's Third Law, you will always find *two forces,* and *two objects.*

You may conduct a living room demonstration of Newton's Third Law if you have a throw rug. As you step forward, the rug leaps backward and does just what its name implies—throws you!

Only if you are nimble as a spider, and have bones of foam rubber do I recommend this demonstration. Stand on a skate board, or roller skates not fastened to your feet. Now try to walk. As you go one way, the skate board, or roller skates, go in the opposite direction. (Remember, this demonstration is *dangerous.* Use caution, or skip it entirely.)

In the summertime, when your garden hose is on the lawn, turn the nozzle so that the water will leap out in a straight, narrow stream. Place the nozzle on the lawn, then turn on the water full force. If the water pressure is high in your city, the hose will squirm like a snake with a stomach-ache. High-speed water shooting out the nozzle shoves the hose in the opposite direction.

Here is a demonstration you don't want to attempt while wearing your Sunday suit. When your canoe is close to the dock, try stepping out of the canoe without first tying it to the landing dock. As you step forward, the canoe will leap backward. I'll leave it to you to guess the results.

A rifle, shotgun, or pistol furnish a superb example of Newton's Third Law of Motion. The expanding gases that result from the explosion of the shell in the barrel do two different things to two different bodies. The force of the gas propels the bullet out of the barrel (action), and at the same time pushes backward on the rifle (reaction).

Each time you fire a rifle, the hot expanding gas resulting from the explosion of the shell does two things—it "shoots" the bullet forward and "kicks" the rifle backwards.

If you had a rifle resting on a table, or suspended from a string, then each time a bullet was fired forward, the rifle would leap backwards.

If bullets could be fired continually, and if the rifle were free to move, it would become a rocket!

In a jet engine or rocket, the "bullets" are the untold millions of burning, high-speed molecules of gas shooting out the tailpipe.

Their "recoils" or "reaction" push the rocket forward; hence, the name "reaction type" engine.

A jet is an "air breathing" machine. It needs a continual supply of fresh air to provide the oxygen to burn with the fuel.

Rockets are jet propelled, but, unlike jet engines, they carry their own supply of oxidizer. Some burn kerosene and liquid oxygen. They have no moving parts except for pumps for the fuel and oxidizer. The fuel burns in a combustion chamber, and the exhaust gases are expelled from the exhaust jet to propel the rocket.

Solid-fuel rockets are similar, except that they do not require a separate oxidizer. The solid fuel is packed in the combustion chamber and is designed to burn rapidly at a steady rate.

To steer a space vehicle in space, we make use of the recoil principle. If we want to turn to the right, we must direct a rocket exhaust to the left.

In space we cannot rely upon friction to slow us down, so we direct a rocket in the direction of our motion. This retro-rocket is a relatively small rocket unit (usually using a solid propellant) installed on a rocket-propelled vehicle. It is fired in the direction opposite to the main motion to decelerate the main unit.

Engineers found a way to put Newton's Third Law to work in landing jets on average-length runways.

The problem was due to speed and weight. When a 90-ton jet transport like the Convair 990 touched down at 135 miles per hour landing speed, it needed far more runway space than propeller-driven craft. Airports either had to spend millions to greatly lengthen existing runways, or more millions to build new airports—unless a third, less costly alternative could be found.

The solution was a "clam-shell" type thrust reverser for the turbofan. As the plane touches down, two blocker doors close around the turbofan exhaust, diverting 40 per cent of the engine's forward thrust in the opposite direction. This creates a counterforce which brings the plane to a stop in half the distance needed without thrust reverses.

For those interested in the magic of mathematics, we can put Newton's Third Law of Motion into the following form (as applied to the bullet and rifle):

(The mass of the bullet) × *(its velocity forward)* equals
(The mass of the rifle) × *(its velocity backwards)*

Or in formula form

$$mV = Mv$$

The product of mv (mass times velocity) is called *momentum*. Newton's Third Law of Motion informs us that

(Little Mass X BIG VELOCITY equals *BIG MASS X Small Velocity)* or,
   Momentum Forward   equals   Momentum Backward

But if the momentum of the rifle backwards is the same as the momentum of the bullet forward, why doesn't the momentum of the rifle kill you—just like the bullet will?

It will, as you would find out, if you attached a sharp icepick to the butt end of the rifle, then held the pointed ice pick next to your heart when you pulled the trigger.

The reason you don't rush to meet your ancestors when you fire a gun is that the broad butt end of the gun distributes the force over a large area. Since pressure equals force divided by area, this means that the pressure on any one spot is very small. If you substituted the sharp end of an ice pick, however, the force will all be delivered to a small area. The pressure would soar, and so would you!

In a rocket, the *mass* of the gas escaping out the exhaust times its *velocity* equals the *mass* of the rocket times its *velocity* in the opposite direction.

DEMONSTRATIONS

String to block

Attach a long, thin, weak string to a heavy block of wood, or to a toy car of sufficient mass. Pull the free end of the string slowly and gently, and the block will move. Give a sudden jerk, and Newton's First Law will keep the block stationary. The thin string will break.

Half-dollar and glass

Place a small square of stiff cardboard over the open end of a glass. Place a half-dollar in the center of the cardboard. Now give the card a sudden snap on the edge with your finger. The card will scoot

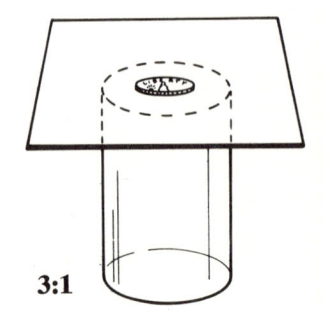

3:1

away, and the half-dollar will drop into the glass, thus showing that a body at rest, the half-dollar, tends to stay at rest and does not suddenly move forward with the cardboard.

Car on plank

For another demonstration of Newton's First Law, place a small plank about 3 feet long on one side of the table, with about 1 foot of the plank extending out over the end of the table. On top of the plank place a toy car of sufficient mass. Now grasp the free end of the plank and pull rapidly. Newton's First Law will keep the car on the table.

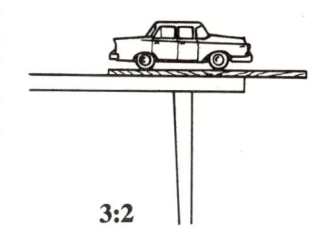

3:2

Goodbye cigar box

Put a 1000-gram weight in the middle of an empty cigar box. Pull box as rapidly as possible in the direction of A.

The back of the cigar box may be blasted apart when it hits the 1000-gram mass, which tries to stay at rest.

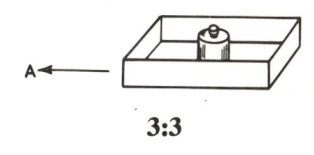

3:3

Overcoming inertia

Hook a spring scale by means of a string, if necessary, to a heavy block of wood, or to a toy automobile. Pull rapidly on the scale. The indicator will momentarily jump to a high reading. As you continue to pull, it will fall back, to show that it takes more force to overcome the inertia of the block when it is standing still, than it does to keep it moving.

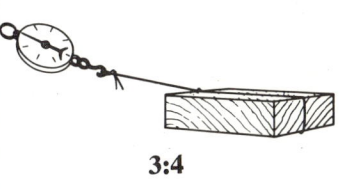

3:4

Leaping basketball

Place a basketball on the table and give it a gentle shove for only a fraction of a second. It moves only a little distance, and slowly.

Now thump the basketball with a vigorous blow. It leaps forward to demonstrate that the force required to accelerate a given mass is proportional to the acceleration produced. A big acceleration requires a big force.

Basketball versus marble

To show how the force required to accelerate an object varies with the mass, place a marble and a basketball on the table. Give each an equal flick with your finger. The marble, having the smaller mass, will move rapidly. The smaller the mass, the easier an object is to accelerate.

3:5

Catcher's mitt

Put a catcher's mitt on your left hand. Pick up a sawed-off broomstick with your right hand, and smack the glove a resounding blow. The glove "gives" with the stick, and thus reduces the impact on your hand by increasing the stopping time.

Foam-rubber cushion

To show how the force required to stop an object is related to the time needed to stop, place a thick foam-rubber cushion on the table. Invite a student to come and hit the cushion full force with his fist.
Then ask the student whether or not he would be interested in hitting the bare table in like manner!
Dramatic proof that the longer it takes an object to stop, the less force is required to stop it.

$$Force = \frac{Mass \times Velocity}{Time}$$

Dime-store jet engine

Blow up a toy balloon, then release it. The air rushing out the exhaust (action) propels the balloon in the opposite direction (reaction).

3:6

Plank on pipes

Get a plank about 2 feet long and 1 foot wide. Place it on top of two pipes as shown. Ask a nimble student to stand on the plank, then attempt to step forward.
Caution student to be careful in demonstrating Newton's Third Law.

Toy water wheel

Drop buckshot into the buckets of a toy water wheel. (Sand or water or anything else convenient may be used.) The reaction will set the

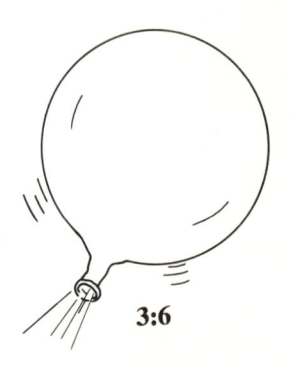

3:7

HOW TO TRAVEL IN SPACE

Walk-around record player

wheel turning according to Newton's Third Law.

If you have an old 78 r.p.m. record player, put it on the table. Let your fingers attempt to "walk around" near the rim. Study the action and reaction.

Spring scales

Hold spring scale #1 in your hand. Ask a student to hold scale #2 whose hook is linked to the hook of #1. Tell student he is *not* to *pull*, but simply *hold* scale #2.

Now you pull with a force of 200 grams. Scale #2 will also read 200 grams! Action equals reaction. The student was actually pulling!

3:8

Transfer

To demonstrate transfer of momentum, try the following. Roll a marble against a stationary baseball or billiard ball, a marble against a marble, a rolling baseball or billiard ball against a stationary marble. Even better yet, if you have one—an old bowling ball and billiard ball on collision course!

Reaction engine

Place an electric fan on a skate board. Use a long extension cord. Turn on the power. The fan may have enough power to stir up a breeze to give you a "jet-propelled skate board."

3:9

"Giveaway" floor

The only reason a student can stand on the floor of the classroom is that the floor reacts with an equal and opposite force, and pushes up against his feet with as much force as he pushes down.

To demonstrate what happens when a floor can't push up with an equal and opposite force, ask a student to stand on top of an empty cardboard box.

Jet-propelled tin can

An old tin can, of the shape shown here makes a good jet engine. Tie the can securely to the top of a

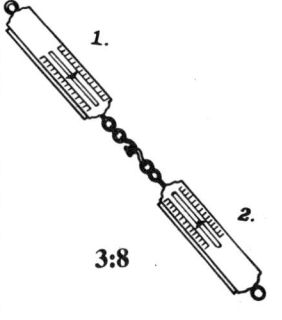

Halls carriage, or to a small toy automobile. Place a small firecracker in the open end of the can, leaving only enough of the fuse exposed to light it. The resulting explosion will shoot a blast of air out the "exhaust" of the can. The opposite and equal reaction will propel your jet across the table.

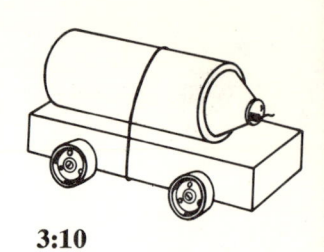

3:10

Jet soda bottle

Working with a firecracker presents an element of danger, so here is a safer experiment.

Tie an empty tin can of the shape shown to a Halls carriage or to a toy automobile, or simply rest the can on two small pipes which will serve as "wheels."

To put "fuel" in the can, turn it upright, and insert five tablespoons of vinegar, and five tablespoons of water. To this add a teaspoon of baking soda (sodium bicarbonate) and cork securely. Turn the can (or bottle) back into its horizontal position, as shown.

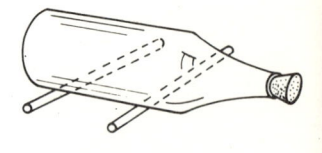

As soon as the carbon dioxide builds up enough pressure, it will pop the cork. The bottle will travel in the opposite direction.

3:11

(Trying to pour a teaspoon of baking soda into the bottle is messy. A more efficient way is to first spread open a little square of tissue paper on the table. Pour the baking soda on the paper, then roll it up into a neat tube. Twist the ends, and insert into the bottle without trouble.)

No-go nail

Here is an excellent demonstration to illustrate that Newton's Third Law is needed to pound a nail into wood.

Hand a student a narrow board about 2 feet long and 2 inches wide into which you have already pounded a nail just far enough to make it stay in place.

HOW TO TRAVEL IN SPACE

The student is to hold the stick in his left hand, with his hand at the bottom of the board, as shown, and the nail on the top side.

The student is to take a hammer in his right hand, and pound the nail into the board *without resting the board on anything*—simply holding the board by the far end.

His futile attempts will prove that to pound a nail, you need more than a hammer. The board itself must be able to push back with an equal and opposite force. Newton's Third Law is needed to drive the nail home!

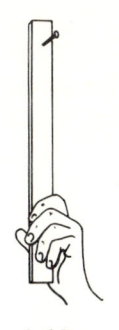

3:12

Rocket goes farther on water!

Here is an interesting demonstration to illustrate that the mass of the particles expelled from the exhaust times their velocity equals the mass of the rocket times its velocity.

To do this demonstration you will have to purchase a plastic toy rocket that comes equipped with a hand pump.

The first time, pump the rocket full of air only. Take the rocket *outdoors* and release it. Note how high it goes.

Now add water to the level shown on the plastic chamber, and pump air into it as before. When you release your rocket now it will go much farther due to the additional mass of the particles of water rushing out the exhaust.

Clothespins and rubber band

Clip clothespins to both ends of a rubber band as shown. Pull on the clothespins until the rubber band is stretched about 6 inches. Release both clothespins at the same time, and note the position in which the pins come to rest. They should be roughly halfway.

Now attach a second clothespin to the left-hand side, and stretch the

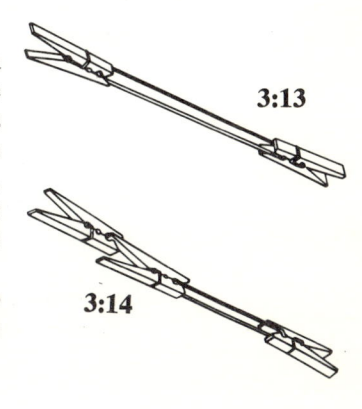

3:13

3:14

Piano stool and pillow

rubber band as before. Release and note the positions of the pins.

Here is an experiment for a student to try at home. Sit on a revolving-type piano stool. In his outstretched right hand, hold a pillow. Then, keeping his right arm extended as far from his body as possible, let him attempt to throw the pillow forward!

Conclusion

On land, on sea, or in the vast cool stretches of space, if you wish to get anyplace, you need a push!

If you walk over to Joan's house tonight after supper, you may think that your feet are responsible for bringing you to 139 Tunison Road. The truth is that you can walk only because the sidewalk pushes against your feet with a force equal and opposite to the force you exert on it.

It may seem odd to say that you can walk only because the sidewalk is pushing on you, but it is the truth.

If you were "standing" out in space, for example, it would be impossible for you to walk. There would be nothing to push against. If a force is to make something move, it must have something to react on. Even the most powerful Thunderbird moves ahead only because the highway is pushing against the car. If the highway is slicked over with glare ice, the "push" is gone. The wheels of the car may spin, but the car does not move ahead. Only when the highway can push does the car move forward.

FOLLOW-UP EXERCISES

1. Can you be kicked by a boulder?
   Just try it. Kick a big rock with a force of 2 pounds. It will "kick back" with an equal and opposite force.
2. If you ever ran headfirst into a stone wall with a force of 20 pounds, you know what happened. You got "smacked" in return—according to Newton's Third Law of Motion.
3. Without thinking, you may inadvertently give a bone-tingling demonstration of Newton's Third Law of Motion when you zoom around a corner of the corridor at high speed, and bump foreheads with a pal coming from the opposite direction. Twin forces (action and reaction) will pound themselves into your skulls.

HOW TO TRAVEL IN SPACE 53

4. Try walking from the prow of a rowboat to the stern. What happens? Why?
5. You can listen to a window-rattling demonstration of Newton's Third Law of Motion when a fire engine roars down the street. The fire engine pushes against the earth (action) and the earth pushes back with a reaction that is sole stirring.
6. Explain how a diving board illustrates Newton's Laws of Motion.
7. You speak of the "pickup" your car has. How is this an application of Newton's Second Law of Motion?
8. The next time you drop in to the gym and visit the swimming pool, watch Newton's Third Law in motion. The swimmer uses his muscles (force) to push the water backward. The backward push causes the swimmer to move in the opposite direction (reaction). The swimmer is pushed forward with as much force as he pushes backward.
9. For a bathtub-size demonstration of Newton's Third Law of Motion, wind up a toy motorboat and note the action of the propeller as the boat goes through the water. If you allow a few drops of ink to fall behind the spinning propeller, you can watch the water's movement with greater ease.
10. You are in a dining car on the train when you drop your knife. Will the knife fall behind the spot from which you dropped it, directly under the spot, or ahead of it? The train is moving forward at 60 miles per hour.
11. Explain how a trampoline illustrates Newton's Laws of Motion.
12. You can give yourself a finger-tingling demonstration of Newton's Second Law of Motion the next time you catch a baseball with your bare hands. As you are aware, you may stop the baseball in one of three ways: You may stop the ball by holding your hands stationary. You may move your hands forward to meet the baseball. You may move your hands slowly backwards at the moment of impact to "give" with the ball.

    Now, apply the formula

    $$Force = \frac{Mass \times Velocity}{Time}$$

    In all three examples,

    - The *mass* of the baseball remains the *same*.
    - The *velocity* of the baseball itself remains the *same*.
    - As you can prove, *the longer the time* required to stop, the *less force* required to stop.

13. Now that you have analyzed the above example, consider the following:
    You dive into a pool full of water. It does not hurt.

You dive into the same pool—without water. The results!?!!??
How come the difference?
Answer: The water increases your stopping time, thereby cutting down on the stopping force.

14. A trapeze artist who misses connections and falls into a net can bounce back for another try. Without a net, he will end up in an ambulance. How come?
Again, the big factor is *time*. The net increases the time required to stop, thereby decreasing the force. Without the net, the man hits the ground, to be stopped in a small interval of time. Results are tragic.

15. Is it possible for a man to jump off the top of a tall cliff just for thrills—and come back to do it all over again?
Certainly! On TV you have watched Olympic skiers zoom down snow-covered slides, then sail out into the wide, blue yonder, high over treetops far below.
By now, you should be able to figure out the "secret"!

16. Why is it easier to be hit with 16-ounce boxing gloves than with a pair of brass knuckles?
The padded gloves "give" and increase the stopping time. Brass knuckles come to a sudden, shuddering stop in a brief interval. Naturally, the area of impact is also involved.

17. Some schools with small basketball courts, suspend padded "blankets" on the wall behind the basket area. Why?

18. Newton's First Law of Motion costs the United States railroads $100 million a year! When an eager-beaver engineer starts up the freight train, he may forget the fact that the merchandise in the boxcar tends to remain at rest. Result, the back end of the boxcar slams into the freight, causing damage to a total of 3 billion tons of merchandise per year.
In an effort to minimize this loss, the Union Pacific railroad built a special boxcar with Plexiglas sides so that railroaders could look in and see what happens when the car is coupled too fast. The U.P. is confident that its one "Package Pullman" demonstration will do more good than all the previous decades' warnings and instructions.

19. Newton's Second Law is used to overcome the effects of Newton's First Law! Spurred on by the climbing cost of damage, the railroads investigated more secure ways to pack boxcars.
Result—in the bag!
An empty rubber bag manufactured by Good Year is inserted between the boxes of merchandise and then inflated. The Super-Cushion Dunnage Bags have reduced damage as much as 50 per cent. Now, if a boxcar starts or stops too suddenly, the air-cushion will absorb the shock by increasing the stopping time.

20. According to investigations, the most successful device to make airplanes safer is an "Air-Stop." In an actual crack-up, a dummy was cushioned by gigantic rubber bags that automatically filled with air. During the crash, the dummy was forced forward and down into a billowy mass that would have saved the life of an actual passenger and probably even have spared him any injuries.

Summary

In this chapter the teacher explained how Newton's Second and Third Laws are put to work at Cape Kennedy to boost giant Saturn rockets off their pads, and send them leaping for the moon.

The teacher was also able to show how Newton's Second Law proves the wisdom of safety belts in cars, and cushions in athletic equipment, and makes for economy in driving a motorcycle rather than a Cadillac.

Most amazing of all, perhaps, will be the realization on the part of the students that a jet or rocket is a "flying machine gun" shooting "molecule bullets"—and it is the "reaction" to the shooting that propels the jet and rocket across the sky.

4

In the previous chapter, you introduced your students to the fact that we are astronauts cruising through space. In place of an "umbilical cord" or rope, such as was used to keep astronaut Eugene Cernan "tethered" to his space capsule, we are "tethered" to planet earth by gravity.

Astronauts "walking" around planet earth, or strolling on the surface of the moon, must wear special suits and headgear to furnish them

Our Canopy of Air

Photo courtesy of NASA

Photo 4. *Many of the difficulties that plague man on the moon are due to the fact that the moon has no atmosphere to serve as an "umbrella."*

OUR CANOPY OF AIR 57

with a life-giving atmosphere, ward off harmful radiation from the sun, and furnish them protection from micrometeorites. We, too, have a special "bubble-dome" that does the same thing for us.

In this chapter, you may introduce your students to the mysteries of that "invisible dome" or "canopy of air" that surrounds planet earth, and makes it safe for us to walk across the face of our spinning sphere.

You can help your students realize some of the many ways our lives depend upon our "umbrella of air." To do this by way of contrast, you can show that the reason the moon is so dangerous and inhospitable is that it lacks an "umbrella of air."

Here now, precisely, is where you can show how beautifully this chapter follows from the previous one. The only reason we "planet people" have an "umbrella of air" is that Mother Earth "holds on to it" with gravity!

You will be able to work many demonstrations to show why our "umbrella of air" is so "tough" and "resists" being "dented."

You may begin the first class on our canopy of air with the following:

> At its distance of some 240,000 miles from us, the golden harvest moon has that well-shaven look. It appears smooth as a graded California orange.
>
> Scientists, however, inform us that the perils that beset man on the moon are intense and formidable.
>
> What makes the moon so inhospitable?
>
> In this chapter, we intend to illustrate that most of the difficulties that plague a man on the moon are due to the fact that the moon has no atmosphere to serve as an "umbrella."
>
> Night and day we are being bombarded by rocks from outer space. When these rocks, or meteors, fly into the earth's atmosphere at high velocity, friction with the air rubs them glowing hot. The surface of the meteor then melts and turns into white-hot gas that streams out behind.
>
> The rocks burn themselves into fine ash, which floats harmlessly to earth. Only the memory of the instantaneous ribbon of light remains.
>
> Meteors are popularly known as shooting stars or falling stars. The term "meteor" is taken from a Greek word and means "things in the air." Since a meteor has no light of its own, and is not a star, this name is far more accurate, though less descriptive, than shooting star.
>
> Meteors are generally no larger than the head of a pin, though they may be larger than an African elephant. Our umbrella of air protects us against all but the biggest of these "things in the air."
>
> But on the moon, with nothing to impede their fall, meteors plunge into its face with velocities as great as 100,000 feet per second!
>
> Over long centuries, the largest of these "rocks from space" have gouged out vast lunar craters—up to 140 miles in diameter!

Since a major meteor impact occurs only about once in 50,000 years, the giant-size "rocks from space" don't worry space scientists.

More hazardous are the tiny space rocks, or micrometeors, which swarm in dense concentrations across the orbits of the earth and moon.

Space-probing satellites, such as our Vanguards, indicate that every square yard of the moon may be struck by as many as 60 micrometeorites a minute. (A meteor is a space rock on the prowl. A meteorite is said rock after being grounded.)

Engineers, anticipating that an explorer's space suit may be pierced by micrometeorites, have planned against sudden decompression by using a liner of gummy sealing materials.

We "planet people" are protected by our umbrella of air. Our cushion of air bounces some of the flying rocks back out into space. The more determined sky raiders that come head-on with billy-goat stubbornness are cannon-balling for trouble. As they nose-dive on us with supersonic speeds, friction with the air burns them to fine ash, and reduces them to dust. Each day our earth picks up many tons of these abrupt visitors from space.

The next time you scan the sky at midnight and see a shooting star turn on the fireworks, you will know it is most likely a pin-size visitor from space burning in the air some 40 miles up. The reason our sombreros aren't ripped to shredded wheat is due to the protection afforded by our umbrella of air.

Since the moon lacks a blanket of air, these tiny rocks from outer space, speeding many times faster than a rifle bullet, could pierce your flesh if you were on the moon. But it would do no good to cry out in alarm. Without air, there would be no sound!

There is no friendly blanket of air surrounding the moon to act as "shock absorber" for sunlight. The sun's fierce rays smite the moon with intense fury to make it a sphere of terrifying contrasts. It is estimated that the temperature on the side of the moon facing the sun rises far above the boiling point of water, 212° Fahrenheit. In the shade it is 250° below zero.

If you could stretch out for a nap on the moon, without the benefit of your space suit, you would find some amazing results. If your feet were in the sun and your head in the shade, you would find that your feet were "hot dogs" for sure, and your head cold as the nose of a snow plough. There is never twilight or half-light on the moon—only dazzling light or total darkness, unless the moon happens to be in a position where it is illuminated by light reflected from planet earth.

Since the moon has no air, the sky, even at high noon, is jet-black as velvet, and sequined with stars that blaze like white-hot coals.

One thing would be to your advantage. Your vision on the moon would not be limited by dust or haze. The entire eerie landscape would be visible right to the horizon, needle-sharp. The Doerfels Mountains, lolling on the horizon, would seem so close that you would think you could reach out and touch their towering peaks.

One of the most thrilling experiences would be to look back at the earth, which is almost four times the diameter of the moon. The vast extent of oceans would make our planet gleam like a huge, blue sapphire. The steaming jungles of the Amazon and equatorial Africa would add a pastel shade of green. The sweep of the Sahara and the vast deserts of our Southwest would lend a tinge of yellow. The rolling prairies of Dakota, Wyoming, and Montana would toss in a splash of russet. The frigid, snow-covered polar regions would give a sparkle of white.

As we toddle around planet earth wearing the water-filled space suits of our skins, we seldom stop to realize that we are "caught" and "held prisoners" in the "middle" of a gigantic tug of war!

The atmosphere is pushing in on us. We aren't squashed because the air inside our body is pushing out with equal force.

If someone suddenly "stole" or "ran away" with the blanket of air surrounding us, the air trapped inside our body would expand and explode our epidermis to all points of the compass.

A man on the moon would have to wear a pressurized space suit. If our man on the moon stumbled and ripped open his pressurized space suit, he would be exposed instantaneously to the lunar vacuum.

His fate was dramatized by a spectacular space experiment. A first-stage Saturn rocket took off from Cape Kennedy. Ninety miles above the earth, 100 tons of water were suddenly released.

Dr. Wernher van Braun reported that the water literally exploded, expanding in all directions at a speed of more than a mile a second.

Thus it seems possible that any substantial tear in a space suit would cause death by explosive vaporization of all the explorer's body fluids.

To forestall such tragedy, engineers designed a suit sturdy enough to withstand any conceivable accident.

So far we have seen the moon is dangerous because it can't hold on to an umbrella of air.

Now the question—*Why* can't the moon hold an umbrella of air?

The answer—lack of gravity. In case you wonder why lack of gravity makes the moon so dangerous, consider the facts.

The air we breathe consists of gas molecules always on the go, like a swarm of gnats. Sometimes they pick up exciting speeds, like miniature tiny rockets.

Fortunately for us, the earth has a strong gravity pull, and thus holds on to these energetic little gas molecules.

In order to escape the earth's gravity pull, the gas molecules would need, like rockets, a velocity of some 25,000 miles per hour. (About 7 miles per second.)

On the moon, however, a speed of 1½ miles per second is enough to carry gas molecules off the surface of the moon and out into the voids of space.

Since the moon's gravity pull is so weak, it cannot hold on to the constantly moving molecules. Consequently, there is no atmosphere.

DEMONSTRATIONS

Air resists being squeezed

Fill a gallon jar about ⅔ full of water, and place it on the table. Now take a glass tumbler, turn it upside down, and push it, open end first, into the gallon jar until the drinking glass is completely submerged.

Note how far up inside the drinking glass the water will rise. I'm amazed every year to find students who expect to see the water rise almost all the way up inside the glass tumbler. They are taken by surprise to find that the water rises only about a centimeter. The air resists being squeezed!

Paper stays dry, even though submerged in water!

Before submerging the drinking glass, ram a piece of paper into the bottom half of the glass. When the glass is turned upside down and submerged, the paper in the upper section stays dry.

After I take the glass out of the water, I let one of the students remove the crumpled paper from the glass, and thus prove beyond a doubt that the paper stayed dry. At this point, I inform the students that the inverted glass in the gallon of water represents the principle of the diving bell or caisson. Because air resists being squeezed, it keeps the water out, and makes it possible for men to work under rivers and lakes, and thus put down the foundations for bridges. Compressed air is forced into the diving bell until it equals the water pressure exerted by the river or lake.

4:1

Float a cork under the water

Can you make a cork "float beneath the surface"? Students find this demonstration of the upside-down glass a fascinating one.

I place a cork on the surface of the water in the gallon jar. When

OUR CANOPY OF AIR

I turn the glass upside down and push it beneath the water, I also "capture" the cork.

Since the air compressed inside the inverted glass allows only about a centimeter of water to rise inside the glass, the cork floats "on the bottom" of the gallon jar!

Basting tube demonstrates Boyle's Law

What happens to air if you "squeeze" it? Boyle's Law gives the answer: The volume occupied by a body of gas is inversely proportional to its pressure, if its temperature remains constant.

Insert the open end of the tube into a glass of water. Now squeeze the rubber ball. By so doing, you decrease its volume, and thereby increase the pressure of the air it contains. This increase in pressure forces some of the air out the open end of the tube.

Release the bulb. Its elasticity will make it spring back into shape. By so doing, however, it increases its volume. This decreases the pressure of the air inside the tube. Now the atmospheric pressure on the surface of the water pushes liquid up inside the tube.

To get the liquid out of the tube, you employ Boyle's Law once more. You squeeze the rubber bulb, thereby decreasing its volume, and consequently increasing the air pressure. This increase of air pressure forces the liquid back out of the tube.

Repeat this experiment several times, so that students will learn that a *decrease in the volume* of a gas (bulb squeezed) means an *increase in pressure* (air goes out open end), and an *increase in the volume* of a gas (bulb springs back to original shape) means a *decrease in pressure* (outside air pushes water up tube).

4:2

4:3

Do you really inhale?

Inform students that they are giving a marvelous demonstration of Boyle's Law every minute.

Our lungs are a bellows, and act the same way, according to Boyle's Law. When you squeeze them into a smaller volume, you increase the pressure of the gas within them, and thereby force out the air.

We say you "exhale" when in reality, all you do is decrease the volume of your lungs. This decrease in volume automatically builds up the air pressure and forces air out of your lungs.

And we don't "inhale." We don't "breathe in" fresh, cool air. In reality, all we do is increase the volume of our lungs. This means lower air pressure inside the lungs. The atmosphere with its pressure of 14.7 pounds per square inch (at sea level) pushes fresh air into our lungs.

Shoot!

An enterprising toy company puts Boyle's Law to work with a rubber pistol that shoots a ping-pong ball. The mouth or muzzle of the rubber pistol is just wide enough to hold a ping-pong ball snugly. When you squeeze the balloon-shaped handle of the rubber pistol, you compress the volume of the air. This decrease in the volume of the gas increases the pressure, and shoots the ping-pong ball from the muzzle.

4:4

Pop goes the cork!

A popgun is still another example of Boyle's Law. Push down on the plunger rapidly, and the sudden decrease of volume builds up enough air pressure to shoot the cork from the muzzle. The compressed air, suddenly released, expands to make the familiar "pop" we hear when the cork flies out of the gun.

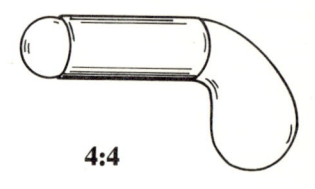

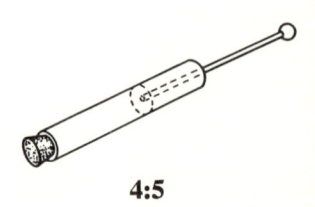

4:5

OUR CANOPY OF AIR

Pressure going up!

A basketball pump affords a dramatic demonstration to prove that the smaller the volume into which you try to compress a gas, the higher the pressure.

Put your finger over the end of the exhaust port to prevent the air from escaping. Now see how far down you can push the plunger. The pressure builds up so fast, you are soon brought to a stop. You can push the plunger no further.

An eyeful

Here is a demonstration to prove that compressed air tries to expand and regain its original volume.

Get a bottle about 6 inches tall and with a mouth of convenient size to take a cork. Drill a hole through the cork just wide enough to admit a long glass tube which you shove down to within about ½ inch or so of the bottom of the bottle.

Now that the apparatus is ready, remove the cork so that you may fill the bottle about half full of water. Replace the cork, and push it down firmly, so that it fits snugly. Invite a student to test his lung power by blowing as hard as he can into the tube.

As soon as he stops blowing, and raises his head from the top of the tube, the compressed air inside the bottle will shoot a fountain of water up into his face.

I put this bottle in a pan on the table before class and invite the students to try it for themselves. This they do with glee. They try to "outwit" the fountain by jumping back from the bottle as fast as possible once they have blown all their air into the tube.

The less water in the bottle, the bigger the fountain. Ask a student to explain why this is so.

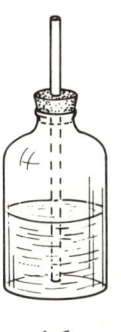

4:6

A balloon you can't blow up

Insert a small toy balloon, bottom down, into the neck of a pop bottle. Slip the mouth of the balloon over the lip of the bottle. Now ask a student to try to blow up the balloon. As soon as he does so, the increase of the air pressure inside the balloon tries to expand the rubber. But when the balloon tries to expand, it has to push against the air trapped inside the bottle. This air resists being compressed. *Result* —no one can blow up the balloon. Leave this demonstration unit on the table for all the students to try for themselves after class.

4:7

What the balloon says

As you blow up a toy balloon it tells a story. It informs the class that an increase in the pressure of a gas tries to increase the volume, if possible.

Keep blowing until the balloon breaks. The noise of the explosion informs the class that a gas likes to return to its original volume and pressure. The sound wave was caused by the "bunched-up bag of air" suddenly expanding back to its original volume.

Secret in the cylinder

If you have an oxygen cylinder or similar container, show it to the class, and ask why such thick walls.

Indicate that the gas contained in the cylinder is under great pressure. To prevent the cylinder from experiencing the fate of the balloon in the previous demonstration, the walls of the cylinder must be strong enough to withstand the tremendous pressure of the confined gas.

4:8

Pop

Uncork a bottle of soda pop, then hold the bottle against the light so that the class may see the sparkling bubbles rising to the surface.

The carbon dioxide dissolved in the pop may be under a pressure of some 12 pounds per square inch. When you remove the cap from the bottle, the higher pressure of the imprisoned carbon dioxide molecules causes them to escape and go dashing out the top of the bottle. This escaping gas gives the pop its sparkling bubbles, and tantalizing fizz.

Do you smoke?

Show students a cigarette, and then inform them that even if they consume a pack a day, they don't really smoke!

All they do is reduce the air pressure on the side of the cigarette in their mouth. Atmospheric pressure then pushes the smoke through the cigarette and into their mouth.

To prove that it takes no brains to smoke, I put one end of a cigarette in the opening of a small hose. I connect the other end of the hose to a vacuum pump. I turn on the vacuum pump, then light the cigarette. Students can see for themselves that as the vacuum pump reduces the air pressure on the end of the cigarette in the hose, the atmosphere pushes the smoke through the machine and out the exhaust port.

I put a clean cloth over the exhaust port of the vacuum pump and "trap" some of the smoke as it pours forth into the room. The amount of the stain and deposit on the cloth from even one cigarette amazes the students.

Squeeze-me tube

Get a plastic squeeze tube, such as honey or mustard sometimes comes in. Place a lighted candle on the table. Hold the nozzle of the tube near the candle and squeeze.

The decrease of the volume of the tube increases the pressure. Air is forced out the nozzle, and blows out the candle.

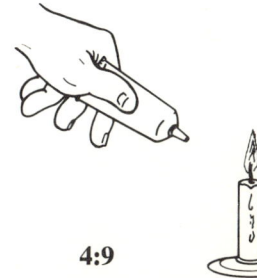

4:9

Relight the candle. This time, squeeze down on the tube before you bring it near the candle flame. Now hold the nozzle of the squeezed-down tube near the flame. As you release your grip on the tube, it will increase in volume, thereby decreasing the pressure of the gas on the inside. Atmospheric pressure will force smoke from the candle into the tube.

Let it snow—in the classroom!

Place a container of artificial snow on the table. Call the attention of the students to the fact that Boyle's Law is put to use in many pressurized containers that bring forth everything from shaving cream to whipping cream, paint, and hair spray.

Now push down on the release valve on top of the metal container, and a "cloud" of "snow" will rush forth to envelop nearby students!

Read the label indicating that the contents are under pressure. When you push down on the release valve, you allow the confined gas to expand and thereby push the contents up and out the nozzle.

Ask the class why some containers advise the user to keep the can in an upright position.

Honk your horn

Another interesting item to illustrate Boyle's Law is a bicycle horn that has a hollow rubber ball on one end. When you squeeze the hollow rubber ball you decrease the volume, and thereby increase the pressure of the air inside it. This forces the air to rush forth and honk your horn.

I leave this item on the table for the students to experiment with after class.

4:10

OUR CANOPY OF AIR   67

> **Conclusion**
>
> We have to thank our "umbrella of air" for keeping us from being ripped to shreds by "flying rocks" from outer space. This same "umbrella" keeps the sun from cooking us by day, and likewise protects us from freezing at night.
>
> The reason planet earth is able to "hold on" to an "umbrella" of air is due to gravity. Hence, in the last analysis, we owe gravity a debt of thanks we seldom think of. Without gravity to wrap a blanket of air around us, we would be left "naked" in space.

FOLLOW-UP EXERCISES

1. Can you ever watch your blanket of air at work protecting you? Yes—simply look up at the night sky, and you may watch the air set fire to a flying rock from outer space and burn it to harmless ashes.

   You refer to the spectacle as a shooting star. In reality, it is a glowing example of air at work protecting you!

2. How much is our "air protection" worth? How much would we have to pay for the safety and security afforded by our blanket of air?

   The astronauts know the answer. Each space suit, custom-fitted for moon wear, costs $100,000. *Life* magazine refers to the astronaut's suit as an "awesome smorgasbord of synthetics."

   On the outside of the 21-layer body suit is a layer of Beta fiber, a fireproof Fiberglas fabric, covered with Teflon, the material used in frying pans. Then come 15 alternating layers of aluminized plastic and Beta cloth. Next come two layers of nylon coated with neoprene (synthetic rubber), a nylon restraining layer, an air-tight bladder of neoprene-coated nylon, and a nylon liner. Underneath this the astronaut wears underwear consisting of elasticized plastic and, finally, next to his skin, a layer of delicate nylon chiffon.

   Each of these layers must be individually cut to order and fitted and refitted by hand. The suit will protect the astronaut from deadly extremes of temperature (from 250° above zero to 250° below), the threat of bombardment by tiny particles known as micrometeoroids, and a complete lack of oxygen and atmospheric pressure. The suit's outer layers are built to take care of temperatures and micrometeoroids. The middle layers, which are interlaced with a network of tubes, will provide oxygen and protection against decompression.

3. Do you ever "chase star dust"?

   The answer is "Yes, every time you help dust the furniture!"

   How can this be?

Reason—when meteorites pass through our atmosphere, their surface heats up by impact with air molecules. The meteorite surface continually boils off and melts off. The molten portion will cool afterward. Surface tension will then pull the material into a spherical shape. These spheres fall slowly to the ground. Some of these spheres are stone (silica) and some iron. Some scientists estimate that over 100 tons of iron-nickel dust falls on the earth each day!

Summary

In this chapter, the teacher introduced students to the fact that we are protected by an "umbrella of air." (And it is precisely because the moon lacks such an "umbrella" that the moon is so dangerous.)

The teacher explained how our "umbrella of air" sets fire to flying rocks from outer space and burns them to dust, thus keeping them from slicing us to shreds.

The teacher showed how this blanket of air stabilizes our temperature, and keeps us from soaring to 250° by day, and plunging to 250° below zero at night—as we would on the moon.

Most amazing of all, perhaps, will be the realization that it is gravity that holds our "umbrella of air" over our heads, and thus, in the last analysis, we can thank gravity for the air we breathe!

In the previous chapter, you introduced your students to our "protective blanket" of air. In this chapter, you can help students find answers to such questions as: "Does air have weight?", "How much pressure does the air exert?"

The importance of this chapter in daily life becomes evident when we consider that every day on radio

5

How to Weigh Air

Photo courtesy of NASA

Photo 5. *Beyond our "thin sky" is the blackness of space. A striking view from Apollo 8 spacecraft showing nearly the entire Western Hemisphere.*

and TV the barometer readings are given. Yet how many people know how a barometer works? And what is meant by a reading of 29.9 inches?

Even less well known is the role air plays in the construction of tunnels under rivers and the building of foundations for bridges.

In this chapter, you can help your students realize why members of the Mt. Everest expedition, who finally conquered the 29,141-foot peak had to carry oxygen with them.

You will be able to show your students how they can measure their lung power, and actually calculate the pounds of pressure they can exert.

You can help students discover the reason why their ears ring or "pop" when they ride a fast elevator to the top of a tall building.

Still other questions you may explore with your students are: "How tall is the sky?", "Why do jet fighter pilots sometimes experience toothaches when they cruise through the tall sky?", "How does a barometer differ from an altimeter?"

You may begin your first class with the following:

> Look at pictures of planet earth taken from the moon. What do you notice?
>
> Since approximately 75 per cent of planet earth is covered with water, most of the photos show our planet as a sphere of blue, speckled with white clouds.
>
> As you and I look "up" from planet earth, we seem to be surrounded by a beautiful blue sky that appears to extend forever outward. Yet, in photos taken from the moon, the earth appears "lost" or "floating" in a void of utter black, darker than the darkest night.
>
> What happened to our sky? How "tall" or "thick" is our sky?
>
> Some folks think we live on top of the world. Actually, we live at the bottom of a great sea, a sea of air over 600 miles high and weighing more than 5 quadrillion (5 million billion) tons.
>
> When you cast a weather eye into the wide blue yonder, the air looks like a gauzy fabric spun of sapphire threads and turquoise gems. Who would ever imagine that all the blue ethereal sky is squeezing down on every square foot of your body with an overwhelming pressure of some 2016 pounds!
>
> The only reason you aren't flattened out with steamroller brusqueness is that air is also inside your body pushing out. The net result is an apparent sense of freedom. If someone were suddenly to remove all the air surrounding your body, you would explode like a keg of TNT. If you are built on a generous scale, a total force of 15 tons or more would blow your epidermis to the four winds of heaven.
>
> Scientists know that there is a thin sprinkling of air 100 miles above the earth because meteors burst into flame at this height, due to friction

HOW TO WEIGH AIR

with molecules of air. At some vague, undetermined spot the particles of air fade away like ghosts in the night. Beyond is the blackness of space. So thin is air in the upper regions of the atmosphere that, even though a few particles may be found 600 miles or so above sea level, half of the earth's atmosphere lies below 4 miles.

The first photograph ever made that showed the actual curvature of the earth was taken from a balloon, manned by two army officers, which rose to a height of 72,395 feet in 1935. Since, at the height of 13 miles, only 4 per cent of the earth's atmosphere was above the camera when the picture was taken, there was practically no dust or other substances to scatter and reflect sunlight. Consequently, the upper sky was very dark and showed up on the photograph as black.

"Trees that look at God all day" already knew that air thins out with increasing height. Even wind-scarred warrior pines that cling with taloned roots on rocky crags, high to the sun, call a halt to their mountain climbing at timberline, some 10,000 to 12,000 feet above sea level, where the oxygen is too thin to support their meager needs.

If you wish personal experience to convince you that most of the lung-worthy air hugs the earth like an onionskin, try climbing Mount Everest, the greatest mountain massif on the earth. Around 16,000 feet, higher than the loftiest peak in the Rockies, you enter a lifeless land—a region of everlasting snow where the air is crystal cold, dancing with frost and cutting as a scimitar. At 20,000 feet you are treading heights so rare that pilots flying at this altitude must breathe 50 per cent oxygen.

Still you climb. Only one living thing is with you still, the lammergeier, the bearded vulture of the Himalayas with a 9-foot wingspread. At 23,000 feet the bearded vulture falls behind, and you go on alone—up the last, long, frozen mile into the upper layers of the troposphere.

Thin air is enemy number one. The slightest exertion leaves you breathless as a roller coaster. At 28,000 feet an axelike headache splits your head. Exhaustion drains your strength, leaving you weak as an amoeba. Your face and lips turn blue as poker chips. Your frostbitten fingers stiffen around the handle of your ice axe in a deathlike grip. Your heart pounds like a kettledrum. It is 40 degrees below zero, and a 50-mile-an-hour gale is shrieking across the peak's cap of reddish-yellow rock, kept bare by constant wind.

Sir Edmund Hillary and "Tiger" Tenzing climbed where eagles fail to soar. Using oxygen tanks to keep alive, they struggled up the 29,002-foot peak and stood on top of the world's highest mountain, whose oxygen-starved peaks are honed by razor-cold winds sharpened on glaciers and ice caps 5 miles in the sky.

The deep blue of the sky extends upwards for only some 12 miles. Beyond this it fades into dark violets and deeper purples. Around 20 miles high, the blackness of space encompasses you, and you can see the stars at high noon.

Is thin air always a disadvantage? No, for the same thin air that proves a drawback to mountaineers is a boon to astronomers. Astronomical observatories are constructed at heights where thin, dustless air allows greater visibility. Shimmering pencils of starlight are less distorted by the earth's atmosphere when the air is thin.

DEMONSTRATIONS

Upside-down glass

Cut a small square of light cardboard or stiff paper wide enough to cover the top of a glass. Fill the glass to the brim with water. Press the cardboard on top of the glass, making sure that it touches the rim all the way around. Now invert the glass and remove your hand. Air pressure pushing up against the paper should hold the water in the glass! (Just in case something goes wrong, I always do this experiment over an empty pan!)

5:1

Squashed container

Pour a little water into an empty 10-gallon can. Be sure to use one that has not contained any kind of flammable mixture. Place the can, uncovered, on a heater. After steam has spouted from the opening for about three minutes, remove the can from the heater and replace its cap to make an airtight seal. Pour cold water over the can to condense the steam and thus produce a partial vacuum. Atmospheric pressure will squeeze in the sides of the can with dramatic results.

Balloon on milk bottle

Blow up a balloon to the size of a tennis ball and tie it securely. Now light a scrap of paper and drop it into an empty milk bottle. As soon as the flame burns out, immediately place the balloon on top of the bottle. A partial vacuum will result as the air inside the bottle cools. Atmospheric pressure may force the balloon into the bottle.
For a variation of this demonstration, blow up the balloon to the size of a large grapefruit. When the partial vacuum is formed, the bal-

5:2

HOW TO WEIGH AIR

loon will be too large to go into the bottle. Watch what happens. Lift the portion of the balloon left outside. What happens?

Put water into an upside-down milk bottle!

Here is a demonstration that always thrills students.

Get a glass bowl about 5 inches wide and 4 inches deep. Pour in water to a depth of about 3 inches. Now take an empty milk bottle. Light a scrap of paper and drop it into the bottle. The very instant the fire goes out, turn the milk bottle upside down and submerge it (neck down) into the water, with the rim of the bottle almost touching the bottom of the glass bowl.

The burning paper consumes oxygen in the bottle. Since oxygen forms about $\frac{1}{5}$ of the air, a partial vacuum has thus been created. As the air inside the bottle cools and shrinks, this will also increase the vacuum. The air in the room, being at greater pressure, will now push water up inside the upside-down milk bottle. Dramatic proof, indeed, that air does exert pressure.

Here is an interesting variation of the above experiment. Insert a candle in a candleholder, and put it in the bottom of the dish. Better use a candle about 6 inches tall. If you do not have a candleholder, let hot wax fall on the dish and force the base of the candle into the melted wax. Pour water into the dish and light the candle. Now take the empty milk bottle, turn it upside down, and hold it over the candle, with the neck of the bottle close to the bottom of the dish. Notice how quickly the candle consumes the oxygen, and then see what happens.

Air pushes

For this experiment you may use a long-necked flask, an empty catsup

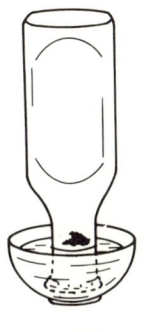

5:3

bottle, wine bottle, or Coke bottle. Simply fill it with water, then turn it upside down so that the rim of the flask is about $\frac{1}{16}$ inch above the bottom of the drinking glass. Students will be amazed to observe that even though the mouth of the flask is not pressed against the bottom of the glass, the water does not spill out. What then, is holding the water up in the flask?

To avoid making a mess, the best way to do this experiment is first to fill the flask with water, then place the drinking glass upside down over the neck of the flask, so that the bottom of the glass makes contact with the mouth of the flask, as shown.

Use your right hand to hold the glass firmly against the mouth of the flask. With your left hand, grasp the flask. Now, turn the entire unit around so that the flask is upside down with its neck inside the drinking glass.

5:4

5:5

Suction cup

Press a suction cup firmly against the smooth surface of the tabletop. Ask a student to come and lift up the cup.

If he is unable to do so, remind him that the only thing holding the cup against the table is "light air"! Can't he exert a force equal to that of the air?

Now slip a fingernail or knife blade under one side of the suction cup. Air rushes in to make the atmospheric pressure the same on both sides of the cup. Now the cup may be picked up with ease—a dramatic proof of the "push" exerted by air!

Two suction cups

Press two suction cups firmly together, and ask a student to pull them apart. Here is dramatic proof that our "thin" air is "heavy" enough to hold the cups together.

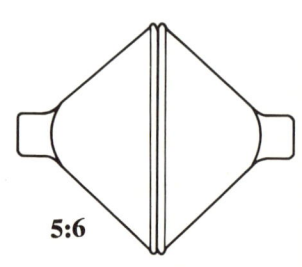

5:6

HOW TO WEIGH AIR

Snap board

In the days when oranges came in crates, I used to perform this experiment with the wood from the side of an orange crate. Perhaps you may still be able to obtain a similar thin piece of wood. If not, get a stiff piece of cardboard about 4 inches wide and 3 feet long.

Place the cardboard flat on the top of the table, so that about 6 inches of it sticks out over the end of the table. Cover the portion of the cardboard on the table with layers of newspapers. Be sure to smooth down the newspapers so that they make snug contact with the board and table.

Now, double up your fist, and with a rapid blow, strike the exposed part of the cardboard sticking out over the end of the table. Air pushing down on top of the newspapers holds the cardboard firmly against the table. Proof, again, that air exerts pressure.

If you were merely to push down on the portion of the cardboard extending out over the edge of the table with your thumb, you would raise the other end of the cardboard enough to allow air to flow in under the paper, and the board would not remain stationary. The sharp, sudden blow, however, makes use of Newton's First Law of Motion as well as the air pressure.

Holes that don't leak

Here is a novel use for an empty peanut butter jar. Use a thin nail or ice pick to punch a number of small-diameter holes in the lid. Now fill the jar with water, replace the lid, and turn it upside down. Note what happens. Even though the lid is full of holes, the water does not come spilling out. Air pressure holds the water up in the jar!

5:7

Pop you can't drink

Here is an experiment you can recommend each student try for himself next time he buys soda pop in a tin can. Punch only one medium-size hole in the lid. Put your lips around this opening, and see how much pop you can drink at one swallow. Even though you keep the can turned upside down above your mouth, you will soon find that no more pop comes out.

Mercury barometer

Here is an experiment to show students how to find just how much pressure the air exerts. Get a glass tube 1 inch in diameter and 36 inches long, closed at one end. Fill the tube with mercury. Now, holding your thumb over the open end, turn the tube upside down and immerse the open end in a bowl containing mercury. When you withdraw your thumb, some of the mercury will run out of the tube, but some 30 inches will remain, if you are at sea level.

What is holding up the 30 inches of mercury? It must be the pressure of the air on the mercury in the bowl.

Once again slip your thumb over the open end of the tube of mercury, lift it out of the dish or bowl, and let the mercury run into a container on a scale so that you may weigh it. The weight of the column of mercury 1 inch in diameter and 30 inches high equals 14.7 pounds. Since the air exerted enough pressure to hold up this column of mercury, we find that the air exerts a pressure of 14.7 pounds per square inch.

If you live in a mile-high city like Butte, Montana, or Denver, Colorado, you will find that the column of mercury will not stand 30 inches high. Dramatic proof of the fact that air pressure decreases with altitude!

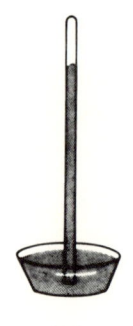

5:8

HOW TO WEIGH AIR

Measure your lung power

Students delight in testing their lung power with this apparatus.
Get a glass jar with a wide cork. Through the cork drill two holes. Into one hole insert a glass tube about 16 inches long, reaching almost to the bottom of the jar or bottle.
Into the second hole insert a smaller tube to which you fasten a small hose or rubber tubing. Fill the bottle to a depth of about 4 inches of mercury. Now let a student blow air through the hose. As he does, the increase of air pressure inside the jar pushes mercury up the long tube, which is set deep enough to be in contact with the mercury. Have a ruler handy so that students may measure the height to which they can push mercury up the tube.

5:9

What's on your head?

To find the force with which the air is pushing down on your head, remember that $Force = Pressure \times Area$.
Estimate the number of square inches on your head, and multiply by 14.7 pounds per square inch.
Since the words force and pressure will come up again and again, we may as well work some demonstrations to indicate what they mean.

Hatchet man

To demonstrate that pressure is force per unit area, or $Pressure = \frac{Force}{Area}$, I bring a hatchet to class and ask a student to stretch open his hand. I place the hatchet, flat side down, on the palm of his outstretched hand. The student experiences no discomfort, since the weight of the hatchet is distributed over a large area.
Now I take hold of the hatchet by the handle, and turn it sharp end down and carefully place the blade

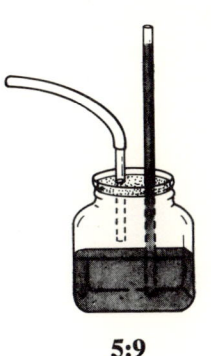

against the student's hand. This time he does feel discomfort. By decreasing the area, I thereby increased the pressure.

Look sharp, feel sharp

I bring a safety razor blade to class, and ask, "Will anyone here volunteer to hold your hand out while I press this blade against your skin with a force of 10 pounds?"

No one offers to help, so I continue, "Since no one is willing, I'll do the demonstration myself."

I place the blade with its broad, wide side face-down on the palm of my left hand. With my right thumb, I press down against the wide blade.

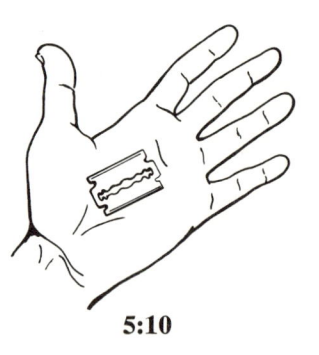

Then I ask, "Since the razor blade does not even cut my skin, how come no one was willing to volunteer for this demonstration?"

A student generally replies, "Because we thought you meant that you were going to push the sharp edge of the razor against our hand."

"What difference would this make?" I ask.

By now most students realize that the difference is due to the area. When the force is distributed over a large area, the pressure is small.

5:10

Get the point

With my right hand I pick up an ice pick by the sharp point, and hold it, handle-end down, about a foot above the open palm of my left hand.

I drop the ice pick. The broad, wide handle hits my palm, distributing the force over a wide area. I experience no trouble.

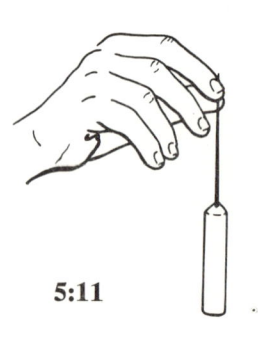

Now I pick up the ice pick by the handle, and keep the sharp end down. I inform the students that since I just dropped the ice pick into my hand, someone from the class should now volunteer to stretch out the palm of their hand,

5:11

HOW TO WEIGH AIR

so that I may drop the pick into it, sharp-end first.

Naturally, there are no "volunteers" so I ask, "Why not?"

By now most students "get the point" of this demonstration and realize that the smaller the area, the greater the pressure. This is a truly dramatic demonstration of the formula $Pressure = \dfrac{Force}{Area}$.

Pin head

Get a pin with a large glass head. Ask a student to push the pin into a little block of cork or softwood. Call attention to the fact that the *force* is the *same* at *both ends* of the pin. The sharp end of the pin, however, enters the cork, since it has a smaller area, and therefore exerts greater pressure.

Although the student's finger is made of soft flesh, the pin does not pierce it, since the big head of the pin distributes the force over a wide area, and thus decreases the pressure.

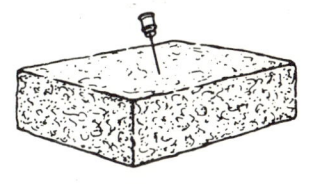

5:12

Ballerina

To demonstrate how pressure increases with a decrease in area, have a student stand before the class.

If he weighs 150 pounds and his two shoes cover a total of 50 square inches, the pressure on each square inch is 3 pounds.

Now have the student stand on one foot only. The area is cut in half. The pressure doubles, and goes up to 6 pounds per square inch.

If the student is wearing soft rubber shoes, and can balance on one big toe over an area of 1 square inch, the pressure soars to 150 pounds per square inch! A job for a ballerina. This makes a ballerina a "high-pressure job"!

Barometer becomes altimeter

Many homes today have inexpensive aneroid barometers. If you live near the mountains, ask the students to take their aneroid barometer with them on the next trip they take up into the mountains. If you live in a city with skyscrapers, ask students to take the barometer with them the next time they take the elevator to the top floor. Observe what happens.

During the first 1000 feet of rise, the barometer will fall about an inch. The drop per 1000 feet becomes less and less as the height increases because the air becomes less dense.

A barometer can, therefore, be used to measure altitude. Under such conditions it is known as an altimeter. The dials are marked in feet.

Can you draw soda through a straw?

When some people put a straw into a soda, they think they "draw" or "pull up" the liquid into their mouth. Actually, all they do is remove the air from the straw. The atmospheric pressure on the liquid pushes it up into their mouth.

To prove it, make a small hole in the top of a can of soda pop. Through the hole insert a soda straw or glass tube. Now pour melted wax around the place where the straw enters the lid, so as to make an airtight seal.

Now place your mouth over the straw and see how much of the soda you can "draw" or "pull" into your mouth. As soon as air pressure inside the can decreases, you will find that no matter how hard you try, no more soda comes.

Now punch a second hole in the lid. Suddenly it is easy to get the soda through the straw. Air entering through the second hole pushes

5:13

HOW TO WEIGH AIR

the liquid up the straw into your mouth!

Hypodermic syringe

Your doctor most likely will be able to give you a used hypodermic syringe. It will make an interesting demonstration to illustrate the "lifting power" of air.

Push in the plunger as far as it will go. Now place the needle in a glass of water. So that the process may be more clearly seen, a couple of drops of ink may be added to the water.

Now pull out on the plunger. As you do so, liquid rises up inside the syringe. The air in the room is pushing on the water in the glass, and forcing it or "lifting it" up inside the syringe.

How high will air "lift" water?

Answer—until the weight of the water equals the pressure exerted by the air. When air pressure is 14.7 pounds it will lift water 34 feet.

5:14

Conclusion

We are surrounded by an ocean of air that pushes down on us from all sides. At sea level this pressure is 14.7 pounds per square inch, enough to lift a column of water to a height of 34 feet.

Our blue sky seems to extend outward into space without limit or boundary, yet half of the earth's atmosphere lies below 4 miles. At a height of some 12 miles, the blue sky fades into deeper purples. At some 20 miles, the blackness of space surrounds you.

FOLLOW-UP EXERCISES

1. Explain why your ears "ring" or "pop" when your car climbs a mountain road or when you ride an elevator to the top of a tall building.
   Hint: *As you go higher the air pressure on the outside of your eardrum falls off. Air trapped on the inside of the eardrum pushes out.*
2. Explain why balloons are sent up into the sky only partially inflated.
   Hint: *Atmospheric pressure decreases with height. As the*

atmospheric pressure falls off, the pressure of the gas inside the balloon makes it expand more and more until the balloon is fully inflated.

If the balloon were fully inflated at ground level, then, as it rose to great heights where atmospheric pressure is low, the gas inside the balloon would expand so much it would break the balloon.

3. Explain what is meant by "aerodontalgia."

Aerodontalgia is a fancy scientific way of saying "a toothache at high altitudes." The Air Force can hardly ground a man because he has a tooth filled. Yet one tooth may conceal a hidden air pocket, painless on the ground, but excruciatingly painful up in the high sky. Dentists are finding that toothache at high altitudes is becoming a serious health problem for pilots. A flyer at takeoff may feel great as far as his teeth are concerned. But let him sail up into the wide blue yonder and a change in atmospheric pressure may give him a painful toothache.

4. Does a vacuum cleaner really clean your rugs?

No, it simply takes away the air from the top side of your rug. The air on the underside of the rug then rushes upward, carrying the dirt with it.

5. Who exerts greater pressure on the ground, an elephant or a girl wearing needle-like heels?

A 120-pound woman wearing a steel-shaft type of heel with a surface area of 0.0276 square inches can exert as much as 3500 pounds of pressure per square inch. The pressure developed under an elephant's foot is only 50 to 100 pounds per square inch.

The Louvre and all other state-owned museums in France have banned stiletto heels to save their floors and carpets. Women touring the sites must wear flat shoes or rent plastic slippers at 25 cents per tour.

By contrast, a 25-ton British tractor exerts a pressure of only 2 pounds per square inch. *Reason*—wide tracks that distribute the weight over a large area.

6. What is the weight of the air pushing down on the floor of your classroom?

Hint: *Estimate the length and width of your classroom. Remembering that the pressure of the air is 14.7 pounds per square inch, figure out the force of air pushing on the floor.*

7. How did Denver's rarefied air affect the U.S. Open Championship golf tournament?

A golf ball hit at mile-high Denver travels up to 10 per cent farther than those hit at sea level. As a result contestants found themselves overestimating yardages. The thin air also caused some players to run short of breath, and sit down on fairways to recover. Tanks of oxygen were made available for those in distress.

8. Why were the Olympics in October of 1968 referred to as "Mexico's Breathless Olympics"?

Hint: *Mexico City rests on a plain that is 7349 feet high, almost 1½ miles above sea level. A breath of air at this altitude contains approximately 25 per cent less oxygen than one at sea level. The "invisible enemy" never before encountered in the history of the Olympic Games was "thin air." Many athletes found themselves "starving" for oxygen long before they pounded down the homestretch of a long-distance run. There was the dreadful sight of the great Australian distance runner, Ron Clarke, gray as dust, an oxygen mask pressed to his face as he lay unconscious by the track for 10 minutes after the 10,000 meters on the first day of competition.*

Summary

In this chapter, the teacher explored with the student the invisible ocean of air in which we live and demonstrated the fact that air exerts pressure.

By means of a mercury barometer, the teacher showed how to measure the weight of the air. With the help of an ice pick, razor blade, and hatchet, the teacher demonstrated the difference between pressure and force.

Finally, the teacher considered various applications of air pressure, ranging from "aerodontalgia" to "Mexico's Breathless Olympics."

6

Increasing Our Knowledge of Weather

The importance of this chapter becomes evident when we realize that "Everybody is talking about the weather." Therefore, to talk about it intelligently, we should know something about it.

You can draw on the personal experience of your students to impress them with the importance of weather in our lives. Fog can shut down airports. Ice-slick highways can increase the number of automobile accidents. A sudden

Photo courtesy of Union Pacific Railroad

Photo 6. *The peaks of the majestic Teton mountains in Wyoming are partly mantled by scarfs of condensed water vapor, alias, the clouds.*

INCREASING OUR KNOWLEDGE OF WEATHER

shower can dampen rye sandwiches on a Sunday afternoon picnic. Swirling snow can bring city traffic to a virtual standstill.

Every day on the radio we hear weather reports, yet how many of your students understand exactly what is meant?

Ask one of your pupils, "Does a report of 50 per cent humidity in the summer mean exactly the same as a 50 per cent reading in the winter?" "Is it true that the only place more dry than the Sahara is apt to be your home in the winter?" "What happens to moisture in the air when the temperature drops?"

In this chapter you will be able to work a demonstration to make it "rain" in the classroom. And you will be able to use ping-pong balls to illustrate how moisture "drops out" of the atmosphere.

Show your class a map of California; then ask, "How come Death Valley is so dry, even in winter, when not too many miles distant, the western slopes of the Sierra Nevadas have an annual average snowfall of 527 inches?"

You may begin your first class with the following:

> Does it ever "rain" in your basement? When was the last time you had a room full of clouds?
>
> The truth is that whether your address is Westby, Wisconsin or Buxton, Montana, your home is a "weather station" in which you can not only "watch" weather but also "make" it.
>
> It is also a "science lab" where you can duplicate the dripping dampness of an Amazon jungle, the parched dry sands of the Sahara, and the fog-smothered banks of Newfoundland.
>
> Look briefly at some of the ways that Nature makes weather, then see how we may duplicate some of these conditions on a limited scale in our homes and in the classroom.
>
> Scientists have learned that large bodies of air, called air masses, are responsible for changes in weather. The atmosphere may remain still for several days over a certain region. During this period, the atmosphere acquires conditions of temperature and humidity that characterize the land or water over which the air mass is developing. An air mass that originates over land near one of the poles is cold and dry; one that comes from the low-latitude waters of the oceans is warm and moist.
>
> Once an air mass has been built up, it begins to move. Although it may be changed in some ways by the land or water over which it passes, the air tends to hold whatever properties it had at its origin.
>
> An air mass that originates over the land is called a continental air mass; one that originates over water is known as a maritime air mass. The three principal air masses that control weather in the United States are: the continental polar air mass (abbreviated cP on weather maps), the maritime polar air mass (mP), and the maritime tropical air mass (mT).
>
> The great expanse of land stretching northward from Hudson Bay to

the Arctic Ocean—an icebox region that takes in almost all of upper Canada—is the breeding ground of continental polar air that is dry as gunpowder and cold as midnight on Mars. As this mass of cold air moves south and east, lumbering like a polar bear with icicles dripping from its jaws, warnings of colder weather are posted in the plains states, the region around the Great Lakes, and the Atlantic seaboard. In summer, the continental polar air mass brings the dry, cool air that refreshes heat-frazzled spirits.

Continental polar air masses generally restrict their "stamping grounds" to the lands east of the Rockies, but occasionally steel-cold daggers of freezing air stab through the mountain passes of California and plunge toward the orange groves. Forewarned by the Weather Bureau, the growers scurry to light the smudge pots in an effort to protect the delicate orange and lemon trees with a blanket of warm air.

The west coast usually gets its weather from the second type of air mass, the maritime polar air. Although this air may be bitter cold and stone dry when it leaves distant Siberia or chilly Alaska, it becomes warmer and gathers moisture as it passes over the waters of the Pacific. This air mass brings the winter rains to the west coast and keeps summer temperatures at a comfortable level. Maritime polar air masses that develop over the cold waters of the North Atlantic bring storms and gales that New Englanders call northeasters.

The third type of air mass, the maritime tropical air, originates over sultry outposts of the equator. As it moves northward and eastward, it picks up moisture from the Caribbean Sea and the Gulf of Mexico. The muggy air creeps up the Mississippi and its tributaries, causing the populace from Saint Louis to New York to mop moist foreheads as they yearn for continental polar air to restore comfort to their warm, humidity-packed atmosphere.

More than any other state, California is a region of contrasts. The reason becomes clear when you study a relief map of this state—one that shows the different elevations (heights) of a surface by shadings or colorings.

As the warm, moisture-heavy maritime polar air that floats eastward approaches the towering peaks of the Cascade Mountains and the Sierra Nevadas, it must rise in order to get over the mountains. Air is cooled as it rises so clouds form, and at higher elevations there is rain. If the mountains are high enough snow falls. Tons of moisture are dumped on luxurious forests of giant redwoods, lordly fir, spruce, and pine. The deepest snows in the United States are found on the western slopes of the Sierra Nevadas. Here the average snowfall each winter is 527 inches (43 feet, 11 inches). No wonder such green, lush forests thrive in these regions.

Finally the air mass reaches the eastern brink of the lofty mountains. Now it plunges down the slopes, sometimes reaching speeds of 4000 feet per minute. When a wind roars down a mountain it becomes warmer and takes whatever moisture it can from land that is already bone dry and parched. Thus the region east of the mountains is very dry, in spots a desert. In southeast California and Arizona, the climate is so warm that

INCREASING OUR KNOWLEDGE OF WEATHER

dates and similar desert crops are grown. In Death Valley, California, the driest spot in the United States and third driest in the world, the temperature has reached 134 degrees Fahrenheit. To the east of Death Valley is Nevada, which has an average rainfall of 8.81 inches only. By contrast, at Monumental in the extreme northwest of California the average rainfall is 109 inches per year.

To understand why warm air can hold more water than cooler air, think of the molecules of air as teams of volleyball players, the molecules of water as volleyballs. If the players are active, they keep the volleyball bouncing in the air. Warm and active air molecules can keep water molecules bouncing like volleyballs. But when the air molecules grow cold and slow down, they can no longer keep many water molecules in action. If you have active volleyball teams, the ball stays in the air. Once the players slow down, the ball will fall to the ground.

The capacity of the air to hold water depends primarily upon the temperature. The higher the temperature of the air, the more water it can hold. As the air cools off, the molecules of air are less active and can keep fewer molecules of water in suspension. Thus at 85° Fahrenheit, 1 cubic yard of air can hold approximately 1 ounce of water vapor; at 50°, it can hold only ⅓ of an ounce. If air is holding all the water it can at a certain temperature, it is said to be saturated.

The amount of moisture in the air is usually expressed in terms of *relative humidity*, which is the ratio between the amount of water vapor actually present in air compared to the amount that air at that temperature can hold. If air is saturated—that is, contains all the moisture that is possible—the relative humidity is 100 per cent. Suppose that the temperature is 50° and there is ⅓ ounce of water in each cubic yard of air. The relative humidity is 100 per cent because that is all the moisture that air can hold at that temperature.

If the air warms to 85°, it may still contain the same amount of water. However, since air at this temperature is capable of holding a full ounce of water vapor, the relative humidity is 33 per cent. Should the temperature fall below 50°, the amount of water that the air can hold will be less than ⅓ ounce. The extra moisture then condenses into visible water vapor, forming dew, clouds, fog, rain, sleet, or snow.

When the relative humidity is 100 per cent, the air molecules can pick up no more moisture. Hence, if you perspire, the moisture will stay on your noble brow, trickle down your cheeks, and cascade off your nose. You feel as sticky as flypaper because there is little evaporation of moisture from the skin. Even a relative humidity of 80 per cent is very oppressive on a hot summer day.

The number of ounces of water present in 1 cubic yard of air is called the *absolute humidity*. For example, the absolute humidity might be ⅓ of an ounce per cubic yard.

The ratio of the quantity of water vapor actually present in any volume of air to the quantity required to saturate the same volume of air at the same temperature is called the *relative humidity*.

Suppose the air at 85° Fahrenheit contains ⅓ ounce of water

vapor. But if the air at 85° Fahrenheit were fully saturated it could hold 1 ounce. Therefore the relative humidity $= \frac{1}{3} = 33$ per cent.

The temperature at which water vapor in the air begins to condense is called the *dew point*. The relative humidity has reached 100 per cent and the air can hold no more moisture. The dew point might be called the debut, or first appearance, of a droplet. It is the magic moment when water steps from the invisible world of vapor to make its appearance in various forms.

When air reaches the dew point, water vapor condenses to form tiny droplets of water—about 1/1000 (0.001) of an inch in diameter. Large numbers of these droplets are suspended in a cloud. Whenever you walk in a fog, you are traveling in a cloud, for a fog is a cloud that is formed close to the ground. Droplets of water only 0.001 inch in diameter are so tiny that they float in the air. If they increase from 0.001 to 0.002 inch in diameter they fall gently to the earth from low clouds as a drizzle. Under certain conditions, the droplets grow more rapidly in size and form drops that are large enough to fall as rain. Raindrops vary greatly in size and in the speed with which they fall to the ground. Large drops fall faster than small drops. To be classified as rain, the drop must fall at the rate of at least 10 feet per second.

DEMONSTRATIONS

Rain in the classroom

To make it "rain" in your classroom, all you have to do is employ the same technique that nature does—cool off a batch of moist, warm air until the moisture falls out.

Put a kettle of water on an electric heater. After the water has been boiling for a few minutes, or even before, remove the lid and notice big drops of water falling from the underside of the lid. Hot, moisture-laden air hitting the colder surface of the metal is condensed to form tiny "raindrops" that fall back into the water.

6:1

"Sweaty" glass

On a hot, humid day in early September, or late May, place a tall glass of ice-cold water on the desk. Note how the outside of the glass "sweats" or drips with moisture. As moist, warm air hits the cold glass, it cools and condenses.

INCREASING OUR KNOWLEDGE OF WEATHER

Foggy mirror

Ask a student to hold a small hand mirror next to his mouth and exhale. Ask him to account for the formation of the film of moisture on the glass.

Ping-pong "rain"

I use a ping-pong ball, tennis ball, or any other handy sphere to demonstrate why it rains. I tell the students to think of the ping-pong ball as a molecule of water. My hands represent air molecules. I pick up the ball, and toss it gently into the air, from one hand to another, back and forth, back and forth.

As long as the "air molecules" (my hands) are "active" they can keep the "water molecule" (the ball) bouncing in the air. But if the "air molecules" slow down, or stop, the "water molecule" falls down. To demonstrate the conclusion, I stop my hands and the ball drops to the table, indicating the fate of a water molecule when air molecules cool and slow down. Moisture "drops" out of the air!

Polar breeze

Obtain a small block of dry ice. Hold it by a tongs or towel to prevent injury to your fingers. Place the block of dry ice on top of a globe of the earth. If no globe is handy, use a basketball, bowl, or any available sphere. Note how the white, "smoking" vapor given off by the dry ice spreads southwards toward the equator. This illustrates how the United States would always have a northern breeze and cold arctic air would always flow toward the equator if the earth did not rotate.

Every wind, whether it is a gentle zephyr, or giant gale shrieking down from the north, is caused by *convection*—the motion of a gas caused by unequal heating.

As the blazing sun beats down upon

6:2

the equator, the earth, water, and air above it are heated to a higher temperature than elsewhere. The warm air expands and rises, and cooler air from regions north and south of the equator moves in to take the place of the warmed air.

If the earth did not rotate, the warm air would divide high in the sky and move towards the poles. Slowly it would cool and sink. A surface wind of cold air, from the north in the Northern Hemisphere, and from the south in the Southern Hemisphere, would blow over the land. But since the earth rotates, there are trade winds which move from northeast to southwest near the equator. Farther north the river of descending air becomes the prevailing westerlies.

Baby-size thermal

To let students see a neat, little thermal, simply light a match, then blow it out. The rising column of smoke is a tidy convection current. The word thermal comes from the Greek word "thermes" meaning "heat." Thermals occur because warm air weighs less than a similar volume of cold air. Smoke from chimneys and smokestacks rise because of convection currents. The warmer, lighter air is forced up the chimney by the cold air rushing in at the bottom.

Conclusion

Our "blanket" of air contains water vapor which can be "squeezed" or "forced" out by a drop in temperature. You can "squeeze" the moisture out of steam coming from a teakettle by letting it hit a cold metal lid, thus dropping its temperature and causing it to "rain."

Absolute humidity is simply a *statement* of the *quantity* of water vapor actually present.

Relative humidity is a *comparison* between what is, and what could be.

INCREASING OUR KNOWLEDGE OF WEATHER

Suppose that on August 15th there were 15 grams of water vapor per cubic meter of air. This is the absolute humidity. It can be measured by the number of grams of water vapor present in 1 cubic meter of air, or in ounces per cubic yard.

Now suppose that on August 30th the temperature is 86° F. At this temperature, if the air were saturated, it could hold 30 grams of water per cubic meter. Hence, the air contains only 15/30 or 1/2 of what it could hold at that temperature. The relative humidity, therefore, is 50 per cent.

Now take the first day of December, when the temperature may be 32° Fahrenheit. Suppose the absolute humidity is 2.4 grams of water vapor per cubic meter.

But if the air were saturated at 32° Fahrenheit it could hold 4.8 grams of water vapor per cubic meter. Hence the air contains only 2.4/4.8 or 1/2 of what it could hold at that temperature. The relative humidity, therefore, is 50 per cent.

Here, now, is a most important point to remember. On both August 15th and December 1st the relative humidity was the same. But there was much more water vapor in the air on August 15th. The absolute humidity was higher on that day—even though both days had the same relative humidity!

Now, perhaps, you know why the air in the ordinary home in winter is more dry than the Sahara.

To continue with the above example, suppose that on December 1st there are only 2.4 grams of water vapor per cubic meter of air. You turn on your furnace and heat this air until it is 76° Fahrenheit. But at 76° Fahrenheit if the air were saturated, it could hold 22 grams of water vapor per cubic meter. Hence, the air contains only 2.4/22 of what it could hold at that temperature. I'll leave it up to you to figure out the relative humidity.

For comparison, remember that the average relative humidity of the air over the Sahara is about 33 per cent, and in Death Valley about 20 per cent.

FOLLOW-UP EXERCISES

1. List a number of thermals you have seen.
   Hints: *When you blow out candles on a birthday cake, rising thermals count the burned-out years. A slice of bread stuck in a toaster sends up a black thermal to signal distress. Watch grandpa smoking his Havana. Smoke rising lazily from the cigar is an aromatic thermal delightful to behold.*

2. Can you name a favorite Christmas centerpiece for the dining room table that works by means of thermals?
   Hint: *It is the "Angel Carousel." Light four little candles and a trio of little angels gracefully take wing to the chimes of singing bells. Pierced metal fins revolve from candle heat, and spin the carousel—music-making thermals!*
3. How does a thermal help keep you alive?
   Hint: *Without thermals and convection currents, you would be suffocated in a blanket of carbon-dioxide gas of your own creation. Fortunately, the warm gas you exhale from your nose rises as a thermal, allowing a supply of cool, fresh air to bring you needed oxygen.*
4. How do thermals help keep food fresh in your refrigerator?
   Hint: *In your refrigerator, air that comes in contact with the freezing unit in the top of the box becomes heavier and sinks to the bottom, forcing the warm air upward and setting up convection currents. When the cold air comes in contact with the food, heat passes from the food into the air, and rises as a thermal. The thermal continues upward until it meets the freezing unit where the air is cooled, and the cycle continues.*
5. Have you ever been kissed by a thermal?
   Yes, if you have a hot air furnace in your home, and you stand by the register on a January day to be caught up in the warm embrace of a thermal.
6. Is it possible to "ride a thermal"?
   Yes—if you wish to glide through the air with the greatest of ease, hook a ride on a thermal with a glider or sailplane.
   Warm air rising over stretches of white sand, and along the seashore, heated by the beaming rays of the sun, provides thermals or updrafts. Over 5000 registered glider pilots speak with glowing enthusiasm of this type of motorless flying that is made possible by thermals.
   Thermals can also provide some extra "thrills" for regular pilots. When a new volcanic cone burst out in flaming fury from Kilauea in Hawaii, an enthusiastic photographer decided to get some aerial pictures. He flew some 500 feet above the leaping fountain of fire in a Piper Cub. Each time the plane staggered through the updrafts of hot, sulphurous gas, it jumped frantically, pushed about by thermals rising from the bubbling pit of bright-red lava.
7. How did thermals smash a dream once cherished for the Empire State Building in New York City?
   Thermals are responsible for the fact that one of the world's most expensive dreams did not come true.

INCREASING OUR KNOWLEDGE OF WEATHER 93

Few sightseers on New York's Fifth Avenue, tilting their heads back to get a view of the top of the Empire State Building, realize that the last 205 feet of that immense building is a steel enshrouded tower originally designed as a mooring mast for transatlantic airships. On the 101st floor, where today's observation platform is located, passengers were expected to cross a narrow gangway leading into the nose of a big airship (either a "zeppelin" or "blimp") to begin their flight across the ocean to Europe.

No airship ever moored atop the Empire State Building, although two made a try at it. Tremendous thermals or updrafts rising from Manhattan's concrete canyons made it impossible to maneuver the airship into position.

8. Is it true that there are thermals in the Grand Canyon?

Yes—instead of using chimneys, nature uses canyons to produce updrafts and downdrafts of tremendous proportions. The sun beats down on steep rocky walls. The rocks, in turn, heat the air, which rises in one place to produce a thermal, and thus cause a downdraft in some other section.

A few years ago a United Airlines DC-7 crashed into a TWA Constellation. Both planes fell into a remote spot in Grand Canyon accessible only by helicopter. All attempts at rescue operations had to be abandoned during the hot afternoon when violent updrafts from Grand Canyon made approach by helicopter impossible.

9. Does it ever "rain" in your house?

On an August afternoon it may "rain" in your basement, even though your roof is leak-proof and there isn't a cloud in the sky!

Warm, muggy, moisture-heavy air comes into contact with cold water pipes. The moisture condenses out of the atmosphere and gathers like beads of sweat along the pipes. When the drops of water get big enough, they fall from the pipes like rain.

And December may do more than bring Santa down your chimney. It may bring a cloud into your house!

Take a hot shower, and you may soon find yourself "lost" in a cloud of condensed vapor. When the walls of the bathroom are cold, so much "rain" may "fall out" of this cloud that the walls, window, and mirror drip with beads of H_2O.

10. How can you create a miniature "Death Valley" in your house?

When you drop a slice of bread into the electric toaster, you use scorching heat from burning hot coils to drive moisture out of the bread, and turn it dry as desert sand, and parched as an ember— if you leave it there too long!

11. Write a composition on: "Our City Depends Upon Convection Currents."

Hint: *When no wind blows, our sprawling industrial cities* *can be blacked out in an evil, gas-filled blanket of smog. In October 1948 in Stan Musial's boyhood town, Donora, Pennsylvania, 20 people died because of air pollution, and 5900 were made ill.*

12. Poets often take liberties with scientific facts. Read Shelley's "The Cloud," a lovely inspiring poem you will cherish. After reading it for enjoyment, make a list of the statements with which you agree and a list of other statements which you might consider misleading.
13. In the winter you may see little thermals of your own creation. As you exhale, your moist breath forms little white balloons that go soaring skywards.

Summary

In this chapter, the teacher helped students increase their knowledge of weather. The teacher showed students how to make it "rain" in the classroom. With the help of a relief map, the teacher showed the correlation between geography and rainfall. With a ping-pong ball the teacher demonstrated why moisture drops out of the atmosphere.

Together with the students, the teacher investigated the difference between absolute and relative humidity.

The teacher urged students to explore a whole new world of their own—a world of "homemade" weather to be found within the walls of their own homes—everything from thermals from birthday candles to "sweaty," ice-cold lemonade glasses, dripping cold water pipes, fog-filled bathrooms, and smoke signals rising from the toaster.

To emphasize the importance of this chapter, you may remind your students of the words of Robert Taber, manager of Westinghouse's Marine Systems Engine-

7

Establishing the Importance of Oceanography and Its Potential Value to Your Students

Photo courtesy of General Electric Research Laboratory

Photo 7. *This "aqua-hamster," penned in a submerged plastic tank, is kept alive by an artificial "gill"—a special synthetic membrane stretched across the top, bottom, and two sides of its underwater home. The "gill" extracts air from the surrounding water, while resisting the passage of the liquid. Carbon dioxide exhaled by the hamster passes out through the membrane, dissolves in the water, and is carried away. Without the "gill," the animal would suffocate. Since sea water is essentially saturated with air to a depth of many hundreds of feet, an artificial "gill" made from the new silicone-rubber membrane could furnish air for the crew of a submarine or the inhabitants of an underwater experimental station.*

ering Division: "At our present population growth rate, the earth's land mass will not be able to support the 7 billion people projected for the year 2000.

"The sea, which covers ¾ of the earth's surface is virtually unexplored, and will become our most important source of food and chemicals."

Other oceanography enthusiasts are sounding a more ominous note, "Man will have to learn to exploit the ocean's depths if he is to survive on this planet."

Show your students pictures of planet earth taken from the moon, or from the orbiting Gemini spacecraft, and they will be able to see why we are justified in speaking of our planet as "Planet Water." Our earth, alone among the planets, is dominated by its water.

You may spark interest by asking your students these intriguing questions: "Despite the success of Sealab, why does man remain a frail alien in the sea?"

"What does a pop bottle with its cap just removed have in common with a person who has the bends?"

"What do sea divers call 'the squeeze'?"

You will be able to work a demonstration to find out the weight of a student's hand, and also calculate the buoyant force of the displaced liquid.

You can help your students investigate problems such as: "Can you find your weight by stepping into a boat?", "Is it possible to build a bridge of concrete that will float?", "Why do whales often die when they are washed up on beaches?", "What is the biggest 'enemy' to underwater exploration?"

Your first class may begin with the following:

> You can't walk on 75 per cent of the earth. Planet earth is almost drowned in water. The great Pacific Ocean alone stretches over almost half the earth. Take a look at a globe from a position over the South Pole. Blue waters of the Pacific, Atlantic, and Indian oceans spread out in all directions from Antarctica.
>
> The average depth of the sea is 2 miles, about 10,000 feet, although in some places the ocean floor drops off to 5 or 6 miles and more. The Pacific Ocean falls away to a depth of 34,578 feet in the Philippine Trench off the Philippine Islands. Near the island of Guam in the Marianas the ocean tumbles 35,800 feet into the Mariana Trench.
>
> If Mount Everest, the highest mountain, were set down in the deepest part of the Pacific Ocean, its pinnacle would disappear a mile below the surface of the water. Actually, the greatest mountain on earth is not Mount Everest; it is the volcanic Mauna Kea in the Hawaiian Islands. The peak of this volcano rises over 13,000 feet in the air; its base lies on the ocean floor, more than 17,000 feet below the surface.

Water pressure increases with depth. Since 1 cubic foot of water weighs 62.4 pounds, at a depth of 10 feet, there would be a pressure of 624 pounds per square foot.

In the 7-mile depths of the Challenger Deep of the Pacific Ocean the water pressure is an overwhelming 7 tons per square inch. So tremendous is this pressure that even water, which is almost incompressible, is reduced in volume.

Water also pushes up. This upward force of water, which acts against gravity, is called *buoyancy*. You have seen objects floating on water; perhaps you have done so yourself on a summer afternoon. Long ago a Greek mathematician named Archimedes discovered that an object immersed in water is pushed upward by a force equal to the weight of the water displaced by the object. *You float because you displace your own weight in water; that is, you push aside enough water so that it can hold you up.*

If you should be taking a swim in Great Salt Lake, you will float with about ⅛ of your body above water. Its salt-filled waters are much more dense than fresh water.

Puget Sound has been called the world's biggest sawmill pond. Through its blue waters towboats guide huge rafts of fir logs. Each log demonstrates *Archimedes' Principle,* for it pushes aside or displaces a certain volume of water which is equal to the weight of the log. If half the log is submerged, the wood is approximately half as heavy as water. Sometimes a piece of wood is left in the water so long that it becomes waterlogged. When it can no longer float on the surface it submerges and may float out of sight.

Did you ever lift a heavy rock underwater, only to find you could hardly budge it when you got it on the shore?

If the rock is 1 cubic foot in volume, for example, it pushes aside 1 cubic foot of water. Since 1 cubic foot of water weighs 62.4 pounds, this is the force that pushes up on the rock when it is in the water. This upward force is buoyancy. As a result the rock seems to weigh 62.4 pounds less when it is in the water than it actually does when it is moved to shore, for it is buoyed up by a force equal to the weight of the displaced water.

A ship floats because the volume of water it displaces weighs the same as that of the ship and cargo. The luxury liner *United States* has a displacement of 53,000 tons, which means that it displaces or pushes aside some 53,000 tons of water.

If a freight train is backing into a railroad yard, all the engine has to do is push the first car. The movement is handed on to all the other cars in turn. Liquids are something like freight trains; when they are enclosed in a container they pass on or transmit any force or pressure applied to them.

Water ordinarily cannot be compressed as air can; any force applied to the water is passed on to all the water in the container. The French scientist Blaise Pascal expressed the law that bears his name in the following way: *the pressure exerted on a confined liquid is transmitted undiminished in all directions.*

Suppose there is a jugful of water and the inside area of the jug is 50 square inches. Suppose the cork is fitting snugly in the top of the bottle, and pushing against the water underneath it. What would happen if someone hit the cork with a pressure of 20 pounds per square inch?

Immediately this pressure would leap throughout the enclosed liquid and push on each of the 50 square inches in the jug with that same pressure of 20 pounds per square inch.

Since the jug has an area of 50 square inches, this means that the total force pushing against the glass walls would be 1000 pounds. The glass jug would shatter, so, please, *read about this experiment only; don't even attempt it.* You may slice open your hand on the jagged glass.

The ocean depths are called the last unexplored frontier on earth. Men who explore these new frontiers are called "aquanauts" or "seamen" or "oceanides."

Proponents of the undersea life point out that putting a man in the sea is even more intriguing than sending him to the moon. "The aquanaut is a free man, not a man in a tin can," says Dr. Greshon Weltman, oceanographer at the University of California at Los Angeles. "The payoff can be immense, and we—many of us—can take a personal part in opening up the new frontier."

The greatest enemy in this new underwater world is pressure. Every time you go down a foot in water, the pressure increases by approximately ½ pound per square inch. At only 45 fathoms (1 fathom is 6 feet), a pressure of some 155 pounds beats in on every square inch of your body.

The main trouble arises from the behavior of gases under pressure. Close the hose end of a bicycle pump, then push down on the handle. The greater the pressure with which you push, the smaller the volume. *Boyle's Law* sums up the matter nicely by saying that *the volume of a gas at any given temperature decreases in direct proportion to the increase in pressure.*

The next time you go swimming, take a toy balloon with you. Blow it up until the balloon is about 6 inches in diameter, then swim with it under water as deep as you can. What do you notice about the volume of the balloon? (If the inflated balloon makes it difficult for you to submerge, tie a big rock to it.)

Did you ever look down into a clear lake and watch bubbles rising from some decaying matter on the bottom? As the bubbles rise, they get bigger and bigger. Why?

Because water pressure decreases with decrease in depth. As the pressure decreases, the gas expands.

Watch how air bubbles from an air hose in the bottom of an aquarium are quite small at first, but grow larger and larger as they rise towards the surface. Why?

Because once again, water pressure decreases with decrease in depth. Since the pressure is less, the gas expands, and the bubbles get bigger.

You may even observe Boyle's Law at work when you remove the cap from a bottle of pop. Hold the bottle up to the light and notice the tiny bubbles that start off from the bottom, increase in size as they rise to the top, and then leap into the air.

No doubt you know that the fizz of soda pop is due to the fact that gas (carbon dioxide) is forced into it under pressure. The English scientist William Henry discovered that the *amount of a gas that will dissolve in a liquid at a given temperature is directly proportional to the partial pressure of the gas.* When you take the cap off the bottle of soda pop, this releases the pressure inside the bottle, and allows the CO_2 to come out of solution in the form of tiny bubbles. The fizzing action may be so violent it spews all over the place.

How does all this apply to a diver?

Suppose you strap on your scuba outfit and dive to 33 feet. At this depth, the water pressure pushing in on you is 2 atmospheres, or twice the pressure of the air at sea level. The air in your lungs is squeezed to ½ its original volume. How can you avoid the painful pressure of this squeeze?

Fortunately the scuba diver has a clever valve mechanism on his tank that supplies air for his body at the same pressure as that of the surrounding water. The air pressure inside the body equals the pressure of the water pushing in on the outside.

Your blood and body fluids act like soda pop. They absorb gas under pressure. Even at normal atmospheric pressure there are small amounts of the various gases present in air dissolved in body fluids.

Since nitrogen makes up about 80 per cent of the air, it exerts the largest partial pressure of all the gases in the air, and more of it dissolves in the blood and tissues.

The loss or gain of the nitrogen takes place in the lungs through respiration. The amount varies directly with depth, time, and circulatory efficiency of the individual.

If you dive to 66 feet, nitrogen at three times atmospheric pressure is forced into solution in your body fluids in much the same way that CO_2 is forced into soda pop in a bottling plant.

What happens if you come to the surface too rapidly?

The situation is similar to the carbonation of beverages, where the carbon dioxide that is dissolved under pressure bubbles off as soon as the cap is removed from the bottle.

Instead of being carbonated, the diver is nitrogenated!

He is, however, deprived of the benefit of a cap like a pop bottle.

When the human body contains dissolved nitrogen at a pressure more than twice the outside pressure, bubbles are formed in the bloodstream and tissues. Bubbles are formed faster than the lungs can eliminate the excess gas.

If bubbles lodge in the joints, muscles, and bones, they produce the "bends" causing excruciating pain. If they lodge in the brain and spinal cord, paralysis and death are the frequent results.

How can you avoid the bends?

Ascend slowly to the surface, so that the dissolved gas will have time to come out of solution and may be exhaled. The time required for this gas to be given off is known as the decompression time. The deeper you go, and the longer you stay, the longer the decompression time.

DEMONSTRATIONS

Cubic foot

One of the most useful teaching aids I have is a box built out of light wood. It is 1 foot long, 1 foot wide, and 1 foot high.

I use this to show students exactly what 1 cubic foot is. I remind students that *if* this were a cubic foot of water, it would weigh 62.4 pounds.

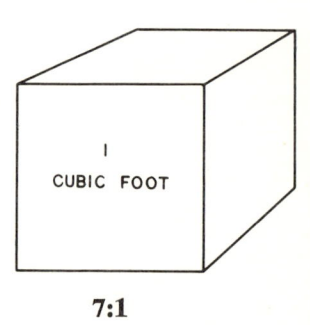

The cubic foot "sits on" or "occupies" 1 square foot of space on the table. The area thus covered is 12 inches long, and 12 inches wide, or a total of 144 square inches.

Therefore, to find the pressure per square inch exerted by a cubic foot of water, we may use the formula:

$$\frac{Pressure}{} = \frac{Force}{Area} = \frac{62.4 \text{ lbs.}}{144 \text{ sq. inches}} = 0.43 \text{ lbs. per sq. in.}$$

Therefore we may speak of a cubic foot of water (weight 62.4 pounds) of exerting a pressure of 62.4 pounds per square foot or 0.43 pounds per square inch.

7:1

Pipe

Here is another method I use to bring home the idea of water pressure. I have a pipe 1 foot long, with a cross-sectional area of 1 square inch. I show this pipe to the students and say that *if* it were filled with water, the *pressure* exerted by the column of water 1 foot high and 1 inch in cross-sectional area would be 0.43 pounds.

7:2

Double it

Now I show the students a similar pipe having the same cross-sectional area, but *twice* as long. Since the height of the water in this pipe

ESTABLISHING IMPORTANCE OF OCEANOGRAPHY

would be twice what it was in the previous pipe, the pressure likewise will be twice as much. Thus, I have a handy demonstration of the formula: *Pressure = Height × Density*

Mercury versus water

The previous demonstration served to illustrate how pressure varies with height.

To demonstrate the second portion of the formula, and to show how pressure varies with density, I get two glass jars about 2 or 3 inches high and 1 or 2 inches wide. I fill one jar with water. The second similar jar I fill with mercury.

I place them on a scale, so that the class may read the weights, and thus figure out the pressure exerted on the bottom of each.

To make the experience more personal, I leave these glass jars of water and mercury on the table, and invite students to come up after class and pick up the bottles, thus getting firsthand evidence of the fact that mercury exerts a greater force on the bottom of the glass than does water.

7:3

Water pushes

To demonstrate that a floating object displaces its own weight, get a widemouth gallon jar, and fill it ⅔ full of water.

Gently place a little pine block of wood in the water.

Now lift the block from the water, and use a ruler to measure how far it sank in the water. (I use a painted block so that I can see exactly how far up the water moistened the side. When I used an unpainted block of wood, I found that capillary action caused a water mark to rise up beyond the actual depth to which the block sank.)

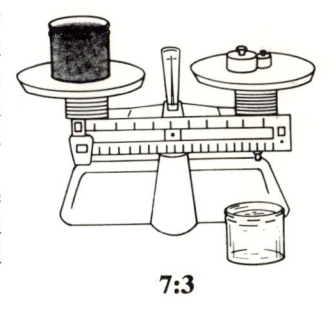

Remind the class that each cubic centimeter of the block that was submerged, pushed aside or displaced 1 gram of water.

Water doesn't like being shoved aside any more than you do. Each cubic centimeter of water that is "displaced" or "pushed aside" tries to get back. It pushes up against the intruder with a force of 1 gram. If 100 cubic centimeters of water are displaced, the buoyant force is 100 grams. This buoyant force counteracts the downward pull of gravity. The block floats.

Now weigh the block on the scale. If the block sank in the water so that it displaced 100 cubic centimeters of water, the weight of the block will be 100 grams.

Vanishing weight!

Here is a demonstration to show that a body which sinks "loses" as much weight as the weight of the volume of liquid displaced.

I have an old billiard ball with a hook fastened to it. I get a 6-inch string, and tie one end around the hook on the billiard ball. The other end I tie to a spring scale. I hold the scale up so that the entire class can read the weight of the billiard ball, 230 grams (7:6).

Now I submerge the billiard ball in a jar 2/3 filled with water (7:7). I have a student read the scale. It reads only 130 grams.

The ball "lost" 100 grams of weight. It is being "pushed up" or buoyed up by the 100 grams of water it displaces.

7:4

7:5

Finding volume

To find the volume of the billiard ball is an easy task. It "lost" 100 grams in weight, and therefore is being "pushed up" by 100 grams of water. 100 grams of water occupy 100 cubic centimeters space, and therefore the volume of the ball is 100 cubic centimeters.

To prove this by a visible demon-

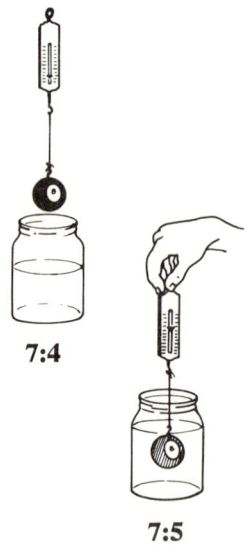

ESTABLISHING IMPORTANCE OF OCEANOGRAPHY

stration, I pour some water into a graduated cylinder which is wide enough in diameter to accommodate the billiard ball.

I now submerge the ball. The water level goes up 100 cubic centimeters. Since I'm using the same ball on the string and scale as in the previous demonstration, I ask students to keep their eye on the scale and the cylinder as I submerge the ball. The scale "loses" as many grams as the number of cubic centimeters the water rises in the cylinder.

(*Note:* I mentioned using a billiard ball. Some other object may be more convenient for you.)

7:6

How much to push a cubic foot?

I have a cubic foot box built simply of six 1-foot squares of light plywood nailed together on the sides. Total weight of the box is about 2 pounds.

I hold the box up to the class and inform them that it is hollow, and weighs about 2 pounds. Could anyone submerge the box simply by pushing it under water with one finger?

I point out that to submerge the box, they will have to push aside or displace 1 cubic foot of water. This "displaced" water shoves up against the box with a force of 62.4 pounds.

Since the box itself weighs only some 2 pounds, it would require some 60.4 pounds to submerge the box.

Metric system

I show the students a little block of 1 centimeter in each direction. Using this cubic centimeter for reference, I mention that if this block were a cubic centimeter of water it would weigh 1 gram. Thus, the density of water is expressed in the Metric System as 1 gram per cubic centimeter.

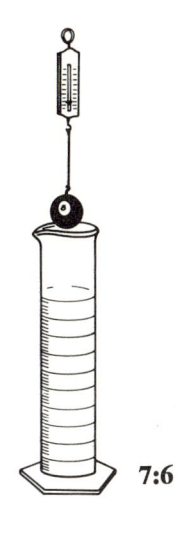

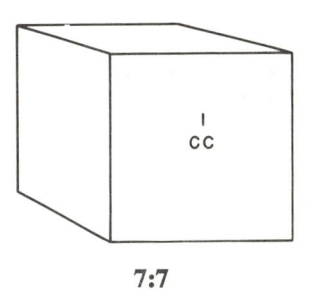

7:7

And if I were to place *10* cubic centimeters of water on top of each other, the pressure on the bottom per square centimeter would be:

$$\begin{aligned}Pressure &= Height \times Density \\ &= 10 \text{ cm.} \times 1 \text{ g/cm}^3 \\ &= 10 \text{ g/cm}^2\end{aligned}$$

Mercury again

I point out that mercury has a density of 13.6 grams per cubic centimeter. Therefore, *if* I had 10 cubic centimeters of mercury, stacked one on top of the other, the pressure would be:

$$\begin{aligned}Pressure &= Height \times Density \\ &= 10 \text{ cm} \times 13.6 \text{ g/cm}^3 \\ &= 136 \text{ g/cm}^2\end{aligned}$$

Buoyancy of styrofoam

Here is a demonstration on buoyancy. You may wish to adjust the details to suit your own convenience.

I have a large graduated cylinder that holds 1000 cubic centimeters. I fill it with water to the 500-cubic centimeter mark. Now I drop the styrofoam ball into the cylinder. Suppose the water level rises by 10 cubic centimeters.

I ask a student to tell me the weight of the ball. By now most of the students realize that any floating object displaces its own weight; hence, the ball weighs 10 grams.

Now I ask a student to come up, take a wooden ruler, and push down on the ball until it is completely submerged.

I ask the class whether they can figure out the additional force pushing up on the ball. Someone generally suggests that this additional force will be equal to the weight of the water displaced. If the water level climbed another 200 cubic centimeters this means that an additional force of 200 grams are pushing up on the ball.

Hence, the *total buoyancy* is 210

7:8

ESTABLISHING IMPORTANCE OF OCEANOGRAPHY

grams. Since the ball is being pulled down by gravity with a force of 10 grams, this means that the force required to hold the ball under the water is 200 grams.

Will it weigh more?

For this demonstration, I place a widemouth gallon jar ⅔ full of water on the platform of a spring balance. If nothing else, a bathroom scale will do.

Now I hold a billiard ball, suspended from a string fastened to a spring scale. (Any heavy object will do.)

I inform the class, "I am going to submerge the billiard ball in the water. I will not let the ball touch the bottom of the gallon jar, nor will I let it touch the sides. Will the spring balance beneath the gallon jar remain the same or will it read more?"

After listening to the various replies, and the reasons for them, I continue, "You are to notice two things. The spring balance beneath the gallon jar and the spring scale in my hand."

As the experiment proves, the spring balance beneath the gallon jar gains 100 grams, while the spring scale in my hand loses 100 grams.

7:9

Weigh your hand

For this demonstration, I use the same gallon jar ⅔ full of water and the same spring balance under the jar.

The first thing I do is ask the students whether anyone can tell me how much his hand weighs.

Now I place my fist into the water and have one of the students read how much the scale went up.

I point out that since the human body has approximately the same density as water, it displaces just about its own weight as well as volume.

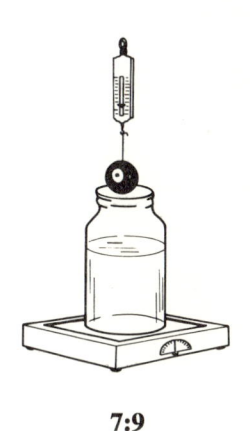

7:10

Volume finder

I show the students a glass insulator (or any other irregular-shaped object), and ask whether anyone can figure out its volume. The insulator's irregular contours make the job a mathematical nightmare.

To show how easy it is to find the volume of any irregular-shaped object by using water as our "mathematical friend," I tie a string to the glass insulator and then submerge it in the water in the graduated cylinder. Students can read how many cubic centimeters of water have been displaced by watching how high the water level rises. From this they can figure out the volume of the insulator.

Archimedes

Here is an interesting demonstration you can do if you have several blocks of different metals—each of the same volume.

Tie a block of aluminum to a spring scale and then submerge the aluminum in the water of a graduated cylinder. Have the class note the displacement of the water and the loss of weight as shown by the spring scale.

Now repeat this experiment with a similar block of copper, then iron, then lead.

Have students note that *all blocks* displaced the *same volume* of water. (As might be expected, since all blocks had the same volume.) *All blocks* also lost the *same weight*. (Since they displaced the same weight of water.)

But—and here is the point of interest. The *ratio* of weight lost by each block (weight lost compared to its total weight) varied for each block. The lightest block, aluminum, "lost" over $1/3$ of its weight. Lead, however, "lost" only about $1/11$ of its weight.

7:11

ESTABLISHING IMPORTANCE OF OCEANOGRAPHY

Judging weight by sinking

Cut the top off a cigar box, then float the empty box in a pan of water. Draw a pencil mark along the water line to show how deep the box is floating.

Now place a 100-gram weight in the box. Mark the new water line. Repeat with another 100-gram weight, and then another. Each time mark the new water line.

The results should convince the class that they can calculate the weight of an object by knowing the amount of water it displaces.

The weight of a cargo carried in a ship can be calculated by knowing how much water it displaces.

Each time another 62.4 pounds of cargo is added, the ship must displace another cubic foot of water. (This is for fresh water. For salt water you can figure on about 64 pounds for every cubic foot of water displaced.)

7:12

Milk carton illustrates pressure

To show how pressure varies with depth, fill a cardboard milk carton with water to the top and place it in a tray. Now take an ice pick or nail and jab a hole near the bottom, one in the middle, and one near the top. The flow of water out of each hole will indicate the amount of pressure behind it. Children may do this experiment at home and write it up.

Apparent loss of weight

To demonstrate how an object "loses weight" when put in water, insert a small screw hook in a little block of wood. Tie a string to the screw hook, and tie the other end of the string to a scale. Lift the entire unit above a gallon jar ⅔ full of water. Gently lower the block of wood into the water. Have students notice how it "loses" weight as the scale goes down to zero. The block displaces its entire weight in

7:13

the water, hence the buoyant force of the liquid counteracts the downward pull of gravity.

Now repeat this demonstration with an aluminum cylinder (or any other heavy object). The cylinder loses only as much weight as the weight of the water it displaces.

Cartesian diver

If you have the *patience* of Job, and are insulated with a bale of four-leaf clovers for good luck, then try your hand at the Cartesian Diver.

The theory of the contraption is as simple as the face of a pumpkin. But trying to get the outfit to work is another story.

Fill a widemouth gallon jar almost to the top with water. Now get a small test tube (or small bottle) and wrap several turns of wire around the tube near the open end. Here comes the tricky job. Submerge the test tube, wire end down, into the water. Tilt it gently and allow just enough air to escape so that it barely floats. If you succeed in doing this, you have it "made." Now drill a hole in the metal lid and put a rubber stopper in it. If you have a rubber stopper with a hole in it, excellent. If not, you can drill a hole just large enough to admit a short section of glass tubing, about 3 inches long. After shoving the glass tubing through the rubber stopper, attach about 6 inches of rubber hose to the top end of the glass tube. If you wish, you may insert a sterilized glass tube in the other end of the rubber hose.

Put the lid on the gallon jar and blow through the hose. The increase in air pressure inside the gallon jar forces more water up inside the test tube, and thus demonstrates

7:14

ESTABLISHING IMPORTANCE OF OCEANOGRAPHY

Pascal's Law that a pressure applied to a confined liquid is transmitted undiminished in all directions.

The increase in pressure on the air in the top of the test tube reduces its volume (Boyle's Law). The test tube can no longer displace its own weight, and consequently sinks.

When you stop blowing, the extra air pressure in the top of the tube makes the gas expand (Boyle's Law again) and thus pushes the extra water out of the tube, thereby making it more buoyant, with the result it floats to the surface again.

The Cartesian Diver gives a wonderful demonstration of Pascal's Law, Boyle's Law, and Archimedes' Principle. It shows that a body which can displace its own weight in water will float. If it can't displace its own weight, it sinks and displaces its own volume.

Sink that boat!

Take a little piece of aluminum foil and bend it into a cup shape or hemisphere so it will float when you place it in a dish of water.

Now wad the aluminum into a tight little sphere. Put it back in the water. It sinks.

When the aluminum was in the shape of the boat it displaced its own weight in the water, and therefore floated. When crushed into a wad, its volume was decreased. When put back into the water it could no longer displace its own weight. Children can do this at home.

Which is the most buoyant?

Blow up a small balloon until it is about 500 cubic centimeters by volume. With your right hand, submerge it all the way down to the bottom of the gallon jar of water. Now remove your hand as rapidly as possible. Have the class judge the buoyancy of the balloon by the

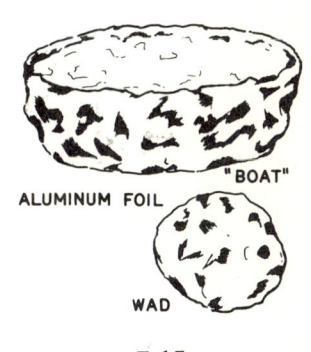

7:15

speed with which it shoots back to the surface.

Now try the same experiment with a block of pine of approximately the same size. Then a block of oak. Finally, if possible, a chunk of ice. Have the class draw their conclusions as to what determines buoyancy.

Dancing mothballs

Here is a demonstration of Archimedes' Principle students love.

Put about a tablespoon full of baking soda in the bottom of a tall glass jar or graduated cylinder, then fill it about ⅔ full of water.

Now pour in about ½ cup of white vinegar. Finally, drop about six mothballs into the solution.

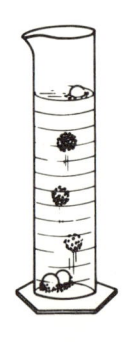

The mothballs are heavier than water, and since they cannot displace their own weight, they sink to the bottom. Soon, however, hundreds of little gas bubbles cling to the surface of the mothballs. This extra buoyancy enables the mothballs to slowly rise to the surface where the gas bubbles break away from them and escape.

Deprived of this extra buoyancy, the mothballs sink once more, only to repeat the process again and again. The up-and-down cycle of mothballs demonstrates quite nicely that a body heavier than water sinks to displace its own volume. If it becomes lighter than water, it will float to the surface and remain there only as long as it can displace its own weight. This is another experiment the children may do at home.

7:16

Pistol for Pascal

A plastic water pistol with clear, transparent sides makes a wonderful demonstration of Pascal's Law. Pull back on the trigger, which is really a plunger that applies a pressure to the confined liquid. The pressure is transmitted undiminished

ESTABLISHING IMPORTANCE OF OCEANOGRAPHY 111

in all directions and shoots a stream of water out the muzzle.

Hypodermic needle

A hypodermic syringe makes another excellent demonstration of Pascal's Law. Many plastic hypodermic syringes are made to be used but once. Perhaps a doctor or nurse friend could pick one up for you. Fill the syringe with water, then push down on the plunger. The pressure is transmitted undiminished in all directions. Liquid shoots out the needle.

7:17

Squeeze bottle

A plastic squeeze bottle, such as honey or hair shampoo comes in, furnishes another demonstration unit for Pascal's Law.

Fill a squeeze bottle with water, then squeeze it to demonstrate that pressure applied to a confined liquid is transmitted undiminished in all directions.

Blow it up

A toy balloon furnishes still another demonstration for Pascal's Law. Blow air into it. The pressure is transmitted equally in all directions. Tie the neck shut. Now press on the balloon with your hands. Note what happens. Again the pressure is transmitted in all directions. Point out that an automobile tire is still another example. When you take the air pressure of the tire, you actually put the air gauge in contact only with one small portion of the tire. Yet, because of Pascal's Law, you know that the pressure registered on the gauge at only one point of the tire is likewise the air pressure throughout the tire.

Conclusion

Man's greatest "enemy" in the underwater world is pressure. With each foot a man descends into water, the pressure increases approximately ½ pound per square inch, or 62.4 pounds per square foot.

This means that at a depth of 10 feet, the pressure on each square foot of your body is 624 pounds. At 100 feet, it is 6240 pounds per square foot.

To keep your body from being squeezed "flat as a pancake" the air pressure inside your body must be kept equal to the water pressure on the outside of your body.

This high air pressure forces nitrogen into your bloodstream. When you make a rapid ascent to the surface, the water pressure on the outside of your body falls off swiftly.

The gas trapped inside the bloodstream can't escape so rapidly. Bubbles are formed faster than the lungs can eliminate the excess gas.

If bubbles lodge in the joints, muscles, and bones, they produce the "bends" causing terrible pain. If they lodge in the brain and spinal cord, paralysis and death are the frequent results.

It is important, therefore, to ascend slowly to the surface, so that the dissolved gas will have time to come out of solution and may be exhaled.

FOLLOW-UP EXERCISES

1. How can you tell your volume and your weight the next time you take a bath?

    If the bathtub is box-shaped, all you have to do is measure how high the water line goes up when you step in and submerge. Multiply the increase in height times the length and width, and you have the volume of the water you displace. Suppose you displace 2 cubic feet of water. Remember that each cubic foot of water weighs 62.4 pounds. Your weight would be 124.8 pounds.

2. You have a pail filled with water. Total weight is 10 pounds. The pail is sitting on a bathroom scale. If you drop a 2-pound fish into the pail, what will the total weight be?

    The same! Since the pail is already full, the fish will simply push aside his own weight, and this 2 pounds of water will run out of the pail, keeping the total weight the same.

3. What is the "squeeze"?

    Captain Arthur W. Ellis, veteran salvage master, can give you the grisly answer. A mile out on Long Beach Harbor the gambling ship Johanna Smith had gone down to a watery grave with thousands of dollars in her vaults—a twentieth-century treasure chest pickled in ocean brine.

    A daring diver known as "Suicide" Johnson fastened on his helmet for a solitary plunge 10 fathoms down to rescue the treasure.

Suddenly his lifelines became entangled in the wreck and his non-return valve jammed, thus causing a loss of life-sustaining air pressure. Instantly the tremendous, overwhelming force of the water stripped the flesh from his bones and packed it up in his helmet like jelly—a terrible example of what sea divers call "the squeeze."

4. How long a time is required for decompression?
It all depends on how deep you go. In 1956 a British Navy diver, George Wookey, dove to 600 feet. It took him *12 hours* to return to the surface. He had to linger every few feet while his body gradually adjusted to the decreasing water pressure.

5. Will man ever adapt to living in the sea?
Yes—according to some scientists. How? By using an "artificial gill" that will exchange oxygen and carbon dioxide directly with the surrounding water, without the use of lungs.

The secret is a man-made gill. It's a film of silicone rubber that is only 1/1000 of an inch thick. Completely free of holes, it retards the flow of water. But oxygen molecules in the water are able to work their way through the film's molecular structure.

Various small animals, such as rabbits and hamsters, have been put in a cage covered with this thin membrane. The cage is submerged beneath the water. The animal's breathing gradually reduces the oxygen content and increases the carbon dioxide in the contained air. This leaves a lower percentage of oxygen in the cage than is dissolved in the water, which causes oxygen to pass from the water through the membrane into the cage.

Similarly, the increased amount of carbon dioxide in the cage will pass out through the membrane into the water. As long as fresh water is brought in contact with the membrane, the atmosphere in the cage will remain breathable.

Summary

In this chapter, the teacher introduced the students to Pascal's Law and Archimedes' Principle. By using a water pistol, the teacher demonstrated Pascal's Law and showed that the pressure exerted on a liquid is transmitted undiminished in all directions.

The teacher showed that a wooden block floats because it pushes aside a volume of water whose weight is equal to that of the block itself. Thus, according to Archimedes' Principle, the buoyant force of the water just balances the downward pull of gravity.

The teacher showed that despite the success of Sealab, man remains a frail alien in the sea. Man's greatest "enemy" in the underwater world is pressure. With each foot a man descends into the water, the pressure increases approximately ½ pound per square inch or 62.4 pounds per square foot.

8

You may begin this chapter by asking your students, "What is it that you are in contact with 24 hours around the clock? Your life depends upon it. Indeed, your body is made of it."

This chapter deals with that wonderful, mysterious thing we call matter. One of the objectives of this chapter will be to show students how we can turn detective, "get on the trail" of matter, and "fingerprint" it. We find its volume and weight, then

Investigating the World of Matter

Photo courtesy of Monsanto

Photo 8. *Shimmering bubbles demonstrate surface tension.*

determine how dense it is. We find that matter is that which occupies space. It has volume and weight, or, more properly, it has volume and mass.

We learn still more about matter by watching how it acts. Ask students how dew forms, how to make buckshot. Why is rain shaped like tear drops, while hailstones are round?

By blowing bubbles you can demonstrate one of the most fascinating properties of liquids.

Ask your students whether they have anything in their home to make water more wet! Suggest a demonstration they can work to prove the advantages of "more wet" water.

You can mix 2 pints of liquids, and end up with less than 1 quart—dramatic proof that molecules are not all the same size.

You can work classroom demonstrations with a "dry" liquid.

Invite your students to explore the world of matter still more. Ask whether or not they have ever noticed "matter moving around by itself"?

A BASKET OF FEATHERS OR A BASKET OF LEAD

I begin my class on density by posing the following question:

"What would you rather carry, a bushel basket full of feathers, or a bushel basket full of lead?"

The universal reply, "I'd rather carry the basket of feathers."

"But why?" I ask. "In both cases you still have the same volume—a bushel basket."

"Yes," comes the reply. "But the lead has more weight."

Thus students themselves develop a feeling for the fact that a comparison of volume to weight leads to a concept we call density.

"Now," I continue, "I need a volunteer. All you have to do is stand in front of the class and let me drop one of two objects from a height of 6 feet on to your big toe."

"In my right hand I have a big block of cork, 1 foot long, ½ foot wide, and 4 inches thick. In my left hand I have a very small piece of lead, only about 1/20 the size of the cork. Which would you rather I drop on your toe?"

"The cork." The response is short and certain.

"But why?" I ask. "The cork is much bigger. Why not take the smaller object?"

"Because it weighs more," comes the response.

By now the students are developing a real feeling for this ratio of volume to weight, which we call *density*.

DEMONSTRATIONS

Pine block

This demonstration is so simple, yet so instructive, especially for students who have had little or no experience weighing objects and measuring them.

I give a small pine block to one of the students, and ask him to find its weight in grams on the balance on the lecture desk.

Now I call up another student and ask him to find the volume of the block in cubic centimeters. Strange as it may seem, I sometimes find a student who seems to have forgotten that you can find the volume of a regular, rectangular object by multiplying its length, by its width, by its height.

At last we have the volume in cubic centimeters, so we can fill in the formula:

$$Density = \frac{Weight}{Volume}$$

After finding the density of the pine block, I give another student a block of oak, another a block of marble, etc. and thus let the class experience how simple it is to determine the density of an object.

8:1

Float iron

When students see this demonstration for the first time, they are truly amazed.

Fill a drinking glass about ⅓ full of mercury. Place an iron bolt, nut, or steel ball bearing in the mercury. Ask the class to note how much of the iron floats above the surface, and thereby judge the density of the steel compared to the mercury.

Repeat the demonstration, putting other small objects into the mercury. See what happens when you use aluminum or wood.

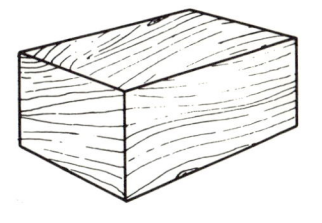

They all float

If you have the time, and materials, here is a handsome demonstration that is an eye catcher.

Get an empty peanut butter jar. Pour 2 inches, or less, of mercury into it. Then about 1½ inches of water, and finally 1½ inches of rubbing alcohol.

Hold the jar up in front of the class and drop a small ball bearing or piece of iron into the jar. It will sink until it floats in the mercury. Next, drop a small piece of wood into the jar. It will sink until it floats in the water.

Finally, drop a small cork into the jar. It will float in the alcohol.

8:2

Specific gravity

To get across the idea of specific gravity, I make use of two empty peanut butter jars and a foot ruler. I fill one jar with water and place it on the table. On top of it I place the foot ruler.

On top of the foot ruler I place the second jar, which I filled with sand. I inform the students that *specific gravity* is defined as the *weight of an object divided by the weight of an equal volume of water.*

A *comparison* involves some kind of equality. The first thing we need are *equal volumes*—and so, we have the two jars with *equal volumes* of sand and water.

The foot ruler represents a dividing line. We divide the *weight* of the *sand* by the *weight* of the *water* to find the *specific gravity* of the *sand*.

Suppose the sand weighs 2 pounds. The water weighs 1 pound. The *specific gravity* of the sand would be 2.

Now I empty out the sand, and fill the top jar with sawdust.

Again, we start off with *equal volumes*.

INVESTIGATING THE WORLD OF MATTER

To find the *specific gravity* of the sawdust, we divide the *weight* of the *sawdust* by the *weight* of the *water*. If the sawdust weighs only ½ pound, and the water is 1 pound, the *specific gravity* of the sawdust is ½.

Tale of two jars

I get two tall jars of the same height. One I fill with water, the other with copper sulphate.

I place a wooden ruler, end down, in the water and have a student tell the class how many centimeters the ruler sank.

Now I place the ruler in the copper sulphate, and have another student record the depth to which the wooden stick sank.

I have the students find the specific gravity of the copper sulphate by dividing the distance the stick sank in the water compared to the distance it sank in the copper sulphate.

$$\text{Specific Gravity} = \frac{\text{Distance Ruler Sank in Water}}{\text{Distance Ruler Sank in Copper Sulphate}}$$

Two jobs in one

I now introduce the commercial hydrometer by saying it does two jobs in one.

Number One—I use the same two jars filled with water and copper sulphate from the previous experiment, and show that the commercial hydrometer does the same job as the wooden ruler or stick. The depth to which it sinks will serve to indicate whether a liquid is heavier or lighter than water.

Number Two—the commercial hydrometer takes over the mathematics the students performed in the previous experiment. The scale on the glass to which the liquid rises gives the specific gravity reading directly.

8:3

Battery tester

Try using a battery tester to find the specific gravity of copper sulphate. Then try using it on water and rubbing alcohol. The small hydrometer in the battery tester won't even float in the alcohol. It was made for testing liquids heavier than water.

8:4

Cohesion

You can roll two lumps of clay into one because the molecules cohere or stick together. This property of molecules of the same substance to cling together is known as *cohesion*.

The cohesive power of soft wax, putty, or moist clay is small. In steel, the cohesive force is strong. Without cohesion there would be no bodies of matter; just individual molecules of different substances roaming around.

Nickel versus gingersnap

Hold a nickel between thumb and forefinger of your right hand and try to bend it. No luck. It has enough cohesive strength to resist you.

Now try a gingersnap. It crumbles due to lack of cohesive strength. A soda cracker has even less cohesive strength.

GINGERSNAP

8:5

No definite shape

Some students are quite taken with this demonstration, which evidently brings home an idea that never hit them between the eyes before.

Get a quart of water. Pour it into a round-shaped container, then into a square-shaped container, and finally into an odd-shaped container. The volume of the water stays the same (1 quart) but its shape does not. The shape changes with each container.

Cohesion in liquids is much weaker than in solids. Thus, molecules of liquids fill any shape into which they are poured. A quart of water

INVESTIGATING THE WORLD OF MATTER

will fit as neatly into a square bottle as into a round one.

Cohesion versus adhesion

Hold up a piece of chalk for all to see. The particles of the chalk "stick together" or "cling to each other" because of cohesion.

Now use the chalk to write on the blackboard. The fact that particles of chalk adhere to the blackboard is proof that adhesion is now the stronger force. In fact, the particles of chalk prefer to "cling to" the blackboard rather than to each other.

Cohesion is the force of attraction between molecules of the same substance. *Adhesion* is the force of attraction between molecules of different substances.

CHALK

8:6

Adhesive tape

To prove how aptly adhesive tape is named, ask a student to volunteer to have a patch of adhesive tape stuck to the back of his hand. Now ask him to pull it off rapidly. Tingling proof of the attraction between unlike molecules!

Adhesive water

Ask students whether they ever heard of "adhesive water"?

To demonstrate what it is like, simply stick your finger in a glass of water, then draw it out.

The water "adheres" or "sticks to" your finger. It is adhesive water. It "wets" your skin.

8:7

Dry liquid

Ask your students whether they have ever heard of a "dry liquid"? To demonstrate what it is like, have a student stick his finger into a dish of mercury, then draw it out. His finger is dry. The liquid does not "wet" his skin. The molecules of mercury prefer to "stick together" (cohere) rather than "stick to" (adhere) or wet a finger. The mercury molecules have strong cohesive, but weak adhesive powers.

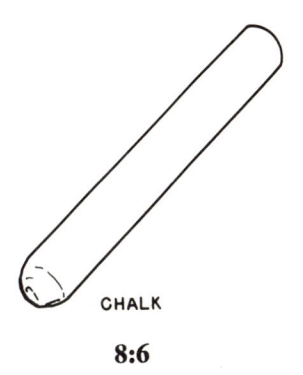

Float a razor blade

Gently place a safety razor blade on the surface of a glass of water. Despite the fact that steel is over seven times heavier than water, the steel does not sink. *Surface tension* will support the blade as long as the surface of the water is not broken. Have the students look closely at the liquid near the razor blade. The surface is depressed, but not broken. To sink the razor blade, simply push one end under the water, or touch the surface of the water with a bar of soap, or drop in a little alcohol or ether. These will lower the surface tension, and the blade will sink.

8:8

"Crazy" chips

Oil has less surface tension than water. You can demonstrate this by putting a drop of oil on water. As soon as it touches the surface it spreads out in a thin film.

For another demonstration of surface tension sprinkle chips scraped from a block of camphor on the surface of clean water in a dish.

Immediately the camphor chips will dash about like Mexican jumping beans. The reason is that water dissolves the camphor most rapidly at the rough edges of the particles. Where camphor dissolves, the surface tension decreases and the camphor particles are pulled to other areas where there is more surface tension. Since the camphor continues to dissolve, the particles jump from one position to another. To stop the motion, jab your finger into the dish of water. There will probably be enough oil on your skin to corral the chips into one corner of the dish.

8:9

"Haystack" of water

Fill a glass with water and place it on the table. Now gently keep adding more water until the surface

INVESTIGATING THE WORLD OF MATTER 123

Cork on the move

bulges up like a haystack or the top of a beehive.

Place a cork in the center of a glass half full of water. Surface tension will slowly move it to one side.

Now fill the glass until the water bulges up like a "haystack." Place the cork on the surface of the water towards one side. Now the surface tension pulls the cork to the middle!

8:10

Float a "boat with holes in it"

Get the lid from an empty peanut butter jar and use a hammer and a very thin nail or brad to punch many holes in it.

Place your "boat with holes" gently in a pan or glass of water. If the holes are small enough, surface tension may give you a "boat with holes" that doesn't leak!

8:11

Goodbye toothpicks

Here is a demonstration to show that surface tension acts like an elastic film. Float two toothpicks close together. I use a widemouth glass bowl to aid vision.

Now place the edge of a bar of soap between them, or simply put a drop of oil on the water. This will reduce the surface tension existing between the toothpicks. The stronger surface tension on the outside of each toothpick will pull them apart. The effect is most dramatic. You may also use a liquid detergent.

8:12

Bathtub admiral

From the dime store you may purchase a small toy boat that has a place to fasten a tiny block of camphor near its stern. As the camphor dissolves, it leaves a thin film behind the boat that reduces the surface tension in the rear. The stronger pull of the surface tension ahead of the boat moves it forward. To perform this demonstration in

Torpedo it!

the classroom, use a long pan of water in which to float the boat.

Float a piece of steel wool in a dish of water. Now pour a few drops of liquid detergent into the water. The steel wool sinks immediately. Your actions have "torpedoed" it by using a detergent to reduce surface tension. You make the water more "wet."

8:13

Water stays inside upside-down milk bottle

Fill a milk bottle with water, then stretch a piece of cloth (a portion of an old sheet or pillowcase will do) over the mouth of the bottle, and secure it in place by tying a string around the neck.

Now turn the bottle upside down. Surface tension combines with atmospheric pressure to keep the water in the bottle.

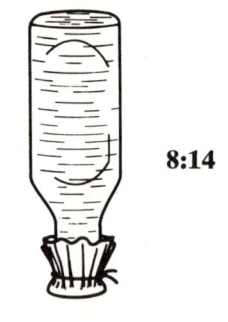

8:14

One stream from three

Get an empty coffee can and make about three holes near the bottom about ½ centimeter apart. Now fill the can with water. Pinch the three streams of water together with your thumb and forefinger. Surface tension will combine them into one.

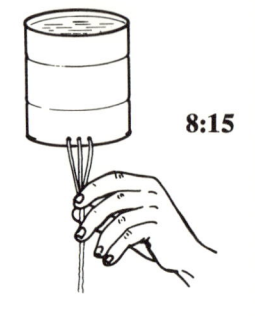

8:15

Bubble, bubbles

Soap bubbles furnish some of the most fascinating demonstrations of surface tension. Get a bottle of the commercial "soap bubble liquid" and use the wire loop to fill the air with the shimmering magic of spinning spheres of fleeting beauty.

Glittering hemispheres

Get an empty peanut butter jar and punch a number of holes in the lid with an ice pick, or nail and hammer. Fill the jar with water, replace the lid, and turn the jar upside down.

Atmospheric pressure will keep the water from gushing forth. Surface tension will mold the water on the bottom side of the holes into beautiful hemispheres.

8:16

INVESTIGATING THE WORLD OF MATTER 125

Silver spheres

To demonstrate surface tension, put a few drops of mercury in a glass dish. Squash the mercury drops with your thumb to make them into smaller and smaller drops. The smaller the drops, the more perfect the spheres.

8:17

Bubble blower

Blow a big soap bubble with a bubble pipe. Remove your lips from the stem, and the contracting soap bubble will force a small "breeze" out the stem. To make the effect of this "breeze" visible, hold the stem near a candle flame.

Whisker cocktail

Immerse a camel-hair paintbrush into a glass of water. The hairs will stand out like whiskers or the hair on a hippie.
Remove the brush from the water. Surface tension will draw the hairs into a neat "tail."

8:18

Floating spheres

Into a mixture of about three parts of water to two parts of rubbing alcohol insert a few drops of olive oil by means of a pipette. Since the buoyant force of the mixture will counterbalance the downward pull of gravity, surface tension will have an opportunity to mold the oil drops into near-perfect spheres.

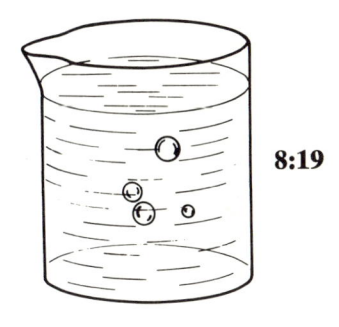

8:19

Climbing water

Many students have never observed the surface of a liquid, so I place a glass ½ full of water on the table and ask a student to come up and inform the class what he notices.
I also have on the table another similar glass ½ filled with mercury. I have a student report to the class on how the mercury looks where it meets the glass wall.
I leave both liquids on the table, so that the students may come around after class and see for themselves the concave surface of the water, and the convex surface of the mercury. They are amazed to

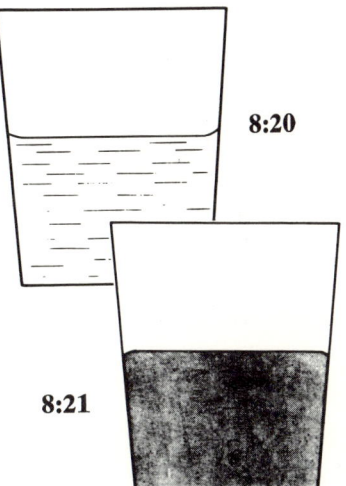

8:20

8:21

find that mercury, instead of "climbing" the glass walls like water, is "depressed" where it comes into contact with the glass walls.

Capillary tube

Capillary action, or the tendency of liquids to rise in tubes which they wet, is a fascinating property of water.

In the previous demonstration, the water in the tumbler does not climb very far. The reason for this phenomenon is that the force of gravity pulling downward on the water is greater than its adhesive power to cling to the wall and the force of surface tension to pull it up to the level on the sides.

If you put a small glass tube into water, however, the tendency of the water to adhere to the sides of the tube is more noticeable. As the concave surface tends to contract, the water climbs until it is higher than the surrounding water in the tube. This climbing continues until the surface tension of the water is exactly balanced by the weight of the column of water. The smaller the tube, the higher the water rises.

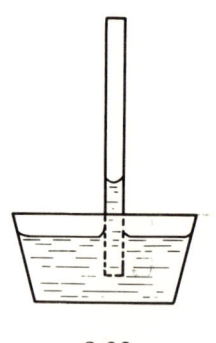

8:22

Up we go

For a demonstration of capillary action, pour a little ink in a shallow dish or use colored water. Hold one end of a blotter in the ink, and have students observe how quickly it rises up the blotter. Hold one end of a wad of cotton, a piece of an old towel, or the edge of a sugar cube in the ink and watch the capillary action which results.

Uphill climb

Put colored water or ink in the bottom of a little dish and place a block of soft pine, end down, in the liquid. Twenty-four hours later the class will observe how capillary action has caused the liquid to rise.

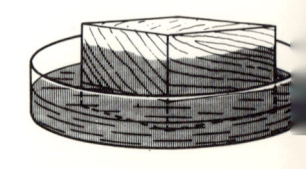

8:23

INVESTIGATING THE WORLD OF MATTER

Cornstalk

If you slice open the stem of a flower or cornstalk, you will see millions of tiny openings filled with liquid. These are cross sections of very fine tubes. Because these tubes are so fine, water from the soil rises through roots and stems to the leaves. Capillary action at work!

Sponges, wicks, towels, mops

Show any or all of these objects to the class to remind students that they are all useful because of capillary action. The spaces between the fibers act as capillary tubes that enable liquids to rise up wicks and take the moisture from your face when you smother it in flexible capillary tubes (the towel).

8:24

Fountain pen

Students are amazed to learn that the slit in the point of a fountain pen is a capillary tube. Even more amazing is the fact that ink doesn't flow from the pen; it is drawn down by the capillary tubes in the paper. To verify this statement, try to make the pen write on a surface without capillary tubes, such as a pane of glass, polished steel, or waxed paper.

Cohesion holds glass plates together

For an interesting demonstration on cohesion, get two glass plates about 2 or 3 inches square. Spread a thin film of water on the bottom plate. Press the top plate firmly against the bottom plate. The cohesive force that now exists between the plates amazes students.

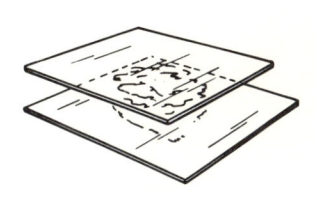

To show the students the tremendous cohesive force involved, I hold the top plate in my left hand. With my right thumb, I push or slide the bottom plate to one side so that it extends out from under the top plate. I can push the bottom plate over halfway out from under the top plate, and still the remaining surface in contact holds the plates together.

8:25

The thinner, the higher

Here is a vivid way to demonstrate that the rise of water is greater where the capillary tube is thinner. It also illustrates that a capillary tube doesn't have to be a cylinder, but may be any narrow space.

Get two pieces of thick, heavy glass about 3 inches square. Ordinary window glass is all right but it is more fragile. Snap a rubber band around the two plates of glass to hold them together. Now, along one edge of the glass slip in a long, thin wire. The plates will now form a "wedge."

Place the glass "wedge" in a shallow dish of colored water and have students see how the liquid rises between the plates.

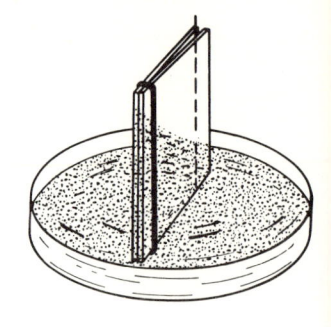

8:26

Smell the ether

In gases, cohesion is so slight that the molecules gallop madly off in all directions to fill all available space. Just remove the lid from a can of ether, and your sense of smell will tell you how fast the ether molecules diffuse themselves through the air. In place of ether, you may find it more convenient to use a perfumed spray or burn incense.

One plus one does not equal two!

Here is an interesting experiment to demonstrate that molecules are not all the same size.

Get 1 pint of rubbing alcohol and 1 pint of water. Pour them into a quart bottle, and behold! You won't fill the quart bottle.

To explain what happens, suppose you had a bushel basket full of baseballs. Now you pour a pound of buckshot into the basket. The buckshot won't make any visible increase in the volume occupied by both baseballs and buckshot. *Reason*—the buckshot is so small, it drops down in between the baseballs.

In somewhat the same manner we

8:27

INVESTIGATING THE WORLD OF MATTER

may consider the smaller alcohol molecules poured in among the bigger water molecules. Like the buckshot, the smaller alcohol molecules tend to nestle in between the bigger water molecules.

Ink in water

To demonstrate *Brownian movement,* simply add a couple of drops of ink to a glass of water, and watch how rapidly the ink spreads out to all portions of the water.

Detect the mothballs

Put some mothballs in a colored bottle or tin can with a narrow mouth so that it is hard to see into the container. Cork the bottle and place it on a table before class.
Uncork the bottle and ask a student to smell and then tell what is inside. Proof again that molecules are in motion.

Tensile strength

Pull on a piece of thin thread about 1 foot long. It breaks easily. Now pull on a stout cord or string, and then on a wire. They will each give a different demonstration of *tensile strength.*

8:28

Elasticity

Stretch a rubber band, then release it and watch it snap back into its original shape. Pull on a spring, release it, and it jumps back to its previous shape. All of these demonstrations will illustrate *elasticity,* or the property of a body to recover its original form when the deforming force is removed.

How much "bounce"?

Air is the most elastic material. It can be squeezed and compressed, but as soon as the original pressure is restored, it jumps back to its original volume.
A toy balloon filled with air can be squeezed, compressed, bulged out, and pressed down. Yet when the deforming forces are removed,

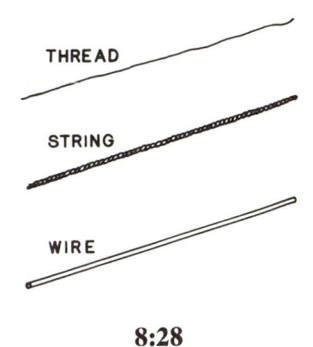

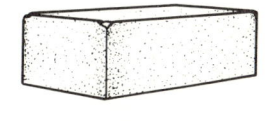

8:29

the balloon returns to its original volume and size.

A block of foam rubber furnishes another interesting example of elasticity, and so do clock springs.

A "Jumping Jack" is a jolly example of elasticity.

By contrast, show how little elasticity is found in putty, clay, and wax. It is the nonelastic property of putty, for example, that makes it useful for putting into place around a window. It "stays put" and won't jump out.

Stretch

Suspend a wire spring from a support rod. Attach a 100-gram weight to the free end. Use a meter stick to measure how many centimeters the spring goes down when the 100-gram weight pulls on it.

Now attach another 100 grams to the spring, and have the class observe the result. Repeat with 200 and then 400 additional grams. The results should convince the class that the change in the spring is proportional to the force applied (*Hooke's Law*).

8:30

Point of no return

If you have an extra old spring, which you can sacrifice for the sake of science, pull it far beyond its elastic limit. Have students notice that once this is done, the spring won't return to its original form.

8:31

Mousetrap and solder

Here is a demonstration for dramatic contrast. Set a mousetrap, then release it by dropping a cork on the trigger to which bait is attached. The spring snaps back into its original position with a bang.

Now get a long length of wire-form lead solder. You can twist it into a pretzel or pig's tail, and it will stay put. It has no elasticity.

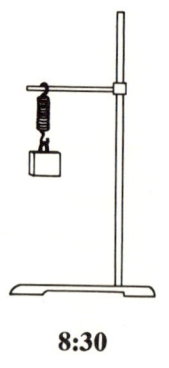

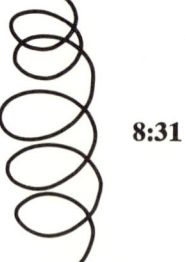

INVESTIGATING THE WORLD OF MATTER

> **Conclusion**
>
> We should be thankful for the wonderful world of matter. If it were not for cohesion, our world would "fall apart"! Our homes and chairs would also "fall apart" and the molecules would wander off like fumes from a bottle of ether.
>
> If water were not adhesive, we could not use it to wash our face. Without capillary action, the towel would not remove water from our skin. A wick could never bring fuel to a hungry flame to give heat and light.
>
> Without the elasticity of the air in our automobile tires, a ride down the highway would be a bone-tingling experience. And how could we catch a mouse without the help of the elasticity of the spring in the trap? And think how devastating it would be to try and sleep without the help of the elasticity of the springs in a mattress. It would be like sleeping on a board.

FOLLOW-UP EXERCISES

1. Small drops of rain that sparkle on your sweater or coat collar on misty days are spherical, and so are the early morning dewdrops that condense on blades of grass. Rain falls in drops, although these are often pulled out of their original spherical shape by air friction as they fall.

2. How come hailstones are round?
   Because of surface tension. Sometimes a drop of water is caught in the tremendous updraft in a huge thunderhead cloud and carried upward to chill heights of some 50,000 feet. Here the raindrop freezes.
   As the frozen drop begins to fall toward the earth, it picks up additional moisture. If the drop is blown back into the high sky, the added coat of moisture freezes, producing another layer of ice. Such drops fall to earth as hailstones. If you slice open a hailstone, you will no doubt see a number of layers of ice, reminding you of the construction of an onion. Each layer tells of a trip to the chill top of a cloud. By counting the layers you can tell how many times the hailstone began to plunge toward the earth, only to be blown back into the freezing sky. Hailstones have been known to grow as large as baseballs before they have sufficient weight to overcome the updrafts.

3. The tendency of molecules of liquids to draw together in spheres is used to advantage in the manufacture of buckshot by means of a

shot tower. At the top of a tower, usually about 150 feet high, is a "shower pan" or sieve and at the bottom a tank of water.

Molten lead, poured into the pan, falls through the holes. As it falls, the liquid assumes the characteristic spherical shape and hardens into small round pellets. The water in the tank cools the shot. One plant alone daily converts 85,000 pounds of lead into almost 300 million pellets of shot.

4. If you absentmindedly leave a bath towel over the side of the tub, one end in the water, you may return to find that the liquid travels by capillary express through the towel to splash water on the floor.

Summary

In this chapter, you introduced your students to the wonders of the world of matter. You showed them why water "clings" to the skin while mercury is "dry." With soap bubbles you demonstrated surface tension and explained why hailstones are round.

You showed how to prove that matter can "move around by itself" and you demonstrated how to find the density of an object.

You used adhesive tape to demonstrate what is meant by adhesion, and now you hope your lesson will stick to the minds of your students.

T he bone-crushing importance of this chapter is self-evident to anyone who has slipped on ice-covered sidewalks, fallen off a stepladder, or stumbled down cellar steps.

To demonstrate how objects are accelerated, all you need is an ice pick and a block of wood. Or, you may use a dime-store toy automobile and a small plank.

Many people who followed the Apollo flights from planet earth to

9

Developing a Practical Appreciation for Acceleration Due to Gravity

Photo courtesy of U.S. Navy, taken by PHI Chip Maury

Photo 9. *The moment the jumpers leap from the plane, gravity accelerates them earthward.*

the moon were amazed to learn that the space capsules, which had galloped away from the earth at approximately 25,000 miles per hour, were slowed down until their speed was less than 2733 miles per hour. How come?

You can show why by conducting a small-scale, perfectly safe classroom demonstration with a ping-pong ball or a tennis ball.

Ask your students whether the earth has a "pulsebeat" and if so, how you could detect it.

You can show how with only a string and a nail!

Since your objective in this chapter is to introduce your students to the acceleration caused by gravity, you may begin by asking questions such as:

"How far does a baseball drop in traveling from pitcher's mound to home plate?"

"Is it true that the Army has a rifle that 'shoots at itself' with round trip bullets?" "How can a dumbbell become a lethal weapon?"

You may wish to include the following introductory discussion in your first class on this chapter:

> A gentleman by the name of Galileo Galilei discovered the "pulsebeat" of the earth. His discovery, in fact, was a "spin-off" or "side effect" or "bonus" for saying his prayers!
>
> Twenty-two-year-old Galileo had entered the Cathedral of Pisa in Italy to say his prayers. As Galileo looked towards the altar, he noticed the Brother sacristan lighting the sanctuary lamp that hung from a long chain that was fastened to the high ceiling. As the Brother sacristan left, he accidentally pushed against the suspended lamp, which began to swing.
>
> Galileo became fascinated by the back-and-forth motion of the lamp, and timed it with the beating of his pulse. He placed the fingers of his right hand on his left wrist, as he had been taught to do in one of his medical classes.
>
> As Galileo watched the swinging lamp, a strange thing happened. The lamp began to swing through smaller and smaller arcs. The distance it covered on each successive swing was less, and yet—and this was the startling thing—the pendulum required as much time to swing through a small arc as through a large one.
>
> Overcome with curiosity, Galileo continued with demonstrations in his home. You, too, may wish to continue to experiment.

DEMONSTRATIONS

Swing it!   Get a piece of string about 3 feet long. Tie one end to some fixed support, so that it will be free to swing.

On the free end of the string tie a weight, which is called the bob.

The weight or bob may be anything handy, a key, a nail, a ring, or even an apple with its stem in good shape. In order to time the pendulum, it will be handy to have a clock or wrist watch with a second hand.

Let position B represent the pendulum at rest. Pull the bob to position A, release it, and the bob will swing from position A to position C. This distance is called the *arc*.

The time required for the bob to swing from A to C and back again to A is called the *period* of the pendulum.

Let the bob swing through an arc of 4 inches. Then let it swing through an arc of 6 inches, 10 inches, etc.

To make it easier to time, allow the bob to make about ten swings on each trial. Check with the second hand on your watch.

What do the results indicate? Are the periods the same for the big arcs as for the small arcs?

The results are truly amazing. Like Galileo, you will find that the size of the arc has no influence on the time required for a swing of the pendulum. In other words, *the period of the pendulum is independent of the arc through which it swings.*

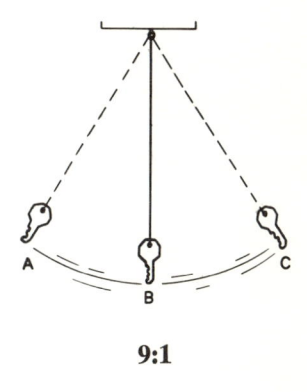

Heavy versus light

For this demonstration, keep the same length of string as the previous demonstration, but fasten a heavier weight to serve as bob. Then use a lighter weight.

Time the number of swings with bobs of various weights, and you will find that *the time required for a complete swing is independent of the weight of the bob!*

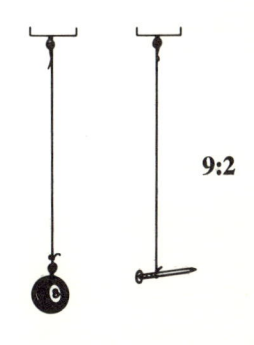

9:1

9:2

Truly amazing. The weight has nothing to do with the speed!

Long versus short

Now let's see whether or not the length of the pendulum has anything to do with its period, or the time required for it to make a complete swing.

Begin with a string about 36 inches long and any size bob you wish. Let the pendulum swing about ten or 20 times. Time it with a watch. Take the average time for the round trip for the period of the pendulum. Now repeat the experiment, this time using a string 9 inches long. You will find that the period of the 9-inch pendulum is ½ that of the 36-inch pendulum. In other words, *the period of a pendulum is proportional to the square root of the length of the pendulum.*

Drop hammer on hand

Gravity is always pulling on you and on all other bodies. The measure of the pull of gravity on a body is called its weight. If you are sitting in a chair, the downward pull of gravity is counterbalanced by the upward push of the chair.

But what happens when nothing is "counteracting" gravity?

The pull of gravity then accelerates or pulls an object towards the center of the earth. The acceleration due to gravity is 32 feet per second per second, which means that at the end of each succeeding second, an object is falling 32 feet faster per second than it was at the end of the previous second.

Here is an experiment to demonstrate that the final velocity of a falling object is equal to the acceleration of gravity multiplied by the time it falls ($V_f = at$).

Ask a student to hold out his hand, palm up. Hold a hammer 1 inch above his hand, then release it.

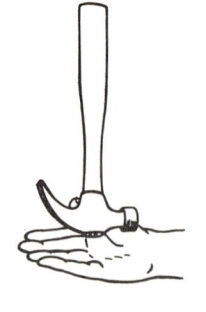

9:3

TEACHING A REAL APPRECIATION FOR ACCELERATION DUE TO GRAVITY

The impact won't bother the student since the hammer accelerates for only a short time.

Now release the hammer from a height of 3 inches, etc. Ask the student to account for the fact that the impact becomes greater.

Ask the student why he won't volunteer to have the hammer dropped on his foot from a height of 6 feet.

Ice pick on block of wood

Here is a similar experiment to show how the final velocity of a falling body depends on the time it falls. Hold an ice pick, sharp point down, about ¼ inch above a block of wood. Release the pick. If it falls for a short time, its final velocity may not be enough to make the point penetrate into the wood.

Now hold the ice pick 4 inches above the block of wood and release it. Note the difference on impact. Now the point goes into the wood. Finally, release the pick from a height of 12 inches or more. The greater time required for the fall means that the final velocity is greater, possibly enough to make the point of the pick penetrate so deeply into the wood that considerable force is needed to pull the ice pick out.

9:4

Hammer a nail

Use a hammer to drive a small nail into a block of wood. At first lift the hammer only 1 inch above the nail. Again, the time of fall is so short that the impact, due to the velocity, will be small.

Now keep increasing the distance the hammer falls. This increase of time will impart a greater final velocity to the hammer, and therefore greater driving power.

Car on plank

To demonstrate that the final velocity depends upon acceleration multiplied by time, secure a long,

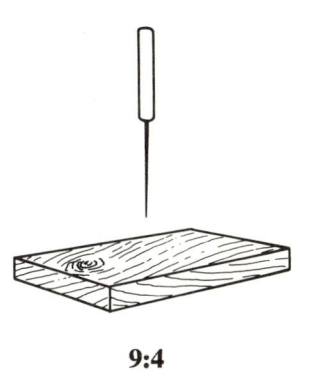

9:5

smooth board or plank about 4 inches wide and 4 feet long. Place one end on a stack of books on your lecture table to give you an inclined plane.

Place a toy car or marble, (tennis ball, baseball, or anything that will roll) 2 inches from the bottom end of the plank, then release the car and notice its final speed; also note how far it rolls across the top of the table.

Now place the car 4 inches up on the plank and repeat. Again, observe the final speed and the distance the car rolls across the table before it comes to a stop.

Repeat the experiment, releasing the car from various heights on the plank. The demonstration will serve to illustrate that *the final velocity depends upon the time the object accelerates, and also that the stopping distance increases according to the speed of the vehicle.*

By removing some of the books from the tall end of the plank, you can vary the amount of acceleration, and thus show how *the final speed is also determined by the amount of acceleration.*

Reaction time

Ask a student to stand by your desk, with his right hand down by his side.

You now hold a marble (or any other object) 1 foot above the top of the table. Release the marble without warning. The student is to get his right hand under the marble before it hits the table.

Since the marble will take only ¼ second to fall 1 foot, the student will have to have reactions fast as a mousetrap if he is to catch the marble.

For a reaction of ½ second, hold the marble 4 feet above the table.

Speedy pendulum

A pendulum serves to illustrate that final velocity depends on the time.

Lift the bob to position B, and release it. Note its speed when it arrives at position A.

Now lift the bob to position C and release it. Note how much greater is its speed when it reaches position A. The longer time of fall gave it the greater final velocity.

Repeat this experiment, lifting the bob to various heights, and noting the speed when it arrives at position A.

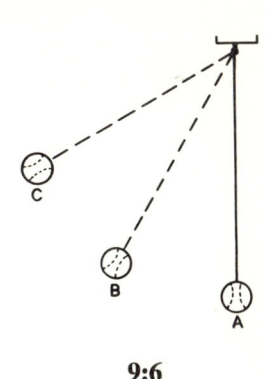

9:6

Invisible brakes

Did your students ever see "invisible brakes at work"?

All you have to do is toss a tennis ball (or any other object) gently up into the air. Swiftly and surely it comes to a stop, then plunges back down.

Gravity "puts the brakes" on any object upward bound at the same rate it speeds things up in the opposite direction.

If you toss a ball up into the air, it will take gravity as long to slow it down to a complete stop, as it will require for the object to fall back to its point of ejection. Time up will equal time going down (neglecting air resistance).

Positive versus negative acceleration

A pendulum furnishes a delightful demonstration of "positive" and "negative" acceleration.

Raise the bob to position A, then release it. Gravity takes over the job of speeding up the bob as it falls from A to B. This gain in speed is called *"positive" acceleration.*

As the bob continues to swing from B to C, gravity "puts on the brakes" and slows the bob down at exactly the same rate it speeded it up. This

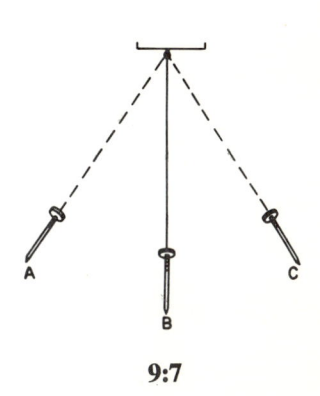

9:7

slowing down is *"negative" acceleration.*

Gravity "speeds up" the bob from A to B then "slows it down" from B to C.

If it were not for friction, position C would be exactly as high as position A.

In fact, we might even go on to say, that were it not for friction, the pendulum would be a perpetual motion machine, for as the bob reverses direction, it would "fall" from C to B, then "climb" back to A again.

Conclusion

We have seen that gravity "pulls" on the bob of a pendulum to speed it up, then slow it down. The conclusion, therefore, is simple. To make a "world clock" or pendulum to take the "pulsebeat" of planet earth, all you need is a string and a nail (or any other weight).

As the weight or bob drops from position A to B, it undergoes "positive acceleration" and speeds up, reaching maximum speed at position B.

From B to C the bob undergoes "negative acceleration" and slows down at the same rate it speeded up on the way down.

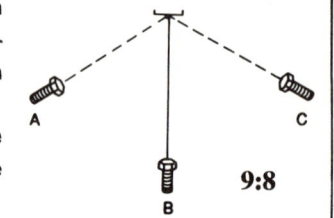

If it were not for friction, the bob would rise to a position C, equally as high as position A, and then reverse itself to swing back to A. We would have a perpetual motion machine!

By raising position A to a greater height, the bob will have a longer time in which to fall, and thus acquire a greater final velocity at B, thereby indicating that the *final velocity* is equal to the *acceleration* X *time*, or $V_f = at$.

9:8

FOLLOW-UP EXERCISES

1. The Army has a gun that shoots at itself with round trip bullets! It is actually a weather gun. Low-altitude wind velocity must be known precisely at the launching site of a guided missile in order to score a bull's-eye, and even relatively low winds have a significant effect. Nicknamed the "Breeze Buster," the new device is a smooth-bore gun which determines wind velocity by firing a small steel ball straight up into the air.

TEACHING A REAL APPRECIATION FOR ACCELERATION DUE TO GRAVITY 141

Easily operated by one man, the unit consists of a light steel gun mount, a protective aluminum shield, a stopwatch, a calibrated measuring chart—and the gun itself.

As soon as a steel ball drops back on the aluminum shield, it makes a dent. By measuring the distance from the gun to the dent, and using a stopwatch and calibrated measuring chart, the wind velocity above may be obtained.

2. As a baseball travels the 60½ feet from the pitcher's mound to home plate at gametime speeds of 70 to 90 miles per hour, gravity pulls it down 3 to 4 feet. To compensate for this, the pitcher's mound is placed 3 to 4 feet higher than the bottom of the strike zone at home plate.

3. At 7:51 AM on Saturday morning, December 21, 1968, a mighty Saturn 5 rocket boosted *Apollo 8* towards the moon. After orbiting the earth for 1½ turns, the third-state engine was reignited and *Apollo 8* was blasted towards the moon at 24,200 miles per hour. At 11:30 AM Sunday, December 22nd, *Apollo 8* was 164,476 miles from the earth and 66,724 miles from the moon—more than ⅔ of the way. Its speed, slowly decreasing under the gravity pull of the earth, was down to 2733 miles per hour.

Then, on Monday, December 23, a climactic moment when man for the first time came into the gravity grasp of another heavenly body. It happened at 3:29 PM EST when *Apollo 8* was 202,700 miles from the earth and about 34,500 miles from the moon.

The pull of the moon then increased *Apollo's* speed until it was moving at a velocity of about 5600 miles per hour.

4. Camera fans will find this an interesting experiment to do at home. Tie a long string to a flashlight, and suspend it about 3 feet above a camera with its lens pointed directly up. For better results remove the glass lens on the flashlight, and use rubber bands to secure a black paper collar to the end of the flashlight. Now start the lighted pendulum swinging back and forth in a darkened room, making various exposures from one to ten minutes. By varying the length of the string, and also by twisting the string, you can secure a variety of fascinating "pictures."

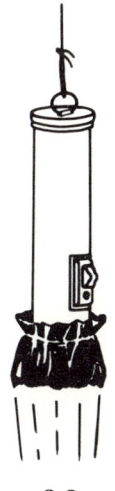

9:9

5. Ask your students to be alert the next time they go skiing or sledding. As they start down the top of the hill, they seem to move slowly, then pick up speed until the rush of wind makes their eyes water. Why?
6. Anyone who has watched a tall tree chopped down knows how the tree begins its descent in majestic splendor, then—under the pull of gravity—speeds up to come crashing down amid a roar and snapping branches. A dramatic demonstration that the final velocity is due to both acceleration and the time of acceleration.
7. To watch acceleration at work, watch a pile driver. The longer it falls, the faster it falls.
8. An icy doorstep, or icy sidewalk may result in a too-sudden acceleration—followed by a too-sudden deceleration—which may give rise to a profound exclamation and/or a pair of crutches!
9. An avalanche is an example of acceleration a mountain climber could do without!
10. Sometimes in the winter the newspapers report people killed by falling icicles. A chilling example of acceleration.
11. If all falling objects would continually increase their speed by 32 feet per second, each second of fall, think what would happen if you were caught in a storm. Raindrops would drop on you like hammers. Hailstones would become bullets. Your roof would be punched full of holes. You would look like Shredded Wheat.

    Fortunately, air offers resistance, or friction, which increases or grows larger with an increase in speed. When the force of air friction equals the pull of gravity, the falling object will no longer accelerate. It will descend with a constant velocity, called the *terminal velocity*.
12. Big, fat, lazy snowflakes silently drifting down from the grey sky are good examples of objects whose air friction is great enough to keep them from accelerating. Instead of speeding up, they maintain a constant velocity.
13. Suppose you jump from a Cessna 180 airplane at an altitude of 5000 feet. Gravity would like to take over and pull you towards the center of the earth with an ever increasing velocity—32 feet faster per second for each second of fall!

    Within about four seconds after you jump, however, the wind resistance will be so great you will have reached maximum or terminal velocity of approximately 120 miles per hour.

    When you get within some 2500 feet of planet earth, you pull your rip cord, and your 28-foot canopy spills open like a splotch of whipped cream on the blue tablecloth of sky.

    The greater air resistance of the chute lowers your terminal velocity to about 15 miles per hour.

TEACHING A REAL APPRECIATION FOR ACCELERATION DUE TO GRAVITY   143

14. To show how the amount of surface exposed to the air increases friction, and thereby cuts down on speed, try this experiment.

Unfold a paper napkin or tissue paper and release it so that the tissue floats to the floor like an erratic parachute. It will dilly-dally, so to speak, with gravity all the way to the floor, like a big snowflake "floating" to earth.

Now wad the tissue paper into a small ball. The more compact ball will fall with greater speed. It has less resistance to offer to the air. Since it has less "braking power" gravity pulls it down more rapidly. Children delight in doing this experiment.

Summary

In this chapter, you introduced your students to the fact that gravity pulls an object towards the center of the earth with an acceleration of 32 feet per second, which means that each succeeding second an object is falling 32 feet per second faster than it was the previous second.

Thus, if an object were to fall for ten seconds, its final velocity would be

$$V_f = at$$
$$V_f = 32\,(10)$$
$$V_f = 320 \text{ ft/sec}$$

V_f = final velocity
a = acceleration (32 ft/sec/sec)
t = time in sec

In our age of air transportation, it is imperative that students understand what holds a Boeing 727, or 747 jet in the sky. Why is the design of the airplane wing of major importance?

With the help of a table fan, you can give a demonstration to show how an airplane gets its "lift."

The same principle that makes an airplane fly also makes it dangerous to stand by the side of a fast moving train. A demonstration with a toy balloon will illustrate why.

10

Establishing the Importance of the Bernoulli Principle

Photo courtesy of the Boeing Company

Photo 10. *Bernoulli's Principle helps keep the Boeing 747 in the sky.*

144

ESTABLISHING THE IMPORTANCE OF THE BERNOULLI PRINCIPLE   145

You will be able to use an aspirator or spray gun for an additional demonstration of Bernoulli's Principle.

Most interesting to the students, perhaps, will be the application of Bernoulli's Principle to winning an auto race by the hair-raising technique of drafting.

Finally, you can make use of Bernoulli's Principle to explain why a baseball can curve as much as 18 inches as it speeds from the pitcher's mound to home plate.

Most amazing of all, Bernoulli's Principle will help students realize a fantastic fact. Tornadoes do not blow houses apart. It is the air inside the house that does the job.

200 YEARS BEFORE KITTY HAWK

You may wish to remind your students that some 200 years before the Wright brothers took to the air at Kitty Hawk, a Swiss scientist, experimenting with fluids, discovered a principle that also applies to air in motion.

Daniel Bernoulli learned that whenever a stream of liquid passes around some object in such a way that its velocity is increased at a given point, the pressure within the stream decreases at that point. In other words, *if the speed of liquid (or gas) is increased, the pressure within the fluid decreases. The greater the velocity, the greater is the difference in pressures (Bernoulli's Principle).*

The wing of an airplane, as you may have noticed, is constructed so that the top side bulges up like a little hill. As air rushes over the wing, part of the airstream goes over the top of the wing, and part below.

The curved top surface of the wing forces the air moving over the top to go farther and therefore faster than the air moving under the wing. According to Bernoulli's Principle, the air traveling over the top at greater velocity will exert less pressure than the air below the wing.

To understand how air pressure can lift the many thousands of pounds in a plane, assume that the surface area of the wing of a certain aircraft is 200 square feet. When the plane is flying near sea level, the air pressure beneath the wing is 14.7 pounds per square inch. Above the wing the faster moving air has less pressure, probably about 14.2 pounds per square inch. Although the difference is only ½ pound per square inch, think how many square inches there are in 200 square feet (28,000). When the difference in air pressure is ½ pound per square inch, the lift is 14,400 pounds. Larger planes require larger wings. This difference in air pressure on the top and bottom surfaces of the wings accounts for about 70 per cent of the lift. The remaining 30 per cent comes from the angle at which the wind pushes against the bottom side of the wing.

DEMONSTRATIONS

How an airplane gets its "lift"

Stand a heavy book in a vertical position, with a piece of light paper between its pages. Allow the free end of the paper to drop down to the top of the table.
On the other side of the book place an electric fan. When the fan is turned on, the air above the paper is set into motion. The air pressure on top of the paper is therefore lowered, and the pressure of the air beneath the paper pushes the sheet up into the airstream.
If you do not have an electric fan, place a piece of cleansing tissue, Kleenex, or paper napkin between the pages of a book so that one end hangs down limply on the outside. If you blow across the top of the book, the tissue will rise.

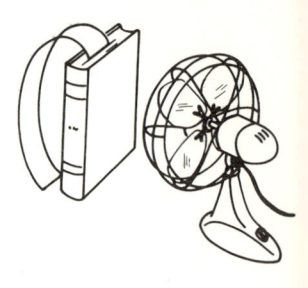

10:1

Apples together

Suspend two apples by strings from a support rod so that the apples are about 1 inch apart. Have a student blow vigorously between them. The apples do not fly apart, but come together. The high-velocity air moving between the apples reduces the air pressure between them. The atmospheric pressure of the air on the outside of the apples pushes them together.

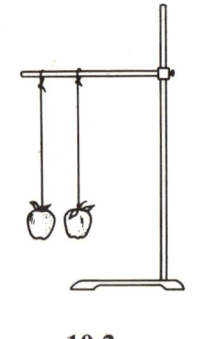

10:2

Balloon in air

Blow up a toy balloon and place it in the airstream from a fan directed vertically upward. Slowly move the fan, or pick it up and carry it. The balloon will move with it. A superb demonstration of Bernoulli's Principle.

ESTABLISHING THE IMPORTANCE OF THE BERNOULLI PRINCIPLE 147

Floating ping-pong ball

You may also place a ping-pong ball in the airstream from a hose hooked to a compressed air unit. Perhaps you have a vacuum cleaner that shoots compressed air out one end. Perhaps you can fasten a soft, flexible rubber hose to the exhaust port. Squeeze the end of the hose into a small area to act as a nozzle. Move the hose, and the ping-pong ball will follow.

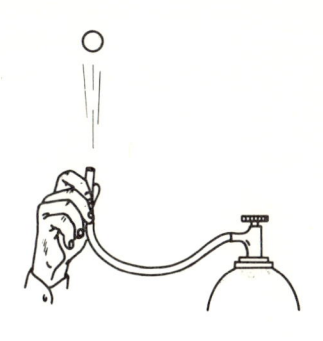

Both the balloon and the ping-pong ball stay up in the airstream because the high velocity of the fast moving column of air reduces the pressure. The ordinary air pressure of the surrounding air keeps the balloon and ping-pong ball "prisoners" inside a "cylinder" of low air pressure.

10:3

Hugging cardboard

Get a piece of light cardboard, and bend its sides to make a "bridge." Have a student try to push the "bridge" over by blowing as hard as possible under it. Better yet, direct a stream of air from the exhaust end of a vacuum cleaner under the "arch" of the "bridge." The fast moving air under the arch reduces the air pressure on the underside. *Result*—atmospheric pressure on the top side holds the "bridge" down and keeps it "hugging" the table.

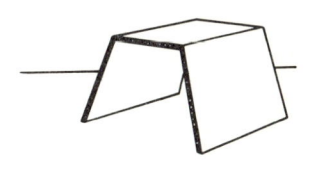

10:4

Spool and cardboard

Get a long thin nail or a big pin, and run it through the middle of a piece of light cardboard about the size of a playing card.

Put the nail inside a spool held in a horizontal position. Place the cardboard snugly against the spool. Now have a student blow through the spool, or direct an airstream from the exhaust port of a vacuum cleaner through the spool.

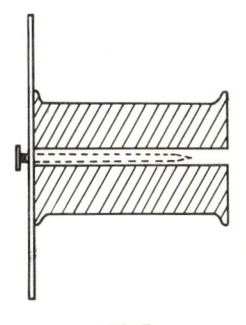

The nail simply keeps the cardboard

10:5

from falling to the ground. Despite the blast of air rushing through the spool, Bernoulli's Principle keeps the card on the end of the spool.

Atomizer

When the rubber bulb of an atomizer is squeezed, air is forced out the nozzle, A, with great velocity. This means that the air moving across the top of tube B has less air pressure than the air inside the container, C.
Consequently, air pressure inside the container, C, forces liquid to the top of the tube, B, where it is caught in the airstream and rushed along with it. Container C must have an air hole in it to allow atmospheric pressure to enter and push up on the liquid.

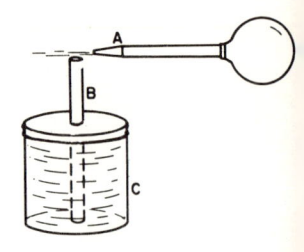

10:6

Bernoulli on your chin

Here is a demonstration for both you and your students to perform. Get a sheet of typing paper or notebook paper and cut off a strip about 2 inches wide. You may also use a strip of newspaper about 2 inches wide and 1 foot long.
Wrap one end of the paper halfway around your right forefinger and hold your finger firmly against your lower lip. Now blow, and the paper will rise up to flutter in the airstream.
By blowing on the top side of the paper, the high-velocity airstream you shoot forth reduces the air pressure. Atmospheric pressure pushes the paper up.

Flying puffed rice

If you have a vacuum cleaner with exhaust hose, direct the airstream over the top of a glass tube about $\frac{1}{2}$ inch in diameter, immersed in a gallon jar of puffed rice or sawdust. See what happens.

Ping-pong ball in funnel

Place a ping-pong ball in a funnel, then, holding the funnel in an upright position, place it over your

10:7

ESTABLISHING THE IMPORTANCE OF THE BERNOULLI PRINCIPLE 149

lips and blow through it.
What happens to the ping-pong ball?

Friendly papers Get two pages from your notebook or two typing pages; hold one in each hand, about 1 inch from each other, and blow down between them.
Watch what happens!

Conclusion

The Bernoulli Principle reminds us that events are often determined by a paradox. It seems strange, for example, to say that a tornado does not blow a house apart. It is the air inside the house that blows the walls apart! The pressure of the fast moving air swirling around in a tornado is less than the pressure of the stagnant air inside the house.

Bernoulli's Paradox informs us that as you increase the velocity of a fluid (such as air or water) the pressure inside the stream is decreased.

FOLLOW-UP EXERCISES

1. Do baseballs really curve? The answer, given in wind tunnels, is "Yes." A ball pitched at moderate speed, with a spin of 30 revolutions per second, can be expected to curve a maximum of some 18 inches enroute to home plate. The slower the pitch, the more the curve.
   When a ball rotates in a stream of air, the air moves faster over one side of the ball than over the other. Because the pressure of air is less where it moves faster, the ball is then moved in the direction of the lesser pressure.

2. Why do you get a better draft up a chimney on a windy day?
   Because when wind is blowing, a chimney becomes a giant atomizer. Wind racing over the chimney reduces pressure on the top side. Then, the air in the basement, under regular atmospheric pressure, pushes up the chimney with roaring delight.

3. Why is it dangerous to stand close to railroad tracks when an express train thunders past?
   The high-speed train tends to move the air along with it. Since this air is fast moving, its pressure is reduced. The ordinary air behind you, at simply atmospheric pressure, may push you under the wheels.

4. Why is it risky for ships running at high speeds to try to maintain positions closely parallel to one another?

According to Bernoulli's Paradox, the water pressure between the boats becomes lower.

5. Did you ever have the frightening experience while riding in a car of coming up close behind a big, fast moving truck. Suddenly your car seemed to be "pulled" forward. You have just experienced "slipstreaming" or "drafting."

    The big semitrailer in front of you is "dragging" some of the air with it. This increase in velocity reduces the pressure of the air.

    Your car benefits from two things. You don't have to fight the air resistance in front of you. The truck is doing this for you. Not only is the truck cutting down the wind resistance in front of you, but the lower pressure or partial vacuum left in the wake of the truck means that the air behind you "pushes" you forward.

    At the Daytona "500" Marvin Panch "drafted" himself to victory. "I'd hitch onto a fast car and stick behind him until either he or I had to make a pit stop. Then I'd pick up another one."

    Carefully conserving his own car so that it could provide the few intense bursts of really high speed he needed, Panch drafted himself into the winner's circle and $20,750 first-prize money.

6. You may give a simple demonstration to show why it is dangerous to stand by the side of a fast moving vehicle. Blow up a toy balloon, tie it shut, and place it on the edge of a table. Now walk as rapidly as you can past the balloon. It will jump off the table to follow you!

    As you walk, you set the air into motion, and "drag" some of the air with you. This increase in velocity decreases the pressure of the air in motion. *Result*—the "stationary" air at atmospheric pressure on the other side of the balloon, pushes the balloon off the table.

Summary

In this chapter, you have shown that such seemingly diverse effects as the curve of a baseball, houses exploding outward in the path of a tornado, a spray gun, and a jet cruising through the sky—all can be explained by the paradoxical law of science discovered by the distinguished Swiss mathematician, Daniel Bernoulli.

Strange as it may seem, the greater the velocity of a fluid (air or water) the less is its internal pressure.

In this chapter, you may introduce your students to the fact that the "Go-Go" generation is the "Energy Transfer" generation. In fact, so important is this "Energy Transfer" that each of us visits a Potential Energy Station at least three times per day to acquire a fresh supply of the mysterious "something" that keeps us on the go—namely, energy.

In fact, we may say that we live in two worlds! One world we see, the other we do not see.

11

Increasing Students' Awareness of the Importance of Energy

Photo by Hal Haney, State of Colorado

Photo 11. *How about a "slice of sunlight" for dinner? A steak is just that— energy captured from the sun! The obliging steer ate grass that had captured solar energy, and then converted this "sun energy" captured by green leaves into a mouth-watering T-bone steak. The energy in meat is truly "sun energy"!*

The world we see is the world of cabbages and kings, gingersnaps, and Saturn V rockets leaping up from Cape Kennedy. By night we see stars poised pale on the fringes of space. By day, we may see the horizon, if there is no smog.

In addition, we are "immersed" or "surrounded" by an invisible world. Our very lives depend on forces we never see.

The world we can see, hammer, pound, measure, and weigh is the world of matter.

The invisible "thing" that enables us to move the hammer and pound the nail is what we call *energy*.

Our life is really a romance with matter and energy!

Potential energy is defined as the ability to do work. *Work* is defined as force acting through a distance, or, in formula

Work = Force × Distance

There are various forms of potential energy. A horseshoe magnet has potential energy that is called *magnetic*. The magnet has the ability to lift up a nail.

The potential energy in a stick of dynamite is *chemical*. The dynamite has the ability to lift a bridge off its foundation.

The potential energy of a mousetrap that is set is *mechanical*. The spring has the ability to catch a mouse!

Potential energy, therefore, is the *ability to do work*. It does not even imply that work is being done. If you are lazy, and sprawled out in deep sleep, you still have potential energy, or the *ability* to do work.

By contrast, *kinetic energy* is called *the energy of motion*. If you wake up from sleep, and begin to walk, you are demonstrating kinetic energy. If you run, you show even more kinetic energy. The faster you run, the greater your kinetic energy.

The moment a stick of dynamite explodes, it becomes kinetic energy, and is *doing work*. It is energy of motion.

As soon as the mousetrap is triggered, its potential energy becomes kinetic energy, as the metal slams down on the neck of a mouse!

DEMONSTRATIONS

Foot-pound

To demonstrate the meaning of 1 foot-pound of work, hold a foot ruler in a vertical position on the table. Lift a mass of 1 pound from the foot to the top of the ruler. You

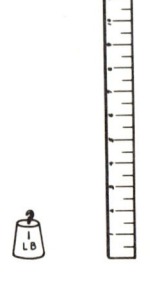

11:1

have just done 1 foot-pound of work.

The 1 pound mass has also acquired 1 foot-pound of potential energy. If it is allowed to fall, it can do 1 foot-pound of work.

Hammer with potential energy

If you lift a 2-pound hammer a distance of 2 feet above the top of the table, it has 4 foot-pounds of work put into it, and has 4 foot-pounds of potential energy, which is there because of the work done to lift the hammer.

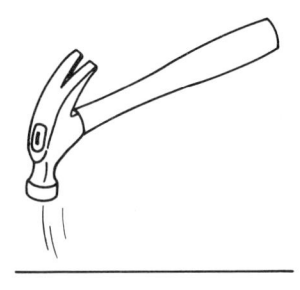

11:2

Have gun— will demonstrate energy

A cap pistol is a superb demonstration of potential energy. The caps have potential energy due to chemical composition. When the hammer is in a cocked position, it has potential energy due to mechanical configuration of the twisted spring.

Pull the trigger, and the potential energy of the hammer turns into kinetic energy of motion. When the hammer hits the cap, this kinetic energy of forward motion is converted into heat energy that sets off the cap, and changes its potential energy into more heat and sound waves.

Bow and arrow

A toy bow and an arrow tipped with a small suction cup make an excellent demonstration unit. Notch the arrow to the string and pull it back. The bow has as much potential energy as the work you put into pulling the string back. Suppose it takes an average force of 20 pounds to pull the string back 2 feet. The bow has 40 foot-pounds of potential energy.

The potential energy of the bow leaps into kinetic energy of motion that slams the suction cup against the wall.

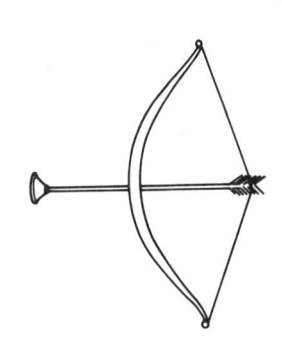

11:3

Hourglass

Turn a toy hourglass so the sand is in the top unit. The sand has potential energy due to position. The falling sand has kinetic energy.

Gram-centimeter

To demonstrate how much a gram-centimeter of work is, lift 1 gram to a height of 1 centimeter above the table. The 1 gram-centimeter of potential energy will transform into kinetic energy as soon as you release the 1-gram piece.

11:4

Pendulum

Lift the bob of a pendulum to position A. It is all potential energy.
As the bob falls, it transforms potential energy into kinetic energy. At B, the halfway mark, the bob has lost ½ of its potential energy. At C the bob is all kinetic energy. As the bob starts to rise, it transforms kinetic energy back into potential energy. At D its energy is part potential, part kinetic. At E it is all potential energy again.

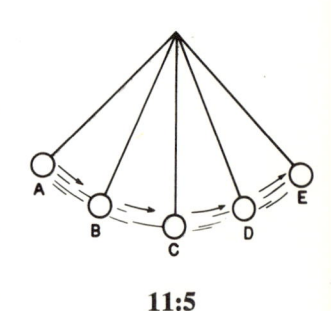

11:5

Mixing bowl and marble

Place a marble in a big glass mixing bowl near the rim. As the marble falls, it converts potential energy into kinetic. At the bottom of the bowl it is all kinetic energy.
As the marble rolls up the opposite side, it converts kinetic energy back into potential energy, then, once again reverses direction. It keeps up this energy exchange until friction brings it to a stop. By this time the potential and kinetic energy the marble once had is transferred into the kinetic energy of the molecules of the glass, which are thus heated.

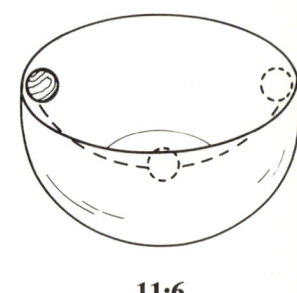

11:6

Yo-yo

A Yo-yo on its way down transforms potential energy into kinetic. On the way up, it reverses this process.

Radiometer

A radiometer furnishes an interesting demonstration on the change of

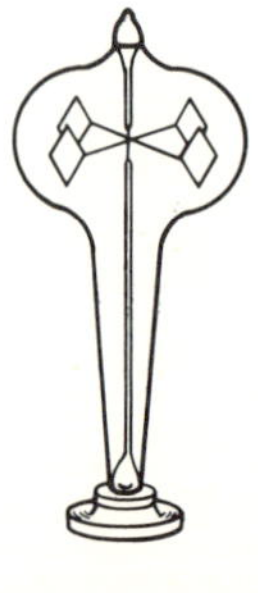

11:7

the energy of sunlight into energy of motion. It is called a "nuclear-powered engine" run by "cosmic energy" from outer space.

Is your wristwatch solar powered?

Wind your wristwatch in view of the class and have them note that the kinetic energy of your moving fingers is being converted into the potential energy of the wound-up spring, which, in turn, transforms its potential energy into the kinetic energy of the moving wheels and thence to the moving hands.

Go back further, and explain that the kinetic energy of your moving fingers came from the potential energy you secured from the food you ate. And the food, itself, obtained its energy by absorbing it from the sun. Hence your watch, in the last analysis, is *solar powered!*

Mousetrap

Set a mousetrap. It represents potential energy. Drop a small piece of cardboard to trip the release. Suddenly the mousetrap jumps with kinetic energy.

Matchstick magic!

Light a match and watch the magic! When the matchstick was part of a growing tree, green leaves on the branches of the tree captured energy from the sun and stored it in the wood.

When the matchstick burns, it is releasing heat from the sun that was captured by green leaves many long years ago, and stored as potential energy—waiting for the magic moment when you would release this "sun energy"!

11:8

The sun will cook your dinner today!

In your kitchen each day you have a demonstration of the transfer of potential energy into kinetic energy. That black rock we call coal is "buried sunshine." Thousands of years ago glorious sunshine cascaded on primeval forests. Its golden energy was captured by leaves in luxurious jungles. Strange, mysterious forces rose up to bury the vast jungles under tons of earth and compressed the vegetation into veins of black coal.

When you burn coal, you are setting fire to an ancient tropical jungle. You are shoveling an ancient swamp into your stove and releasing energy from the sun that lay deep and dark in the earth for long eons, until dusty-faced miners blasted the precious cargo loose and hoisted it to the surface.

If you have converted to gas or oil, then liquid sunshine cooks for you and warms your home. Oil comes from the remains of marine animals which ate vegetation that had absorbed energy from the sun.

What is your horsepower?

James Watt found that a horse could do 550 foot-pounds of work in one second. Even though Old Dobbin no longer pulls an ice wagon down Main Street, we still use this unit of power or rate of doing work.

$$Horsepower = \frac{Foot\text{-}pounds}{Seconds \times 550}$$

Suppose you weigh 110 pounds and you climb a 10-foot ladder in four seconds. What is your horsepower?

$$Horsepower = \frac{110 \text{ lbs} \times 10 \text{ ft}}{4 \text{ sec} \times 550} = \frac{1}{2}$$

11:9

Conclusion

We spend our lives obtaining potential energy (food for our bodies, fuel for our automobiles) and converting it into kinetic energy.

We can't hope to get matter into motion without potential energy "standing by" ready to "push" molecules into action.

Here, now, is the strangest fact of all—*the potential energy required to get matter into motion is found "stored" or "locked" in matter itself!*

This means that every gasoline station is, in reality, a Potential

Energy Station. In every gallon of petrol lurks the energy needed to speed your Buick down the highway at 60 miles per hour.

Your dining room or breakfast nook is likewise a Potential Energy Station. In one frankfurter is enough energy for a 1 mile walk.

Sugar Information, Inc. reminds us, "Sugar puts 'can do' in candy, and in you." They go on to say, "Energy is the first requirement of life and sugar is the purest energy food there is."

FOLLOW-UP EXERCISES

1. Write a composition on potential energy.
   Hint: *Although we define potential energy as the ability to do work, the truth is that you and I have never seen this creature. We can't roll it up like a raincoat and tuck it under our arm. We can't extract the energy from a lump of coal like we remove a rabbit from his skin, and hang the carcass up for public view—naked energy as such.*

   The fact is, we never see plain, naked energy as such. In this respect, energy is like a leprechaun—we talk about it a lot, but never see it. Energy is an invisible, mysterious thing that seems to come "hidden" or "disguised." It "hides" in a box of Wheaties, in a lump of coal, or in a glass of tomato juice.

   We *don't* see energy itself. All we see are *chunks of matter that have energy*—a gallon of gasoline or a slice of bread (potential energy).

   Or, we see matter in motion—a car speeding down Highway 101, a baseball flying over the fence (kinetic energy).

   We don't pour naked potential energy into the tank of our Ford, but *matter that contains energy*.

   Likewise, from this gallon of gasoline, we don't get simply "pure" ethereal kinetic energy of motion, but, rather, *matter* (an automobile) that *has kinetic energy*.

   We have mentioned that energy is not seen "naked" or "alone" but is manifest in *connection with matter*.

   Or, looked at another way, we may say that matter, seemingly so "lumpy" and "inert"—like a lump of coal—is really possessed of some "mystic" almost "magical" power that can set molecules into a mad dance to cook your steak or warm your home.

   All of us have experienced heat. But, again, we don't find just "pure, simple" heat all by itself. Rather, we experience matter, *molecules in motion*—be they burning winds, steaming waters, or sizzling branding irons. The heat energy of any body is the sum of the kinetic energy of all its many molecules.

   What a strange world! You can't hope to get matter into motion

without potential energy "standing by" ready to "push" molecules into action (potential energy in gasoline ready to propel your Ford down the street).

Yet, this potential energy necessary to get matter into motion is found "locked" or "waiting" in matter itself.

2. Write a composition explaining how the potential energy we use became "imprisoned" in matter.

Hint: *By far the greatest amount of energy we make use of on planet earth is "captured" from a star!*

The "star" in this case is our friend, the sun, some 93 million miles distant in space. We call it our daytime star. It is really a nuclear power plant in full operation around the clock.

Each second your watch ticks, some 4 million tons of the sun's mass is converted into energy and radiated out into space. Of the total energy radiated out by the sun, only one two-billionth of it strikes the earth.

Would you believe it? Hoover Dam (and others like it) are run by solar energy—indirectly, to be sure, but nonetheless surely. Energy from the sun causes water to evaporate from the oceans. The evaporated moisture falls to earth as rain.

Some of the energy the water acquired in evaporation can now be used to turn a water turbine. The kinetic energy of falling water rotates a turbine connected to the shaft of a generator which furnishes electrical power. The electric light in your home is "burning" with energy "snatched" from the sun!

In the above case, the "matter" that helped "capture" the sun's energy was water.

3. Explain why you are a solar-powered, internal combustion engine.

Hint: *Three times a day you eat sunlight!*

When you eat apples, oranges, or potatoes, you are eating energy packaged for you by a blade of green. Each green leaf—be it a leaf on an apple tree or a blade of wheat—transforms "lumpy," inert chunks of matter into energy-packed food.

Tender green leaves in the exuberance of their green magic capture the energy of the sun and store it for future use. Plants package sunlight. Each year the amount of the sun's energy fixed in this fashion amounts to the equivalent of 300 million tons of coal.

We know of no other practical process which can fix the sun's energy in chemical compounds.

Man is an energy-consuming creature. And we get our energy packaged in units of matter we call apples, raisins, cabbages, and crackers.

It is a stabilizing thought to realize that man, though he be the apex of creation, owes all he has in a physical way to blades of green.

When we want energy, we get it by eating "packaged sunlight" alias food.

The only reason you can laugh, run, and read this print, is that your energy is "sun energy." The sun reaches out through 93 million miles of space to catch you in its warm embrace, and kiss you with its life-giving powers—not directly, but in the magic of its masquerade in green.

Each Sunkist orange is just that. Each drop of liquid it contains is "kissed" with energy from the sun.

When you drink orange juice, or tomato juice, or pineapple juice, you are drinking "sun power." You are benefiting from radiant energy from the sun.

Man rules the seven seas. He builds a Boeing 747 to leap from New York to Paris in a span of short hours. He makes a Saturn V rocket to launch an Apollo mooncraft—but he cannot make a radish!

The little blade of green, however, can do just that. It can reach out and grab iron and phosphorus from the soil, drink in water through its roots, take carbon dioxide from the air, plus energy from the sun, and combine them all to give you the tang of the tangerine, the sugar of the cane, the aroma of coffee, the fuzz on a peach, and the shirt on your back.

Magic! This is tantalizing mystery that even Sherlock Holmes couldn't solve. With the searching eye of the microscope and the sleuthing of chemical analysis, scientists have been trying to pry open the secret of the blade of green, to learn its formula, to find how the energy of sunlight which falls on a green leaf is stored in the sugar which is made there.

When the golden rays of the sun shake hands with the green pigment (chlorophyll) in a leaf, magic is in the making. In this building-with-light process, called photosynthesis, the carbon dioxide you exhale is combined with water to form oxygen and sugar. There is magic in each drop of moisture you exhale! Magic in your breath.

How marvelous is this process. Carbon dioxide, which you exhale, is combined with water to form sugar, which you eat. Oxygen is returned to the air. Animals take oxygen from the air and exhale carbon dioxide; plants absorb carbon dioxide and give off oxygen.

Thus animals and plants supply necessary substances for one another.

Summary

The thing we need to get matter into motion is energy. Potential energy is defined as the ability to do work.

By far the greatest amount of energy we make use of on

planet earth is "captured" from the sun. We are "sun powered." Our energy comes from the sun.

No wonder ancient people considered the sun to be a god and worshiped it. Although their way may seem strange to us, these ancient people were not wrong in recognizing the sun as the most important thing in their lives.

You may introduce this chapter by asking your students whether or not they can make a piece of steel "grow longer" and then "shrink" it.

Ask them whether they have ever taken a container filled with a liquid, then, without removing any of the liquid, made the liquid "vanish" to less than 1/10 its original size.

Magic? Yes—the magic of expansion and contraction; the magic of heat!

12

Establishing the Importance of Heat

Photo courtesy of TWA

Photo 12. *Pompeii, the most celebrated ruin of a big city, was the victim of a thermal in 79 A.D. when Mt. Vesuvius (in the background) erupted. Hot clouds of gas rising from the volcano drifted south, and dumped some 20 feet of dry ashes on this ancient Roman city, insulating it down to modern times.*

Your objective in this chapter is to explore the realm of heat and see what happens to objects when they warm up and cool.

To stress the importance of this chapter, ask your students whether they can explain how their lives depend upon the fact that metals expand as they get hot.

Ask, "Just where in your home do you make use of this 'Lifesaving' trait of metal?"

"How does your comfort depend upon the cooperation of metals changing size with temperature?" "What giant business is built on this behavior of metals?"

DEMONSTRATIONS

Put on the teakettle

To show how heat makes molecules move faster, simply put water into a teakettle or Pyrex flask and place it on an electric hot plate or gas burner. When the water heats up, some of the molecules will move fast enough to leap out of the flask or out the spout of the teakettle as steam. (Strictly speaking, what the students *see* coming out the spout of the teakettle is *not* steam but water. Steam itself is invisible as the water vapor above any dish of water. As the invisible steam strikes the air, some of its molecules give up their heat and return to the liquid state. It is this condensed "steam" in the form of fine particles of water we see. There generally is a clear space between the spout of a vigorously boiling teakettle, and the cloud of condensing steam. This clear space is where you will find the steam.)

12:1

Picnic bus

We may use the previous demonstration of steam coming out the spout of a teakettle to remind students that heat does not make molecules any bigger. It simply speeds them up, so that they jostle against each other harder and move farther apart.

ESTABLISHING THE IMPORTANCE OF HEAT

When 1 pound of water evaporates or turns into 1 pound of steam, it expands about 1700 times. The molecules of water in the liquid state are like a group of teen-agers packed into a bus. Their motion is limited. Their kinetic energy is low. When the bus unloads at the picnic grounds, the teen-agers tumble forth and run all over the landscape. They are like molecules of water jumping from a liquid to a gas. Their individual size is still the same, but they occupy an area 1700 times that of the bus. They are warmer. They have more kinetic energy. They dash about like mad gremlins.

Kinetic energy produces heat

To show how heat may be caused by kinetic energy and friction, drag a wooden match (old-fashioned, kitchen-size match) over a rough surface. It will break into flame.
People waiting for a bus on a cold day in winter rub their hands to increase the motion of the molecules. Indians of old learned how to kindle a fire by briskly rubbing two dry pieces of wood. Perhaps you have a Boy Scout in class who can demonstrate this for you.

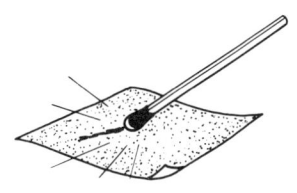

12:2

Pound a nail

Pound a nail into a big, tough block of wood. Let a student put his finger on the nail after you finish pounding the nail, and notice how hot the metal is. The kinetic energy of the descending hammer is transferred to the molecules at point of contact. Both the molecules in the nail and in the head of the hammer speed up when they collide, and thus increase their kinetic energy.

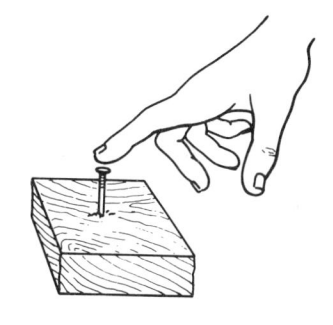

12:3

Pump heat

Get a basketball or football pump and push down on the plunger vigorously several times. Then let a student grasp the pump. He will find that the bottom part of the pump is quite warm.

Point out that some of this heat is produced by friction of the plunger in the pump. But most of the heat comes from the compression of the air in the pump. You force the air molecules into a smaller space, thus causing the walls of the cylinder to be bombarded more often.

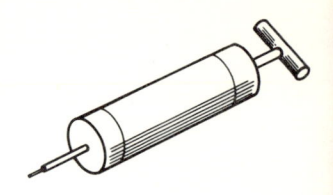

Pushing a great number of air molecules into a smaller space is like chasing wild horses into a small corral. So many madly galloping mustangs are herded into a small space, they continually bump into the sides of the corral. The more horses you cram into a corral, the more often the walls will be bombarded by flying hooves and thumping bodies.

12:4

Pop balloon

To demonstrate that a gas expands when it gets hot, simply blow up a balloon to maximum size, then place it in a window in direct sunlight. For more speedy results, hold it over an electric hot plate, or place it in front of an electric radiant heater, or focus a sunlamp on it. The results will speak for themselves.

You might point out that automobiles cruise down the highway because of explosions. The expanding gas inside the cylinder pushes down on the piston and turns the crankshaft, which, in turn, makes the wheels spin.

Operation deep freeze

To demonstrate the opposite effect, namely the result of cold temperatures on the volume of a gas, simply blow up a toy balloon to maximum size. If it is a very cold day in winter, leave the balloon outside the window for ½ hour. Otherwise, ask the students to do this demonstra-

12:5

ESTABLISHING THE IMPORTANCE OF HEAT

tion for themselves. Place a fully inflated balloon in the deep freeze. See what has happened to its size 24 hours later!

Sterno

Show students the warning printed on canned heat containers: "Don't replace lid until contents have cooled."

Point out that if the lid is put on while the gas inside the can is still hot, it will cool, shrink in volume, and thus cause a partial vacuum, or low pressure area. The atmosphere will then push against the top of the lid so hard as to make it very difficult to open.

If anyone doubts this, let him try the demonstration for himself.

Peaches

Inform students that if someone will bring a pint-size Mason jar of canned peaches (or anything else) to class, you can demonstrate how heat—or the lack of it—affects the volume of a gas.

Place the Mason jar on the table. Remove the threaded cap, which is simply a ring or circle of metal. The main cap is still on the jar.

Even though the main cap is simply a thin wafer or circle of metal, it hugs the jar so tightly, you can't take it off with your fingers. You must use a device to pry it loose. At the very moment you pry the lid off the jar, students will hear a hissing noise, as air rushes into the jar. Point out to the class that the Mason jar was capped while the peaches were still hot. As the contents inside the jar cooled, the air pressure inside the jar decreased. The atmospheric pressure pushed the lid tightly against the rim of the glass. Thus, the very air in the room holds the lid on a Mason jar—because the pressure inside the jar

12:6

"Pop" bottle

was reduced by a decrease in temperature.

Take a warm bottle of pop. Shake it vigorously before you open it. The moment you remove the cap, it will take off like a miniature Old Faithful straight from Yellowstone National Park.

Indicate that you gave the soda pop extra kinetic energy by shaking the bottle. Truck drivers who deliver pop in open trucks in the summer sometimes find that the bottles explode. Heat from the sun, plus the shaking of the truck gives the confined gas too much kinetic energy. The pressure soars, and "pop" goes the bottle!

Lilac mist

Get a container of "Lilac Mist" or any other type of "room freshener" and read the warning to all the class. "Danger. Do not store in warm place or in direct sunlight." If you do, the increase in temperature will mean an increase in pressure and a possible explosion.

12:7

Wet lies

To show how unreliable the body is as a temperature gauge, try this demonstration.

Place three pans on the table. The first is filled with ice water, in which ice cubes are floating. The second dish is simply lukewarm water. The third container has water as hot as you dare make it.

Now have a student come to the lecture table and place his left hand in the ice water and his right hand in the hot water. After keeping his hands immersed for two minutes, he is to place both hands in the lukewarm water.

His right hand will tell him that the water is cool. His left hand will tell him that the water is warm. Neither is true. You are handed a couple of wet lies.

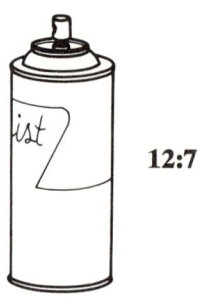

12:8

ESTABLISHING THE IMPORTANCE OF HEAT

Air thermometer

Here is an air thermometer.
Get a tall, clear glass bottle with a mouth about 1 inch in diameter. Put a cork in the bottle, having previously drilled a hole through the cork just wide enough to admit a glass tube. Insert the tube so that it extends almost to the bottom of the bottle.

Fill the bottle about ⅓ full of water, and put a few drops of red ink in the water to make it easier to see and more dramatic.

Now shine a heat lamp through the top part of the bottle. The air will become warm and expand, pushing the red liquid a slight distance up the thin glass tube stuck through the cork.

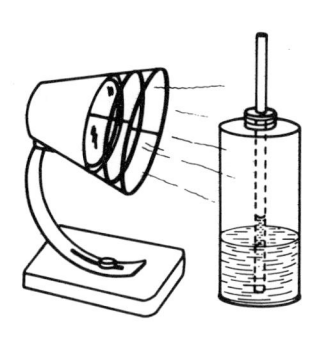

12:9

A mistake makes heat!

Point out to the class that if anyone makes a mistake while writing, and then uses an eraser, both paper and eraser warm up in the process. The kinetic energy of the moving hand is transferred to the kinetic energy of the molecules in the paper and in the eraser.

Colt .45

I like to bring to class a toy model of a Colt .45 and explain that a pistol is in reality an internal combustion engine!

When the hammer of the pistol impacts against the shell, the heat caused by the collision makes the gunpowder burn rapidly or explode. The expanding gases in the cylinder or barrel of the pistol push the bullet out the muzzle.

A Colt .45 is thus a heat engine which converts heat into work.

Burn steel

Ordinarily we think of steel as "fireproof." We put precious documents and papers in safes to protect them. The reason the steel safe doesn't burn is the same reason it is hard to burn a Sears, Roebuck catalogue. If you apply a lighted match to the cover, you may burn a few of the outside pages, but the interior of the catalogue will most likely remain untouched.

If you wish to burn the entire catalogue, you will first have to tear out each page, crumple it, and make a big pile of crumpled pages, so that the oxygen can get at each sheet of paper.

If you wish to burn iron, you have to do the same thing. Expose enough of it to oxygen.

To demonstrate this, simply get a tongs, pick up a wad of steel wool, and hold it over a candle flame. The sparkling "stars" of burning steel wool result from tiny bits of steel combining with oxygen in the air. This "combining" of steel and oxygen (called oxidation) gives us a compound called iron oxide.

To keep the steel in the body of your automobile from combining with the oxygen in the air (i.e., rusting or oxidizing), the car is given a coat of paint to keep it from making contact with the oxygen.

We paint steel, therefore, to prevent it from "burning up"; i.e., "rusting" or oxidizing by combining with oxygen. Rusting is slow oxidation. Fire is rapid oxidation.

12:10

Flash bulb

You may show the students a flash bulb and indicate that oxygen is required for combustion in the bulb. The bulb contains shredded aluminum or magnesium, which is visible to all, plus oxygen, which is invisible.

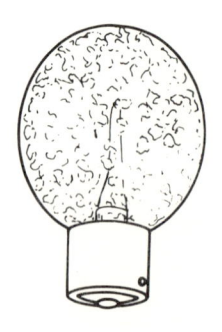

When you set off the flash bulb, you prove that metal will burn—if it offers enough surface to oxygen.

Light bulb

Now show the class an ordinary tungsten lamp with a clear lamp. Point out that the air has been taken from this bulb for the express pur-

12:11

ESTABLISHING THE IMPORTANCE OF HEAT   169

	pose of keeping the filament from burning up. Argon gas has been introduced into the bulb to act like a "blanket" around the filament and to keep it from vaporizing too fast.
Burnt-out flash bulb	Show the students a *fresh* flash bulb. It contains *two separate elements,* aluminum and oxygen. The aluminum the students can see. The oxygen is invisible. The used flash bulb still contains the same two elements, but *combined* into a *compound,* aluminum oxide, which coats the inner surface of the bulb. A magnificent demonstration of *metal combining with oxygen.*
Falling stars	Put some iron filings into a salt shaker and then sprinkle them over the flame of a burning candle. A bright demonstration of metal combining with oxygen.
How to stop burning!	To stop burning (*oxidation*) is simple. Shut off the supply of oxygen. To demonstrate this, hold a glass tumbler upside down over a candle flame. The smaller the glass, the sooner the flame goes out. That is why you, too, would "go out" if someone placed a plastic bag over your head, and kept it there.
Dry ice puts out fire	To demonstrate how CO_2 can put out a fire, simply get a large piece of dry ice, and hold it in a pair of tongs over a candle flame. As the dry ice sublimates, white clouds of heavy gas will sink down over the flame, cutting off its supply of oxygen, and thus putting out the fire.
4th of July	Use a 4th of July sparkler to demonstrate the difference between heat and temperature. Although the brightly glowing sparks that fall on your hand have the same tempera-

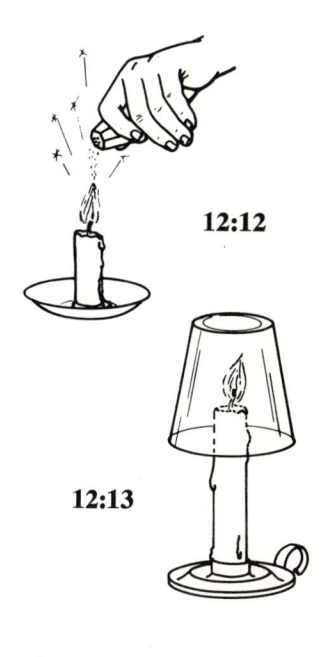

12:12

12:13

12:14

ture as the glowing wire, they have so little mass, they have very little heat. The glowing wire, however, having a greater mass, has a much greater amount of heat.

You can let the sparks fall on your hand, and they won't harm you, but a warning printed on the box cautions you against touching the glowing wire.

Paper won't burn

To demonstrate the conductivity of copper, get a copper pipe about 6 inches long and 1 inch in diameter, or less. Wrap a piece of paper snugly around the middle of the copper pipe. Hold this paper directly over the candle flame. It may blacken, but it won't burn, if you have the paper fitting tightly around the copper. Be sure to use only one thickness of paper and keep it tight as you possibly can. The copper picks up the heat from the candle so fast, and rushes it the length of the pipe to dissipate it in the air, the paper can't acquire enough heat to burn.

12:15

12:16

Now it burns!

Repeat the previous experiment, only this time wrap the paper around a wooden stick instead of a copper pipe. A sawed-off portion of an old broomstick makes a good stick. Since wood is a poor conductor (or good insulator), it does not take the heat away, but lets the heat stay where it is. *Result—*scorching!

12:17

Safety screen

Get a piece of copper screen, such as is used for screen doors. A screen about 4 x 3 inches or more will do nicely.

Gently lower the screen into a candle flame. Note that the top portion of the flame does *not* go through to the top side of the screen. The copper screen conducts the heat away so fast, there is not

12:18

enough heat left to ignite the gas that escapes to the top side of the screen.

If you are lucky enough to have a Bunsen burner, you can perform even a more dramatic demonstration. If the gas is allowed to rise through the copper screen, and then ignited above it, the heat is carried away so rapidly by the screen that the gas on the bottom side of the screen does not receive enough heat to catch fire.

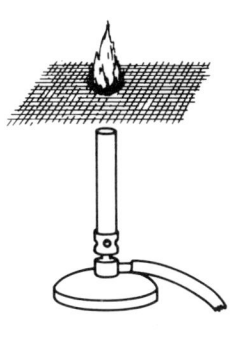

You may also do as you did with the candle. First light the Bunsen burner, then lower the copper screen into the top of the flame. The fire will not go through to the top side.

12:19

An application of the copper screen is the Davy safety lamp. It is an oil lantern with a cylinder of copper screen around it. The wick is lighted before the lamp is taken into the mine. If there is gas in the mine, it will enter into the copper cylinder and flare up as it burns, but no fire can escape to the outside of the screen to ignite the gas in the mine. To find out whether or not an iron screen would be equally satisfactory, hold an iron screen over a Bunsen burner for a few minutes, and see what happens. The iron can't carry the heat away as fast as the copper. If the flame is high enough, it may get the iron wires red hot and ignite the gas on the top side.

Glowing cigarette won't burn cloth

This is a "parlor trick" to demonstrate the high conductivity of silver. Stretch a portion of your handkerchief, or a small cloth, over the face of a half-dollar, which you hold in the palm of your left hand.

With your right hand, pick up the glowing cigarette and press the burning end firmly against the cloth.

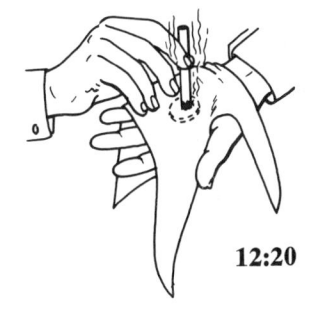

12:20

	The silver will conduct the heat away from the cloth so fast, it won't burn.	
Heat race	Here is an interesting demonstration the students may try for themselves before or after class. Have two equal strips of iron and copper. Pick up the iron with the right hand, the copper with the left hand, and hold them over a candle flame or a Bunsen burner. Place only the far ends of the metals in the flame. Find out which metal will conduct the heat to your fingers first.	12:21
Air-cooled engine	Perhaps one of the students has a small toy airplane motor which he can bring to class and show the students the fins on the air-cooled motor. The conductive power of aluminum is used to take heat from the cylinder of the engine and rush it away into the atmosphere.	12:22
Lazy conductor	To demonstrate what a poor conductor wood is, get a pan with a wooden handle, put a little water in it, and place it on an electric hot plate until the water boils. Ask the student to pick up the kettle of boiling water. He will do so by means of the wooden handle. Point out that thereby he proves what a poor conductor wood is.	
Cook hot dog by conduction	Put a little cooking oil in the bottom of a small frying pan, and place the pan on an electric hot plate. Put a hot dog in the pan. The meat cooks by *conduction,* by *contact* with the *hot metal* of the pan.	12:23
"Convect" a marshmallow	Run a long stick through a marshmallow and hold it over the red-hot coils of an electric hot plate. It roasts by *convection,* by means of the *hot air* rising upward from the coils.	12:24

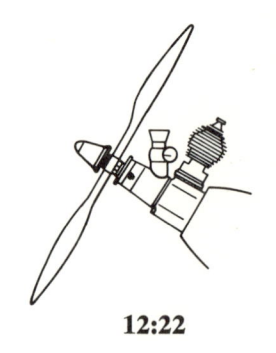

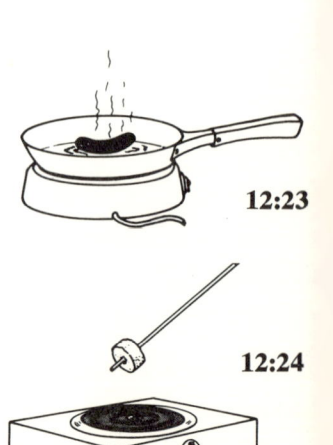

ESTABLISHING THE IMPORTANCE OF HEAT

Convection currents

Smoke curling lazily out the end of a cigarette or drifting upwards in aromatic clouds from a smoker's pipe, show how warm currents of air rise.

For a more dramatic demonstration, place a piece of burning incense in a dish. The smoke rises gently, like a white cloud, until it meets the ceiling.

Jack frost

Point out to students that Jack Frost helps them see thermals on cold winter days. When they exhale, the vapor in their breath condenses into frosty balloons that rise rapidly in the frigid air.

Convection engine

Get a piece of stiff paper, draw a spiral on it about ½ inch wide. Cut out the spiral and suspend it by a string run through a pinhole punched in the top of the spiral. Hold the spiral over a radiator when the heat is on and watch the results. You may also try holding it over a 100-watt lamp.

Some stores feature unique lamps with a spiral similar to the one pictured here. Heat from the lamp causes the spiral to turn, thus causing a beautiful variety of fascinating patterns.

12:25

Hot box

Get two, ½ gallon empty "cardboard" milk containers. Cut off the tops. Turn each box upside down. Punch a hole in the bottom of each box with a pin. Through this hole run a string. Secure the string with a knot on the inside of the box, so the box won't slip down.

Suspend each milk container from the end of a meter stick, which is balanced by a string tied at the 50-centimeter mark.

When the entire unit is balanced, place a lighted candle under the open end of the box on the right-

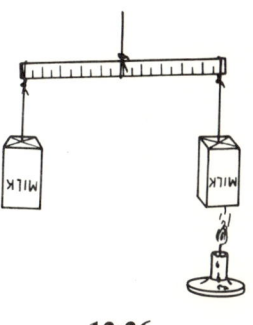

12:26

hand side. The air inside warms up, becomes less dense, and expands, thereby making that side lighter. The rising convection current forces this container up.

Box of cold air

Take the top off a cardboard box and leave it outdoors on a very cold day for about 20 minutes or more. A deep box about 2 feet long, 2 feet deep, and 1 foot wide will do nicely.

Bring the box from the cold outdoors into the classroom. After the box has been sitting on the lecture table for about 15 minutes, have students come up and place their hands down inside the box. They will find that even though there is no lid on the box, there is still cold air inside it.

Point out that deep-freeze units in supermarkets make use of this same fact—namely, that cold air sinks; hence, they do not need lids to keep the contents cold. Unlike hot air which "jumps up" and "floats away" the cold air sinks to the bottom. Children can do this experiment at home and also bring the box to class on a cold day.

Sawdust trail

To demonstrate convection currents in water, place a beaker of water on one side of a hot plate, so that only one edge of the beaker is directly over the hot coils.

A little sawdust added to the water will help make visible the fascinating convection currents.

12:27

Block that cold!

A glass block, of the type used in glass-block windows, makes a fine demonstration unit to show how heat loss is reduced by using glass (a poor conductor) plus a pocket of dead air. The air held captive inside the block is not only a poor

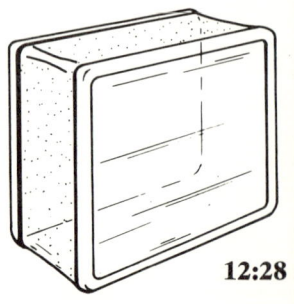

12:28

ESTABLISHING THE IMPORTANCE OF HEAT 175

conductor, but since it is "imprisoned" it cannot carry away heat by convection.

Watch convection currents

On a cold day in winter, when the heat is turned on, students may tell you that they are "watching convection currents" rise above the hot radiator.

Inform students that what they see is the effect of the convection currents—the bending of rays of light by layers of air of different densities. The convection currents themselves are invisible.

Radiate a hot dog

To cook a hot dog by radiation, impale the frankfurter on a wooden stick, and hold it in front of an electric heater that has a reflective metal behind it. Some electric room heaters are built with a concave reflector behind the coils. If so, hold the hot dog at the focal point of the concave reflector, and cook it by radiation.

Point out that the hot dog is *not* being cooked by conduction. (Air is a poor conductor.) Also indicate that the hot dog is *not* being cooked by convection. (Hot air rises.)

The infrared rays from the electric heater are traveling through space to heat the meat, just like the rays from the sun travel through space to heat planet earth.

12:29

Radiate a student!

Ask a student to stand by a radiator. If the radiator is not too hot, he may gently place his hand on it, and be heated by *conduction*.

If he holds his hands *over* the hot radiator, in the path of the rising warm air, he is being heated by *convection*.

If he stands about 3 feet to one side of the radiator, the heat that reaches him directly is by *radiation*.

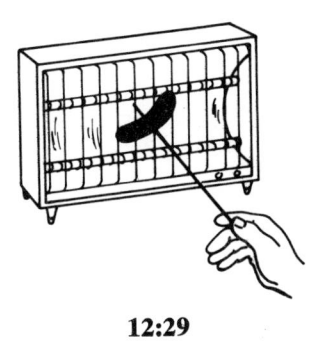

12:30

ESTABLISHING THE IMPORTANCE OF HEAT

Radiant heat

An electric heater with a concave reflector makes a fine demonstration piece to use for radiation. Have a student briefly move his hand past the focal point and observe the heat being radiated into his epidermis.

Or simply hold the electric heater in your hands and slowly turn the reflector around the classroom. Many, if not all the students, will be able to feel the radiant energy as soon as you direct the infrared rays their way.

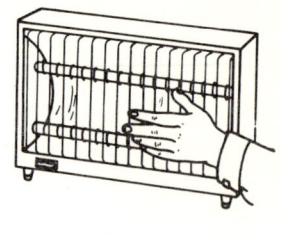

12:31

Spotlight on radiation

12:32

Place a radiometer on one side of a glass building block. On the other side of the glass block place a heat lamp or spotlight. Shine the light from the lamp through the glass block on to the radiometer. It begins to spin immediately.

Point out that the heat coming to the radiometer can't be due to conduction, since both the glass block and the dead air space inside it are poor conductors.

And the heat reaching the radiometer can't be due to convection. Convection currents travel up, not sidewise in the direction of the radiometer.

Heat goes through cool block

Use the same apparatus as above. After the radiometer has been spinning a couple of minutes, have a student come up and place his hand on the side of the block near the

ESTABLISHING THE IMPORTANCE OF HEAT

radiometer. His hand will be warmed by infrared rays coming to him by radiation.

Now turn off the heat lamp. Ask the student to pick up the glass block or simply place his hands on it. He will most likely be amazed to find that the glass block is not even warm.

Point out that radiant energy can pass right through a transparent object without heating it.

**Hot sun—
cold window**

If sunlight is streaming through a classroom window on a cold day in winter, ask a student to stand next to the window. The sunlight falling upon his body makes him feel warm. The radiant energy he absorbs makes him feel warm and comfortable.

Now ask him to place the palm of his hand on the windowpane, and report its temperature to the class.

When he says the glass is cold, point out, once again, that radiant energy can go through a transparent body without heating it much at all.

Radiant energy

Use the previous demonstration to point out that radiant energy will produce heat only if it is absorbed. Between us and the sun is some 93 million miles of space. Yet this space is not "hot" for the simple reason there is nothing there to absorb the heat.

On the other hand, if a spaceman were caught out in space between us and the sun without his protective aluminum suit to reflect its rays, he would absorb so much radiant energy he would be cooked in no time.

Sun starts fire

Use a convex lens to focus the rays of the sun on a piece of rough black paper. It will break into flame rapidly.

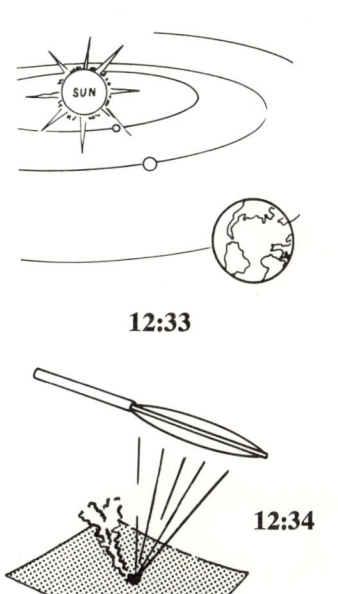

12:33

12:34

Now focus the rays on a smooth white paper. It may not burn at all or do so only after a long time.

This demonstrates that black objects absorb radiant energy more readily than do white objects.

Cool aluminum

Place your hand 4 or 5 inches in front of a heat lamp. You will soon have to move it. It is too close for comfort.

Now wrap your hand in a sheet of aluminum foil, or simply place your hand in an aluminum-lined sack such as is used for bringing ice cream home from the store. Now, even though your hand is in front of the lamp, you feel comfortable. The bright, shiny surface of the aluminum reflects the radiant energy. Leave this unit on the table for the students to try for themselves.

12:35

Thermos bottle

A thermos bottle, from which you can remove the bright, silvered interior flask is a most useful demonstration unit.

Point out that the bright, silvered surfaces limit heat loss due to radiation. The silvered walls reflect the heat back into the liquid, and thus keep your coffee warm.

The vacuum between the double glass walls prevents heat loss due to both conduction and convection, since both these methods of heat transfer depend upon molecules. The few stray molecules that are left in the partial vacuum are not sufficient to transfer much heat.

About the only place for heat to escape by conduction is through the cork and through the glass neck of the bottle, but since both cork and glass are poor conductors this heat loss is slight.

When you reassemble the thermos bottle, point out that there is also a dead-air space formed between the

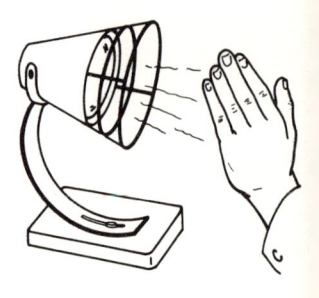

ESTABLISHING THE IMPORTANCE OF HEAT   179

glass bottle and the outside metal walls of the container. Likewise, there is another dead-air space between the cork and the top of the threaded cup. All of which helps to cut down on heat loss by conduction and convection.

Thermal on the table

To demonstrate how warm water rises upwards in thermal currents, obtain a big gallon jar with a wide mouth and fill it about ⅔ full of cold water.

Get an old ink bottle and fill it with warm water. There may be enough old, dried-up ink in the used bottle to color the water. If not, add a few drops of fresh ink to the water. Place the ink bottle of warm colored water in the bottom of the gallon jar, and watch inky convection currents swirl up to spread a mantle of inky blackness across the surface like a witch's cloak. Finally, the ink-colored liquid will cool, become more dense, and slither downwards like a snake uncoiling itself from a stick.

12:36

Grandfather's time

Perhaps you may be lucky enough to have a pendulum from an old grandfather's clock. Point out that in hot weather the long brass rod expands, and this would cause the clock to lose time. The bob must be adjusted by means of a threaded bolt and nut.

In winter, the brass rod shrinks and the clock gains time. Again the bob must be adjusted, and this time let down by the threaded bolt.

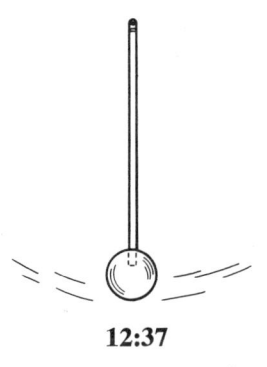

12:37

Warm-up

To show how fast a liquid can expand, throw the beam from a heat lamp on a thermometer. (*Danger*: Don't expose the thermometer to the heat too long!)

Students are amazed at the rapid increase in the volume of the liquid. I use a thermometer with colored

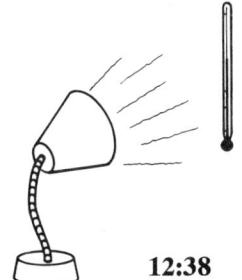

12:38

alcohol. It is easier to see than mercury.

If you have a thermometer made of Pyrex glass, you may now plunge the thermometer into cold water. Again the students are fascinated by the rapid change in volume.

Ball and ring

This is always a dramatic demonstration. I submerge the brass ring in a beaker of ice water, while I place the ball over the coils of an electric hot plate or in the flame of a Bunsen burner.

The expanded ball won't pass through the shrunken ring.

Now I plunge the ball into the ice water and put the ring over the heat. With a change of temperature in each and a corresponding change in volumes, the ring now easily fits over the ball.

12:39

Watch it expand

To show how heat causes metal to expand, stretch a long piece of copper wire, about 6 feet long, between two insulators tied to vertical support stands.

Connect the ends of the copper wires momentarily to a 6-volt storage battery and watch the wire sag. Shut off the current and the wire will pull up again. (*Caution—DON'T* touch wire when current is running through it.)

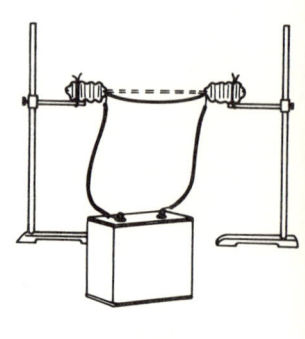

12:40

Regelation

To demonstrate that ice will melt under pressure, and freeze again when pressure is released, wrap the ends of a thin copper wire around the middle portion of two pencils. With the pencils serving as handles, place the top of the loop on the top of an ice cube, and bear down hard on the pencils.

As the wire presses against the cube, the ice will melt, only to freeze again once the wire has passed

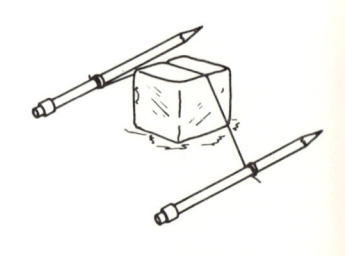

12:41

ESTABLISHING THE IMPORTANCE OF HEAT

through, leaving a block of ice as solid as when you began.

Point out that pressure causes the ice to melt directly beneath the wire. As the ice melts it takes heat from the wire, which, in turn, takes heat from the water directly above it. This water above the wire, no longer under pressure, freezes when it gives up its heat. This process of melting under pressure and refreezing when the pressure is released is called *regelation*.

Expanding world

During the coldest days of winter you may be able to demonstrate how water expands when it turns into ice. Fill a milk bottle (or any other large bottle) with water and leave it outdoors overnight. The next day the students may see the results for themselves.

If you have access to a deep freeze, you may try this experiment anytime.

Make matter "vanish"

You can cause matter to "vanish" by making it change states! To demonstrate this, place an ice cube in a small pan placed over an electric hot plate. In short order, the ice cube will melt; then, finally, the water will boil away as steam. You have made one ice cube "vanish."

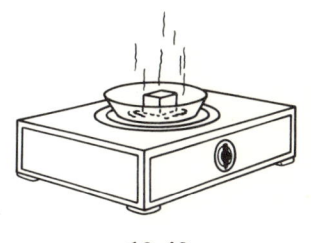

12:42

Ice that never melts

Dry ice, which is carbon dioxide in the solid state, evaporates directly from a solid to a gas. It does not go through the liquid state.

To demonstrate this process of *sublimation*, place a big chunk of dry ice into a large glass dish filled with water. This is a most fascinating demonstration.

As the dry ice turns into a vapor, the giant-size bubbles of carbon dioxide rise to the surface of the water, where they break with a bubbling sound that reminds you of the

DRY ICE

12:43

land of the sky-blue waters where rippling mountain streams babble over glossy boulders.

Most fascinating of all are the dense, white clouds of carbon dioxide that tumble out over the top of the bowl, then fall to the top of the table. The clouds "flow" along the flat surface of the table like a river. When they come to the edge of the table, the "river" of white "smoke" falls to the floor. Truly a most beautiful and captivating demonstration.

After a few minutes, the intense cold of the block of dry ice will freeze the water in direct contact with it. Thus covered with a layer of thick ice, the carbon dioxide will not be able to escape as a gas and the bubbling will stop—but only for a time.

Before long, the gas pressure builds up inside the layer of ice. With a loud bang, the gas finally breaks open the shell of ice and the process continues.

12:44

Boil it

Every year I'm amazed to find how fascinated the students are in watching water boil.

The reason—for many of them, this is the *first* time they have actually examined the process.

Place a beaker of water on a hot plate or over a Bunsen burner. The first thing to notice are the small bubbles of gas that seem mysteriously to appear from nowhere. Many of them cling to the sides of the beaker. These are bubbles of air. Heat is driving out air dissolved in the water. The absence of air from freshly boiled water is responsible in part for its flat taste. For a brief time the water "purrs" and "rumbles" like a pussy cat after a full meal. Finally, bubbles of steam form on the bottom of the

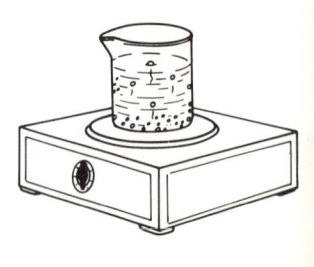

12:45

beaker and start to rise like round skyrockets. But suddenly they vanish. When they bump into colder layers of water above them, they condense and go back into liquid. As water rushes in to fill the space previously occupied by the bubbles, it makes a humming sound, as though it were softly singing a soft lullaby of dreamland.

All this time, bubbles are launching forth bravely from the bottom of the beaker, only to stagger, grow smaller, then vanish as they are condensed by cooler water.

Despite their continued defeats, the bubbles slowly succeed in working their way closer and closer to the surface.

About this time we notice thin, gauzelike clouds trailing across the surface of the water as some of the water vapor escaping from the surface condenses into visible droplets of water.

At last bubbles of steam rising from the bottom of the beaker steadily increase in size as they rise to the surface, where they break to produce the turbulent motion we associate with boiling.

Cool hand

Ask for a volunteer to stretch forth the back of his hand so you may pour a little ether or rubbing alcohol on it. Have him wave his hand a couple of times and the liquid vanishes.

Request the student to inform the class how the liquid felt. When he says "the liquid was cold," you can indicate why he experienced this effect.

For the ether to become "airborne" it had to acquire enough energy to jump from the liquid into the gaseous state. It did so by "stealing" heat from the student's hand and

Fire alarm

thus cooling the skin. Each student will enjoy this experiment—if you have enough alcohol to rub on all the hands.

Shine a heat lamp (not shown in diagram) on the bimetal strip AB. It will expand and come down to touch the contact point, C, thereby completing the electrical circuit, and the alarm will ring.

This simple "fire alarm" shows how the expansion of metals can be put to work to protect our homes, factories, etc. The above device can also be used as a thermostat. In your icebox, for example, when the temperature gets too warm, a bimetal strip makes contact. Electricity flows through the circuit and turns on a motor that runs the unit that cools the icebox. When the refrigerator has cooled, the bimetal strip contracts, breaks contact, and the motor turns off.

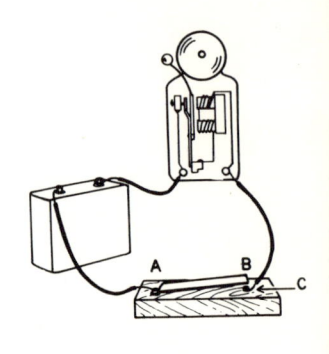

12:46

Furnace control

From the local furnace man I obtained an old wall thermostat used for controlling the temperature in the home. This makes a wonderful demonstration unit. You can show the students that the length of time the furnace stays on is determined by the distance between the contact points, which can be adjusted by the dial setting to any desired temperature.

Conclusion

Our lives depend upon heat. We use it to keep warm, to cook our food, to change iron ore into steel for automobiles, and to melt sand into glass. Yet, too much heat makes us uncomfortable, may even kill us and destroy our property. The secret, then, is to control the amount of heat so that we have only the proper amount. To do this involves a study of the three methods by which heat is transferred—

ESTABLISHING THE IMPORTANCE OF HEAT 185

> conduction, convection, and radiation. We also must examine what happens to objects when they are heated. Armed with a knowledge of the above heat principles, we can make the expansion and contraction of objects work for us rather than against us.

FOLLOW-UP EXERCISES

1. Explain how the thermostat in your hot-water heater is a "lifesaver."
   Hint: *When the temperature of the water reaches a certain point, the bimetal strip expands and breaks contact, thereby shutting off the heat to the water. Otherwise, the water would get so hot, it would turn to steam and explode, and take you and your house along with it!*

2. Explain how the comfort of your home depends upon a thermostat.
   Hint: *On cold days a thermostat turns on your furnace, then, when your room is the proper temperature, the thermostat turns off the furnace.*

3. Can you name one business built on the contraction and expansion of metals? The answer—among others—is Minneapolis Honeywell Control.

4. Does your overcoat keep you warm in winter?
   Strictly speaking, no. You keep yourself warm. All the coat does is prevent heat loss by conduction and convection. The coat traps untold millions of dead-air pockets, and thereby prevents the warm air from leaving your body.

5. How does convection keep you alive?
   When you breathe, the hot air you expand, loaded with carbon dioxide gas, rises and thereby allows the fresh air, with its load of oxygen, to enter your lungs.

6. Why do fruit growers and plant lovers like to have a heavy snow on the ground when the deep cold of winter arrives?
   Because the deep snow traps the air, and thus "insulates" the roots of the trees and plants from the terrible subzero cold that might otherwise harm them.

7. How do pigeons make use of dead-air space to keep warm in winter?
   Just look at them, and find out. They puff out their feathers, thus "trapping" more air, which acts like a "blanket of insulation" to keep the warm air from their bodies from leaving them.

8. Did you ever see a thermometer made of a bent piece of metal like a watch spring?
   This springlike strip of metal is a bimetal strip whose contraction and expansion turns the dial or needle on the thermometer to indicate the temperature.

Summary

What a fantastic world surrounds us! Heat is a "magic wand" that can make water jump into steam. If you want to make ice disappear, you first apply enough heat to melt the ice and then add more heat to the water to change it into invisible vapors.

How strange it is to realize that the molecules in a strand of wire, your desk, or your ball-point pen are in constant motion. If you could look into this miniature world of molecules and atoms you would find motion everywhere.

Every molecule, each atom, is spinning, vibrating, and whirling. Every substance known—even ice cubes, frozen peas, and ice-cold watermelon—is actually aquiver with the invisible motion that produces heat. Things that you call cold are just objects that have less heat than other objects.

13

The importance of this chapter will be brought home with a bang to anyone who slips on ice or fails to corner his car around a snow-slick curve.

You many introduce this chapter by asking, "Is friction a friend or

Investigating the Importance of Friction

Official photograph, U.S. Navy

Photo 13. *At this moment the parachute jumper can say that friction is his best friend.*

foe?" Have students draw up a list of pros and cons.

In this chapter, you can show what friction is, how to calculate its force, and illustrate how important it is in our daily lives. As you will see, "Friction supplies us with the stops that keep us going!"

On the other hand, friction can be a dangerous hurdle facing astronauts returning from the moon. As the spacecraft slams into the atmosphere at 24,700 miles per hour, the heat around it builds up to a sizzling 5000° Fahrenheit—hotter than a blast furnace!

Most important for the pocketbook, you can show why it is economical to drive at reasonable speeds—all because of air friction.

DEMONSTRATIONS

Friction match

A "friction match" is well named. You light it by dragging it across a rough surface. Friction comes from a Latin word meaning "to rub." It is the resistance to relative motion between two bodies in contact with each other.

13:1

"No light" match

The amount of friction depends on the kinds of surfaces in contact. To demonstrate this, try moving the match tip across a plate of smooth glass or one covered with smooth ice. The smooth surface will offer so little friction, the match won't ignite.

By contrast, drag the match head across a piece of sandpaper.

13:2

Rough hands

Here is a demonstration the students may try for themselves, to show how the amount of friction depends on the kinds of surfaces in contact.

Have them place their palms on a smooth surface, the top of a table, a block of ice, or oily surface, and push. Their hands will slide across the smooth surface easily. Now, by contrast, spread a large piece of sandpaper on the table. Have someone hold the sandpaper in place

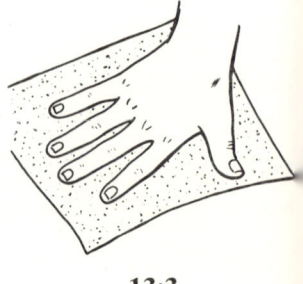

13:3

INVESTIGATING THE IMPORTANCE OF FRICTION

while a student places his palm on the rough surface and tries to slide his hand over the sandy surface.

Winter wonderland   Every winter students give superb demonstrations on how the amount of friction depends on the kinds of surfaces in contact. A sidewalk coated with glistening ice is so smooth it offers little resistance to forward motion. As a result, a student can slide for a long distance. No one tries to slide in like manner on a dry concrete sidewalk with bare feet.

13:4

Basketball shoes   A basketball player wears a shoe that will provide him with maximum friction, so that he may start and stop rapidly. Ask students to look at their shoes. Cleats are fastened to shoes to increase traction.

13:5

"Hot rope"   Every student who attempts this demonstration should be cautioned about the danger, but it makes a superb demonstration to show how friction depends both on the different surfaces in contact—and on speed. Have one student pick up one end of a long rope. A second student is to allow the rope to run through his hands while the first student runs with the rope across the room. (Caution student to grasp the rope only lightly, and to let go the moment the heat becomes too great.) Try different ropes at different speeds. *Warning—rope burn is easily possible. Use extreme caution.*

13:6

Floor burn   Anyone who plays basketball may have noticed the heat caused by friction when, after stumbling, they slide along the hardwood floor and acquire a "floor burn."

13:7

Toothbrush   Show students a toothbrush and remind them that it is friction pro-

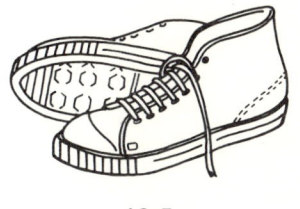

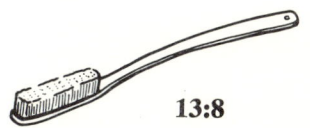

13:8

Warm hands

Rub your two bare hands together or rub your hand across your face and note the heat produced by the friction.

Coefficient of friction

The coefficient of friction may be defined as the *pull* (the force of friction) divided by the *load* (the force pressing the surfaces together).

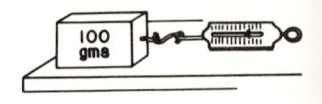

$$\text{Coefficient of Friction} = \frac{Pull}{Load}$$

13:9

Fasten a hook into one end of a block of wood, so that you may attach a spring scale and drag the block across the surface of your desk. Suppose the block of wood weighs 100 grams and it takes 20 grams of force to pull the block; then the coefficient of friction would be $\frac{20}{100}$ or $\frac{1}{5}$ or 20 per cent.

Drag the block over a rubber mat and notice the scale reading. Note how the force of friction (the pull on the scale) will depend on the surfaces in contact.

Double it

If you have another 100-gram block, place it on top of the first block, then pull the scale and notice that the reading is twice what it was before; but—and here is the interesting thing—if the blocks are in contact with the same desk surface, the coefficient of friction will remain the same. In other words, as long as the same type of surfaces are in contact, the force of friction (the pull) is always the same fraction of the load pushing on the surfaces. In this case, the coefficient of friction would be $\frac{40}{200}$ or $\frac{1}{5}$ or 20 per cent. The same as it was before!

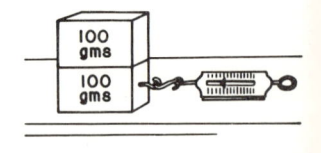

13:10

INVESTIGATING THE IMPORTANCE OF FRICTION

Roll it! Put two pipes, or simply two round pencils under the 100-gram block of wood, and pull on the scale. Note how little pull is now required to move the load.

You have changed "sliding" friction to "rolling" friction. No wonder the wheel is called one of the greatest inventions of mankind!

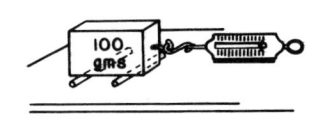

13:11

Conclusion

When you slip on the ice next winter and find yourself looking at the sky from a horizontal position, remember to exclaim sweetly, "All this is due to lack of friction." You can make use of friction to warm your hands or start a fire, but friction is also responsible for putting holes in your shoes, holes in the elbows of your sweaters, holes in tires, and holes in your socks!

FOLLOW-UP EXERCISES

1. How can you "sharpen up" with friction?
   Just use an emery wheel to put a sharp edge on your knife or an axe. And note that the glowing sparks are the result of friction between the fast moving wheel and the steel.

2. What advantage is there to having jewels in your watch?
   The jewels in watches are highly polished rubies, which serve as bearings and reduce friction to a minimum, increasing the efficiency and accuracy of your watch.

3. Sioux Indians once carried their sick in a "pony drag," a buffalo skin stretched between two poles tied to the sides of a horse. The free ends of the poles dragged on the prairie. When the palefaces rolled west in wagons, the Sioux learned that rolling friction is less than sliding friction, and so they took to wheeled transportation. You can see this for yourself if you visit the Pine Ridge Indian Reservation, Pine Ridge, South Dakota.

4. Do you know why you don't like to visit the dentist?
   The answer is "friction." It is friction caused by the spinning drill that makes heat, and this is what bothers you. To eliminate this heat problem, modern dental drills are equipped with water sprays that shoot cold water on the tooth while it is being drilled. This eliminates the heat which causes so much pain.

5. Write a composition on "Without Friction, Civilization Would Be Brought to a Smooth Standstill."

Hint: *If you fell down, you couldn't get up. No trains or buses would run. Continue to develop this theme.*

6. Here is another title for a theme: "Friction Supplies You with the Stops That Keep You Going." The only way to stop a car is by getting rid of its kinetic energy of motion. One way is to run into a tough tree or a stone wall. A better way is to change the kinetic energy into heat by using friction.

   When you slam on your brakes, the *energy* of *forward motion* is transferred or *changed* into *heat* in the brake drums, tires, and pavement. Friction helps you change *forward motion* into *heat!*

   But heat itself is described as the motion of molecules. Therefore, friction helps us change the *motion of a car* into the *motion of molecules* in the *brake drum*. What a tantalizing world we live in!

   The next time you ride in a car, remember that your trip is based on friction. To get moving, you make use of friction to overcome inertia. To stop, you must use friction to overcome the momentum that tends to keep you going. Slowing down is just as important as speeding up.

7. It is one thing to fling an object into space and keep it there. It is another—and equally difficult job—to bring it back to earth.

   When Russia launched the space age in October 1957, no one had to worry about the 184-pound *Sputnik* falling 550 miles and crashing through the roof of his split-level house. All the early satellites met a fiery death in the sky. Friction gave them hot noses.

   The near vacuum in space offers little friction as a missile plunges downward, but on re-entering the earth's thick blanket of air it meets increasing friction and heat.

   A missile with an ordinary nose cone meets destruction in the dense air about 14 miles above the earth. One of the most difficult problems in using ballistic missiles is to get the warhead back to earth and on target. It was understood all too well that an ICBM re-entry body of cone and warhead would crash back into the earth's atmosphere at a near-meteor speed of 15,000 miles per hour, with enough motion of energy to vaporize five times its weight of iron.

   Piling up ahead of the re-entry body would be a high-pressured air layer reaching up to 15,000° Fahrenheit. Any vehicle returning from space to earth must change its enormous energy of motion into heat. Fortunately for our Apollo astronauts returning from a trip to the moon, scientists found a way to reduce this intense heat considerably. One way involves the use of a broad, blunt nose for the space vehicle. The snub nose acts as a potent insulator. The violent shock wave, produced when the nose cone hits the atmosphere at high speed, scatters a much higher percentage of the intensely hot gases than would one of the thin, streamlined noses formerly thought to be better.

Another way is to cover the nose with ablating materials—substances designed to be destroyed by heat. The ablating materials vaporize and blow away, leaving a cooler surface.

The first space-age conqueror of the hot-nose problem now rests in the Smithsonian's National Air Museum, Washington, D.C. The black, heat-seared, rough metal skin of the RVX 1-5 gives evidence of the tremendous heat energy encountered by the first re-entry nose cone to be recovered. The RVX 1-5 was projected into space on April 8, 1959, at Cape Kennedy, by a Thor-Able flight vehicle and traveled on a set course to a point near Ascension Island in the South Atlantic at a speed of more than 15,000 miles per hour.

Upon re-entering the atmosphere, the cone was subjected to an air friction of more than 6500° C.

Summary

Friction is both friend and foe. It supplies us with the stops that keep us going, but it also means a blazing return to earth for spacecraft coming back from the moon. It keeps rocks from outer space from ripping us to shredded wheat by burning them to ashes as they plunge into our atmosphere. Friction also helps your walk, polishes your teeth, and wears out your clothes!

14

Y ou may begin this chapter by asking, "What surrounds you every moment of the day? What flows through you, like an invisible river, yet you are not even aware of it?"

Even as you read this sentence, this mysterious force is going through your head, hands, and feet,

Developing an Awareness of Our Magnetic World

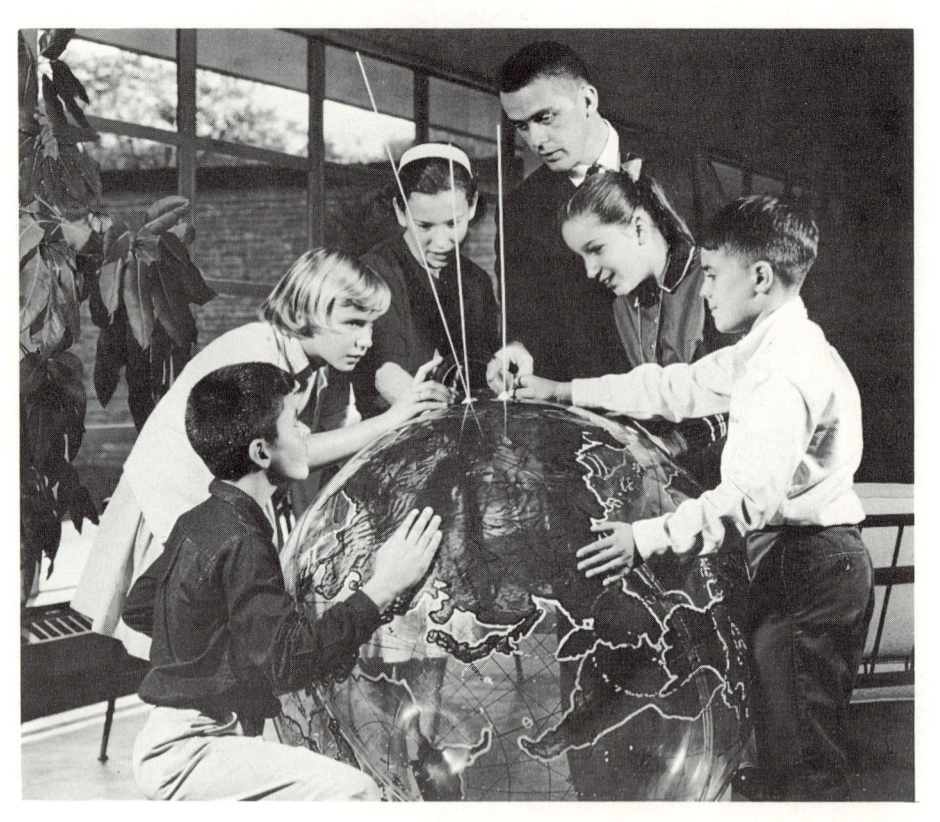

Photo courtesy of "The Chicago Tribune."

Photo 14. *Why does the earth act like a giant magnet? White sticks on top of globe represent electrical particles from the sun that are attracted by the magnetic pole. As these particles from the sun hit the upper atmosphere, they produce the northern lights or aurora borealis.*

DEVELOPING AN AWARENESS OF OUR MAGNETIC WORLD 195

zipping through your body like a bullet going through a cloud bank, and you aren't even aware of it?

How can we detect the presence of something we cannot see, or hear, or smell, or touch? In fact, we cannot detect this mysterious force with any of our senses.

Your objective in this chapter is to introduce your student to the unseen, invisible world of magnetic forces that surround us on all sides.

DEMONSTRATIONS

Invisible mover

Ask your students, "Can you take a piece of steel, and with it move another piece of steel—without touching it?"
Demonstrate how easy it is with two bar magnets. Suspend one magnet by a string tied to a support stand. Now bring the other magnet near the one suspended from the string. Bring unlike poles together, then like poles, and observe the results.

14:1

Now you see "invisible things"

To show how we may detect things we cannot directly see, touch, or hear, you can sprinkle iron filings on a paper resting on top of a bar magnet. The iron filings will form a pattern that "follows" the invisible lines of magnetic force "flowing" from the north to the south pole. A glass plate is excellent, if you have one.

14:2

Poles

If you have a rock known as magnetite (magnetic iron ore), roll it in a pile of paper clips. The places where the paper clips cling are at the concentrations of magnetic strength. These places are called the poles.

14:3

Paper clip "bridge"

Dip a bar magnet into a big pile of paper clips or small nails. When you lift the magnet from the clips or nails, you may find a "'bridge" or "chain" of clips or nails extending from pole to pole.

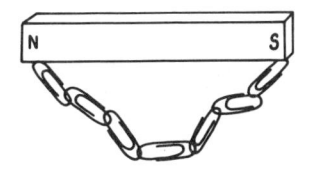

14:4

Attractive poles

Hold the unlike poles of two bar magnets about 1 or 2 inches apart and dip them into a pile of paper clips or small nails. When you lift up the magnets, you will have a "bridge" of paper clips, indicating that unlike poles attract.

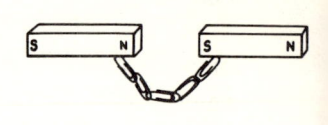

14:5

Repulsive poles

Now hold like poles about 2 inches apart and dip them into paper clips. This time when you lift up the magnets there is no bridge. Instead, the paper clips on the end of each magnet are repulsed apart, thus showing that like poles repel.

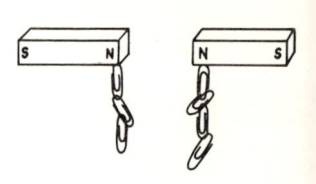

14:6

Magnet-propelled car

Tie a bar magnet to the top of a small toy automobile. Hold the north pole of another bar magnet near the north pole of the one fastened to the toy car, and you can "chase" the car across the table. Use the south pole of your hand magnet and you can "pull" the car.

14:7

Magnetic field

To demonstrate the magnetic field surrounding a magnet, place a compass needle on its support stand near a bar magnet that is suspended by a string from a support stand. Give a slight push to one end of the bar magnet so that it will turn slowly. As it does, the compass needle will turn first in one direction, then another.

14:8

Rockabye

Place a U-shaped magnet on the table with its open end up. Hold another such magnet about 2 or 3 inches above it. By moving the top magnet back and forth, you can make the magnet on the table rock. A pleasing demonstration of magnetic fields.

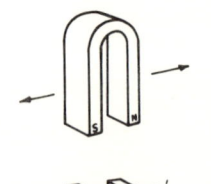

"Floating" ping-pong ball

Here is an interesting demonstration to have set up on the table when the students enter the classroom. Make a small cut in the side of a ping-pong ball with a safety razor

14:9

blade. Through this opening push a paper clip, to which you have tied a long black thread.

Tie the other end of the black thread around a small brick, block, or book, to act as anchor. Place the ping-pong ball under a strong alnico horseshoe magnet, that is suspended by a thread from a support stand. The ping-pong ball "floats" in the air.

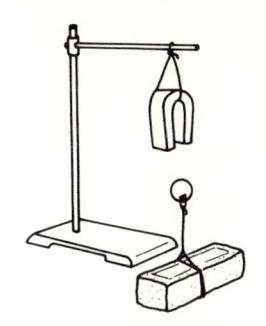

How many metals are magnetic?

Place small pieces of copper, brass, zinc, tin, nickel, lead, aluminum, steel, etc., plus an assortment of coins, on the table. See how many can be picked up with a magnet. Note that you can pick up a Canadian nickel, but not a U.S. 5-cent piece.

14:10

Through your hand

If you have a strong alnico magnet, place your hand over the poles. "Sprinkle" paper clips on the back of your hand, and if your magnet is a powerful one, it will hold the clips snugly against your skin, thus indicating that magnetic lines of force are going through your flesh even though you don't feel them.

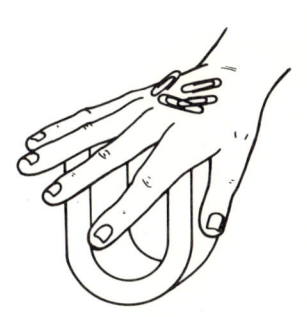

"Dancing nails"

Place a few small nails in a shallow wooden box or empty cigar box. Hold the box in your right hand. With your left hand, move a strong alnico magnet back and forth along the underside of the box. The nails will tumble around, some of them will "stand on their heads" while others will balance on their points, as though they were "dancing" under the influence of the powerful magnetic field.

14:11

For variety, place some small steel ball bearings in the box, and give them the "runaround" with the magnet beneath the box.

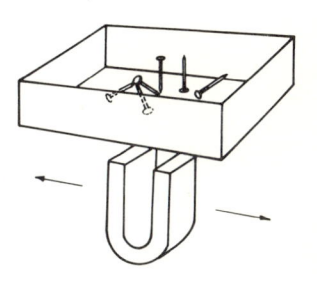

14:12

Holding power

Can you pick up a piece of wood with a magnet? Not by itself, since wood is not magnetic—but if you place a piece of iron on the far side of the wood, it is caught in a "squeeze play" and held tight by the attractive force between the magnet and the iron. Instead of wood, use brass, aluminum, glass, and paper. Note that magnetic lines of force go through these materials.

14:13

Pendulum stopped by magnet

Get a copper or brass pipe about 1 inch in diameter and about 3 or 4 inches long. Drill a hole through one end of the pipe so that you can run a thread or string through it, and suspend it like the bob of a pendulum.

Hold the string so that the copper pipe may swing between the poles of a strong alnico magnet. Pull the pipe slightly to one side, then release it, so that the pipe may swing like the bob of a pendulum.

Instead of swinging for a rather long time, like a pendulum, the pipe is brought to an abrupt halt.

Repeat the experiment with an aluminum pipe. It will most likely stop even sooner. Most likely it won't even make one complete swing. Since aluminum is antimagnetic, the magnetic field has a "dampening effect" on it, and "opposes" or "fights against" its passage between the magnetic poles.

Tie a thread to one side or near the rim of an aluminum pie plate and let the pie plate hang in a vertical position. Try to get the pie-plate pendulum to swing back and forth through the magnetic field. Note what happens.

Or simply hold the pie plate between your fingers and try to force the aluminum through the magnetic field. You will be surprised at the "opposition" the magnetic field of-

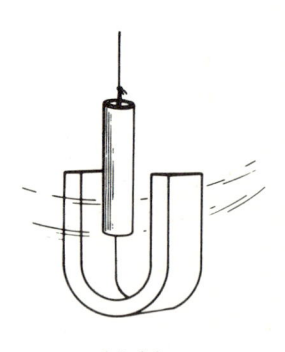

14:14

DEVELOPING AN AWARENESS OF OUR MAGNETIC WORLD 199

fers to the passage of the aluminum pie plate.

Keeper

Suspend a horseshoe magnet from a support stand and see how many nails or paper clips the magnet will hold.

Remove the nails, and place an iron bar across the poles of the magnet to serve as keeper. Now see how many nails the magnet will hold. The keeper does just what it says. It "keeps" the magnetic lines of force flowing through the iron bar, rather than through the surrounding space. *Result*—only a few nails, if any, will cling to the bottom side of the iron bar.

Conclusion—to shield objects from the effects of a magnet, cap the magnet with a keeper.

14:15

Test tube magnet

According to theory, the difference between a magnetized piece of steel and one that is not magnetized is that its molecules, which act like tiny magnets, are "lined-up" or "pointing" in the same direction. Here is a marvelous demonstration to illustrate the theory.

Pour iron filings into a glass test tube. Cork the tube. Turn the test tube on its side, and bring it near a compass needle mounted on a pivot, so that all the class may see the results. Either end of the test tube of filings will attract either end of a compass needle, as will any piece of unmagnetized steel.

Now pick up the test tube with your left hand and hold the tube in a horizontal position. With your right hand, pick up a strong bar magnet and move the north pole of the magnet along the length of the tube. Do this several times, always making sure that you stroke the tube in the *same direction each time*.

By now, the iron filings, which we

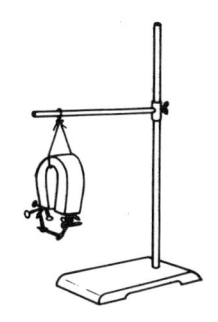

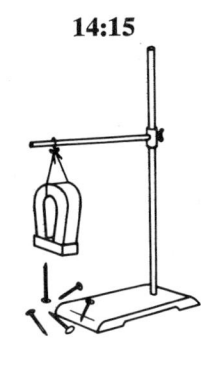

14:16

14:17

may consider to represent molecules in a bar of steel, are "lined up" with their north poles pointing in the same direction.

Bring the test tube "magnet" near the compass needle. One end will repel the north pole of the compass. The other end of the compass will be attracted.

You have "made a magnet" by lining up the particles in the same direction.

To "unmake" your test tube magnet, simply shake it. You thereby throw the iron filings "out of line." Now either end of the test tube will attract the compass, thereby proving you have "lost" your "magnet." This should prove to students that one way to weaken a magnet is to "shake up" its molecules by violent pounding, jarring, and dropping on the floor.

"Space magnet"

To demonstrate how to magnetize by induction, hold a strong bar magnet in your left hand. With your right hand, hold a nail about ½ inch below the south pole of the bar magnet. Dip the far end of the nail into a pile of paper clips and note how many it will hold.

Now remove the bar magnet. The nail will lose practically all of its magnetic power and the paper clips will fall off. Soft iron loses its magnetic property when taken out of a magnetic field.

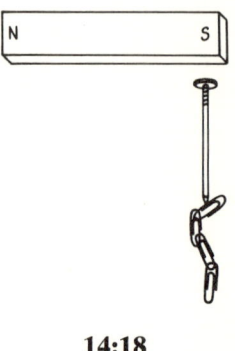

14:18

Contact

Repeat the above experiment, only this time place the head of the nail in direct contact with the south pole of the bar magnet. Do you pick up more paper clips than before? Why?

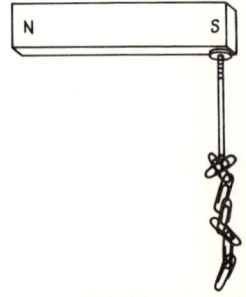

Make a magnet by hammering!

Get a steel rod about 3 feet long. To find out whether or not it is magnetized, hold one end first at the north pole of a compass needle,

14:19

then at the south pole of the compass needle. If the rod attracts both poles, it is not magnetized. (Any piece of unmagnetized steel will attract any pole of a compass.)

With your left hand, hold the steel rod at an angle of about 70° with the horizontal and in a north-south plane. With your right hand, take a hammer and pound the top end of the rod vigorously.

Now hold one end of the steel rod at the north pole of the compass needle, then at the south pole of the compass. If the rod repels one of the poles, it is magnetized. You have proved it is possible to turn a steel rod into a magnet by jostling its molecules with a hammer and then letting the molecules rearrange themselves under the influence of the earth's magnetic field.

Finally, hold the steel rod in your left hand so that the rod does not line up with the earth's magnetic field. In fact, keep turning the rod, as once again you pound it with a hammer.

Now hold the steel rod near the compass. Any end of the rod will now attract both poles. You demagnetized the rod by jostling its molecules in such a way that they could not line up with the magnetic lines of the earth.

Magnetic radiator

Students are amazed to learn that any steel object that has stood for a long time in the earth's magnetic field, itself becomes a magnet. If you have an old-fashioned steel radiator in your classroom, you may try a devastating demonstration.

Bring a compass needle (a big compass needle mounted on a pivot for all to see) near the top side of an iron radiator. It will attract the north pole of the compass needle. Lower the compass needle to the

STEEL ROD

14:20

bottom of the radiator. The south pole of the compass will swing around!

Heat destroys magnetism

Magnetize a steel needle by stroking it. Hold it near a compass to test its polarity or dip it into iron filings to prove it is a magnet.

Use a pair of pliers to hold the tip of the needle in the flame of a gas burner until it is red hot. When the needle cools, bring it near a compass again and see whether it is still magnetic. See whether it will pick up iron filings.

"Hand motor"

By means of a string, suspend a bar magnet from a support rod. Pick up another bar magnet and hold its north pole near the north pole of the suspended magnet. The like poles will repel. You can "chase" the suspended magnet around and around and thus demonstrate the principle of an electric motor—one magnet chasing another. (Instead of using bar magnets, electric motors make use of electromagnets, but the reason the motor spins is that one magnetic field is reacting on another magnetic field.)

14:21

Stand-apart magnets

Get a string about 10 inches long. Tie the ends around the north poles of two bar magnets and suspend the string over your finger. The magnets will "stand apart" from each other as like poles repel.

14:2

"Fingerprinting" magnetic lines

We mentioned earlier how fascinating it is to sprinkle iron filings on a paper placed over a bar magnet. For variety, use two horseshoe magnets or two bar magnets. Place like poles together, then unlike poles. Try using combinations of bar magnets and horseshoe magnets.

Ping-pong tester

The ping-pong ball setup mentioned earlier can be used to test for

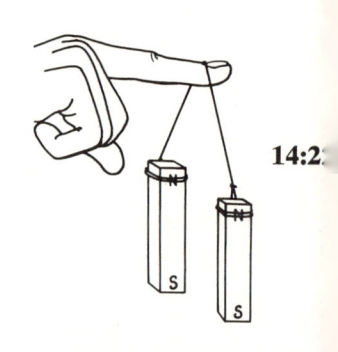

14:23

DEVELOPING AN AWARENESS OF OUR MAGNETIC WORLD

magnetic and nonmagnetic materials. Hold a piece of paper, cardboard, thin wood, or strip of copper under the magnet. The lines of force go through these materials. The metal clip inside the ping-pong ball will not be affected.

Now hold a sheet of soft iron under the magnet. The soft iron will concentrate the magnetic lines of force within itself. With the lines of force thus deflected, the ping-pong ball will fall.

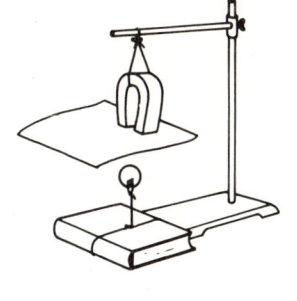

14:24

Floating magnet

Place a strong alnico bar magnet in the bottom of a shallow glass bowl and pour in water to a depth of about 2 inches.

Run a magnetized steel needle through a flat cork so that the north end of the needle pierces the water. Place the north pole of the needle above the north pole of the bar magnet. The needle will move along a magnetic line of force extending from the north to the south pole of the bar magnet.

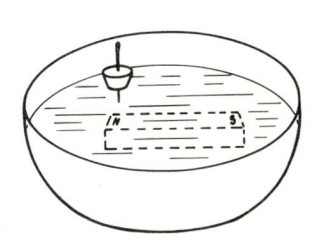

14:25

Conclusion

We live in an invisible world we cannot see, touch, hear, taste, or contact directly by any of our senses. In this world of magnetic forces, a piece of magnetized steel (a compass needle) is more sensitive than our fingers, more discerning than our eyes. It picks out the invisible magnetic lines of force and shows the direction in which they flow past us. Even inert iron filings become more "alert" and "sensitive" than we are, and when sprinkled on a paper covering a magnet they will show the beautiful pattern described by the invisible magnetic lines that escape our direct detection.

FOLLOW-UP EXERCISES

1. Some dime stores feature small plastic boy and girl dolls with revolving heads that contain alnico magnets. When brought close together, they turn heads and "kiss." A striking example of the mutual attraction of unlike poles!

2. Another interesting item carried in many dime stores are small plastic toy automobiles that contain alnico magnets. When like poles face each other, one car can "chase" the other without ever catching it.
3. Your family car may have begun its life with the help of a magnet. Taconite is a low-grade ore once considered worthless. This flint-hard rock contains about 30 per cent iron. The rock is crushed to the consistency of face powder. It is then carried to magnetic separators which separate the iron particles from sand.
4. Although we can't touch or feel magnetic forces, people have wondered whether or not they can affect living things. During the last century, certain "healers" claimed miraculous health cures from magnetism, but they were denounced as "magnetic charlatans" by the medical profession.

    Today, however, scientists are finding that magnetic fields can affect life—but not exactly in the ways early quacks had thought. Scientists have found that mice placed in strong magnetic fields eat less, but get more energy from the food they do consume.

    When young mice were exposed to magnetic fields 6000 times as great as that of the earth's magnetic field, the creatures stopped growing and the males died.

    Scientists in many laboratories around the world have discovered that magnetism will cause changes in blood, slow the growth of bacteria, and disrupt the central nervous system of some animals.

    How do magnetic fields produce these varied changes? The scientists themselves aren't quite sure.
5. The magnetic poles wander. In the early 1940's, for example, the magnetic pole in the northern hemisphere was located on Prince of Wales Island, some 150 miles south and slightly east of its present position. In fact, the poles may move as much as 700 miles a century.

    Now for the most amazing news of all. Nine times in the past 4 million years or so, the earth's magnetic field has completely reversed or "flip-flopped." The North Pole became the South Pole, and the South Pole the North.

    What actually took place was this. For long centuries the magnetic field of magnetism of the earth grew weaker and weaker, until at last it disappeared entirely!

    If a compass had been placed anywhere in the world at that moment, its needle would have had no place to point.

    Five thousand years later the imaginary compass needle stopped spinning. Once again the earth had become magnetized. But now the compass needle was pointing in the opposite direction. For some unknown reason the earth's magnetic field had done a complete flip-flop.

How and when do the scientists know that this reversal in direction took place?

The answer to this question is found in the nature of volcanic rocks and in the change that takes place in one of the elements found in these rocks.

6. The earth's magnetism is decreasing. Some 2000 years from now, it is expected to reach zero!

7. According to a theory advanced by Dr. Bruce Heezen of Columbia University, the mutation and extinction of species in the evolution of life may be attributable in part to periodic disappearances and reversals of the earth's magnetic field.

This decline in intensity, Heezen said, means the loss of the magnetic field as a shield helping to protect the earth from bombardment by cosmic rays. The cosmic rays thus strike earth species with dangerous force.

"The result of this cosmic-ray bombardment is the complete killing off of some species," the geologist declared. "Other species are created through mutations, and some of these mutations are successful and create new dominant species."

Summary

What is it you live in all the time? What surrounds you every moment of the day? What flows through you like an invisible river, yet you are not even aware of it?

Even as you read this sentence, this mysterious force is going through your head, hands, and feet, zipping through your body like a bullet through a cloud bank, and you aren't even aware of it!

But wait a minute. If we can't see it, taste it, or touch it, or even hear it, how do we even know it is there?

The answer is that since we can't detect this ever-present force with any of our senses, we have to get information from rocks and bars of steel.

Does this mean that a rock or bar of steel is more sensitive than our fingers?

In this case, yes. A rock of magnetic iron ore called magnetite or a bar of steel that has been magnetized, can be used as a compass that will detect the invisible lines of magnetic force that surround us.

You may introduce this chapter by asking, "Can you turn your head into a broadcasting station?", "Can you 'listen' to the sun on your radio?", "What is it that you can hear on your radio almost immediately via radio waves, then, in a few short seconds, hear directly again via airwaves?"

This chapter is important in many aspects. It will help you demonstrate the principles behind radio broadcasting. You may introduce

15

Understanding Static Electricity

Photo courtesy of Westinghouse Electric Corporation

Photo 15. *A bolt of lightning directly overhead usually spells serious trouble, but not if you're sitting in your car. To demonstrate that the automobile provides passengers complete safety from lightning bolts, this 1960 Mercury was hit by an artificial stroke at the Westinghouse Corporation's high-voltage laboratory where electrical apparatus is developed and tested. Occupant at wheel is untouched even though he's sitting beneath a 3-million volt stroke. The charge usually flows to the ground by arcing over one of the tires. In this case, the arc is visible at the right front wheel.*

UNDERSTANDING STATIC ELECTRICITY

your students to radio stars and to broadcasts sent out by the sun!

Most important of all—this chapter may save a life! With but a modest amount of equipment, you can bring home an important lesson which will mean safety during lightning storms, as well as safety when a car strikes a utility pole and high-voltage wires drop down to entangle it.

DEMONSTRATIONS

Repulsive newspaper

We can't "see" electricity "standing still" with the naked eye, but a device called an electroscope helps us to detect the presence of electricity by its actions.

To make a simple electroscope, take a page from a newspaper and cut out two strips, each about 2 or 3 inches wide and 1 foot long. Hold the top ends of the paper strips between thumb and forefinger of your left hand. With your right hand, pick up a woolen cloth or piece of fur.

Place the fur around the top of the strips of paper, just under your left thumb. Gently but firmly pull down the fur with your right hand. After two or three strokes, the "leaves" of your electroscope will spread apart.

What has happened? The friction of the fur caused electrons to leap from the fur to the paper. Both strips of paper were "swarming" with electrons. Since like charges repel each other, the like charges on the two strips of paper made them push apart or repel each other.

To "shake hands" with the paper electroscope, place your right hand between the leaves while they are spread apart. Notice how rapidly they swing over to "shake hands" with you. The excess negative charges on the paper strips are attracted by the positive charges on your hand.

15:1

Note: All experiments with static electricity work best in dry, cold weather. For this reason I do all these experiments in January. In moist weather you may get no results at all.

No-kissing balloons

This is the most dramatic electroscope I show my students every winter. I tie two strings, each about 2 feet long, to the end of a meter stick. On the free end of each string I tie an inflated balloon. I rest the meter stick on my desk, and rub each balloon in turn briskly with a piece of fur or wool. Now I pick up the meter stick, and behold! The negative charges on the balloons repel and the two balloons spread apart.

15:2

Kissing balloon

Here is a way to be kissed by a balloon. Blow up a toy balloon, tie it with a string about 2 yards long, and suspend it from a light fixture or any other convenient spot. Rub the balloon briskly with a piece of fur or wool.

Now walk close to it. The balloon will gently swing over to "kiss" you. The excess of negative charges on the balloon are attracted by the positive charges on your epidermis.

15:3

Wallflower balloon

Here is a balloon that is truly a "wallflower." Briskly rub a balloon with a piece of fur or wool. Now place the balloon against your slate blackboard or wall. Opposite charges will hold it captive.

15:4

Chasing rulers

Two plastic rulers make an excellent electroscope or "device to see electricity in action." Suspend one plastic ruler by a string tied to its middle so that it is free to rotate. Rub one end of this ruler with fur or wool to give it a negative charge. (Remember that friction causes the

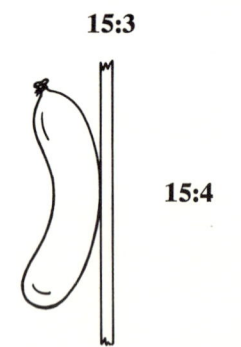

UNDERSTANDING STATIC ELECTRICITY

negative charges to leave the fur and jump onto the ruler.)

Rub a second plastic ruler in the same manner. Now bring the charged end of the second ruler towards the charged end of the suspended ruler and watch what happens. Since like charges repel, the electrons on one ruler will "chase" the second ruler away.

Electroscope

To make a more elaborate electroscope, use a big jar with a cork or block of wood for a stopper. Through the cork insert a big nail or bolt, and wrap a light wire around the end of the bolt to serve as a stirrup through which you insert a light strip of aluminum foil.

The glass bottle protects the foil from air currents and allows maximum visibility. It also serves to insulate the bolt with its aluminum foil leaves. When the electroscope is neutral (equal number of protons and electrons on the leaves), the foil strips or leaves hang straight down. Touch the head of the nail or bolt with a plastic ruler that has just been rubbed with fur or wool. Excess electrons in the ruler pass into the head of the bolt. Because metal is a good conductor, the electrons will not remain on the head of the bolt but will run down into the foil. Since the two strips of aluminum attached to the stirrup now have extra electrons, they are negatively charged. Since like charges repel, the leaves fly apart.

Paper-catching ruler

Here is a simple demonstration the students like. Tear up some thin paper into very small pieces and place them on the table. Now rub a plastic ruler with a piece of fur or wool. Hold the ruler near the small pieces of paper and observe

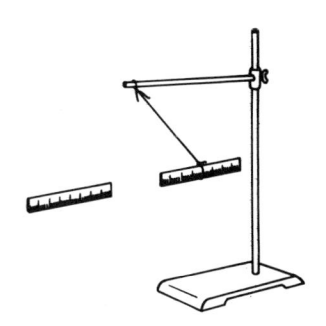

15:5

15:6

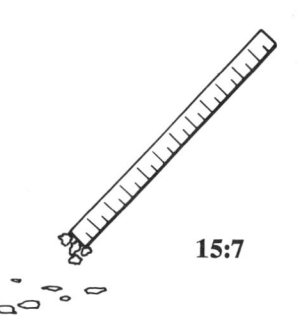

15:7

the results. The charged ruler will attract the uncharged bits of paper. If bits of paper pick up some of the electrons, then they will become negatively charged also and then be repelled!

"Electron" balloons

Rub an inflated toy balloon with fur or wool and place it on the table. Do the same with another such balloon. Place the second balloon about 2 feet from the first balloon. Use a meter stick to shove the second balloon towards the first one. Observe the antics as the like charges on the balloons make them repel each other.

15:8

"Come hither" ping-pong ball

Use a darning needle to run a stout thread through a ping-pong ball. Tie the end of the string in a knot so it won't go through the ball. Tie the free end of the string to a support stand. Rub a plastic ruler or comb with fur or wool and bring the ruler near the ball. The attraction between opposite charges will cause the ping-pong ball to swing over to "rub noses" or "shake hands" with the ruler.

15:9

Friendly aluminum

Cut out a piece of aluminum foil about 1 inch wide and 1 foot long. Tape one end to a support rod.
Rub a plastic ruler or comb with fur or wool. Bring the ruler near the free end of the aluminum foil. It will jump over to "shake hands."

1

Is glass always an insulator?

Rub an inflated balloon with fur or wool and bring it near the knob of an electroscope. Watch the leaves diverge.
Now take the charged balloon and hold it near the base of the glass walls of the electroscope. As you move the charged balloon back and forth near the glass, you may notice the fascinating motion of the leaves

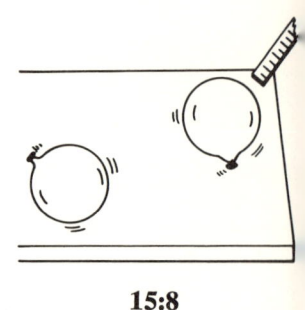

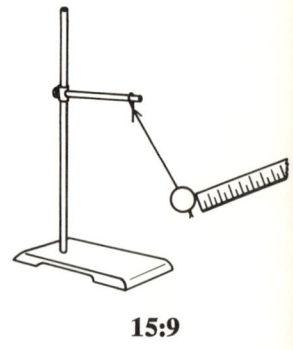

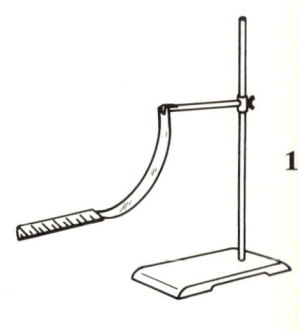

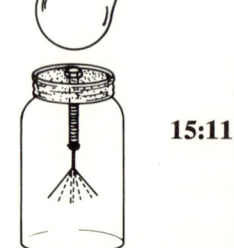

15:11

UNDERSTANDING STATIC ELECTRICITY

Use your head to broadcast!

showing that the electric field is going through the glass.

When you run a plastic or rubber comb through your hair, electrons rush onto your comb to charge it with electricity. Your hair holds on to its electrons less securely than does a plastic comb. When you run the comb through your hair, electrons leap from hair to comb.

When electrons are in motion, they let the world know it by putting out electromagnetic disturbances called radio waves.

You may start broadcasting right now and demonstrate how jumping electrons cause radio waves. All you need is your head, with hair on it, one plastic comb, and a radio. You can do this experiment at home.

In this demonstration, your head is a "broadcasting station." Your radio will catch the private program coming from station "DOME"!

Your "program" will be better on cold winter days when the air is very dry. Place your radio on the table and move the dial to a spot where there are no stations, then turn up the volume. Now stand near the radio and run a plastic or rubber comb through your hair. As the comb glides through your hair, it will cause electrons to jump between hair and comb. The jumping electrons will "broadcast" that they are in motion by sending out radio waves.

As the electromagnetic waves leap out from your head, they cut across the wires in the antenna of your radio. In so doing, their energy is converted into electrical current, which is then amplified and made to vibrate the diaphragm of the loudspeaker. You will hear static.

15:12

The faster and more ferociously you comb your hair, the greater the static.

To find out how far you can broadcast start with your head close to the radio, then slowly walk away from the table. You will finally reach a distance where the broadcast fades out. The energy of your radio waves will have been absorbed by the air before it reaches the radio. Static is caused by "untamed" electrons jumping around and giving out waves of untamed energy. When you run a comb through your hair, the untamed electrons hop around wildly like Mexican jumping beans. In regular broadcasting the electrons are "tamed" and made to vibrate in harmony, keeping "in step" with the sound waves that push against the diaphragm of the microphone. The frequency of their "jumps" is thus adjusted to the lyric song of a girl soprano or a dramatic news commentator.

SOS via rulers

Here is an interesting variation of the above experiment. Get a plastic ruler and a piece of fur or wool. Hold the ruler near the radio and rub the ruler with the wool or fur. Each time you do, you will get a blast of static on the radio. By rubbing the ruler at proper time intervals, you can control the static to give a dot-dash effect. With a little practice, you may even use the Morse code to send an SOS.

"Super sparks"

This is not a classroom demonstration. You will have to wait until the next electrical storm to see it, but at least we can cue you in on what to expect.

Lightning is static electricity's big, burly, red-eyed brother—rough and reckless. When lightning flashes, nature gets into the business of making radio waves—with a bang. Every time a group of electrons jumps from a cloud to the earth (or to some other cloud) during a lightning storm, they broadcast the fact with a burst of radio waves that causes your radio to roar and rumble.

Many theories have been advanced to explain the cause of lightning, but none of them is entirely satisfactory. In essence, the electrons that terrify the earth in vivid, scarlike flashes of gleaming light are the same as those that leap in tiny sparks from your hair.

Lightning is the jumping of tremendous quantities of electrons from cloud to cloud or from cloud to earth. Clouds can build up either positive or negative charges which mount to undreamed of power. When the force of attraction between opposite charges becomes powerful enough, a tremendous surge of electrons, an electric current which we call lightning, leaps between the charged bodies.

Lightning bolts between clouds and ground may travel 3 miles or more. Between two clouds, they may flash a distance of 10 miles or more. Since it takes about 67,000 volts to leap 1 inch, a 10-mile flash indicates a tremendous power.

The average flash of lightning has about 500 times as much horsepower as all American automobiles put together. This vast power, however, is turned on for intervals as short as 35 millionths of a second. In a lightning flash, you do not see electricity itself—only a burning spark channel or burning air column about an inch in diameter. The searing, red-hot 30,000° Centigrade heat of the flash causes the channel of air to expand or explode with tremendous force. The airwave thus produced pounds against your eardrum to cause the sensation we call thunder. If the discharge is close by, the thunder comes as a sharp, whiplike crack.

You can determine the distance of lightning if you start counting the moment you see it or hear it on your radio. Since light waves and radio waves travel 186,000 miles per second, you see the burning column of air (or hear the static on your radio) almost the instant it leaps into being.

The sound wave it produces, however, travels more slowly—only some 1100 feet per second. If five seconds tick by before you hear the sound of the thunder, the lightning bolt was approximately a mile away. The sound of thunder generally does not travel more than 18 miles. What we call "heat lightning" is ordinary lightning, but it is so distant that the rumbling thunder of its voice does not reach you.

Safety first

The safest places to be during a lightning storm are in a garbage can, in a furnace, in a refrigerator, in an automobile, or inside a steel skyscraper.

Why? Because electric charges distribute themselves over the outside of a metallic conductor.

To demonstrate this, I place my right hand inside a tin can, which I have grounded by running a wire to a water pipe or radiator. Use an alligator clip to fasten the wire to the can.

With my left hand, I turn on a portable induction coil and bring it to the outside of the can. Sparks leap over from the tip of the induction coil to the metal can, but I feel nothing.

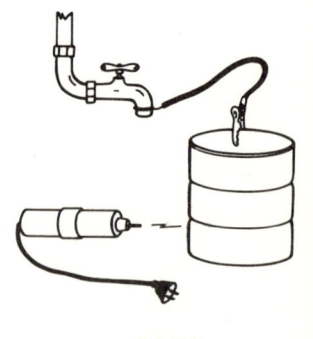

15:13

Even more dramatic is to wrap a piece of copper screen, about 6 inches long, around your hand. You can secure the copper screen in place by interweaving the loose ends of the wire into the screen mesh.

As previously, attach a ground wire by means of an alligator clip. Make sure the other end of the wire is fastened to a good ground such as a radiator, cold water pipe, etc.

Now bring the coil near the copper screen. A sizzling, hot stream of sparks turn the air blue, but you feel nothing. To the students it appears as though surely your flesh must be jabbed by the fast flying sparks. The magic mesh protects you. It is a modern application of the Faraday ice-pail experiment to show that charges distribute themselves over the outside of a metallic conductor.

Conclusion

The "secret" behind broadcasting is simply this—electrons are "tattle-tales." Whenever they are in motion, whenever they jump they "tell the world about it." When electrons leap into motion, they put out electromagnetic disturbances or radio waves. As these radio waves cut across the wires in the antenna of a radio, they create in the wires or set up, an electric current. This current is weak and feeble like your pocketbook just before payday. Your radio now takes this tiny electrical current and amplifies it, making it powerful enough to cause the diaphragm of your loudspeaker to vibrate like the vocal cords of Paul Bunyan.

FOLLOW-UP EXERCISES

1. How shocking are you? You can find out on a crisp winter day when you walk across a thick rug, then stretch out your fingers to shake hands with a visitor. Or to get the same effect, touch a radiator or light switch.

2. Perhaps you shocked yourself by sliding across the plastic seat covers in an automobile, then touching the handle of the door.

3. On a dark winter's night when the air is dry, you can manufacture your own "lightning bolts" by standing in front of a mirror and combing your hair. If the air is sufficiently dry, you will see sparks playing leapfrog in your hair and you will probably hear faint crackling noises.

4. You may also hold a small fluorescent tube in your hands as you slide your feet across a thick rug. The tube will quiver with flashes of light. Rub the tube on your wool sweater when you are in a dark room, and notice how the tube quivers with light.

5. While driving your automobile down a highway parallel to high-voltage transmission lines, you "lose" your musical program and get only static on your radio. This is because electrons are "jumping" or moving back and forth in the overhead wires 60 times a second, and putting out electromagnetic waves that leap through the antennae of your radio causing the static.

6. The National Safety Council advises against letting little children play with plastic bags, such as those the dry cleaner uses to return your clothes in.

   The reason is this: The static electricity created by the friction as the child pulls the bag over his hair will make the plastic cling close and snug to his face, shutting off the vital supply of fresh air.

7. Write a composition entitled, "Whenever Electrons Jump, They Put Out Electromagnetic Waves." The following are "hints" for developing this theme:

   (A) We already mentioned how to broadcast from station DOME and how to use plastic rulers to "broadcast"—but how about this? Try to listen to Petula Clark on your radio while Dad is using his electric shaver that gives off sparks. His hand-size broadcasting station will make you think you have a radio tuned in to a convention of snapping turtles and mad tomcats.

   (B) How about fluorescent lamps, vacuum cleaners, etc. Have they ever bothered your radio reception? If so, explain why.

   (C) Remember that the biggest demonstrations of electrons "jumping" come with the flashes of lightning that sear the midnight sky.

8. Whenever you hear static, you know that somewhere electrons are "jumping" or moving. But, remember, that all the static on your radio is *not* produced by static electricity. Not all electrons "jump" or "move" for the same reason.

   1. In dad's electric razor, electrons jump because they are being "pushed" through the wires by the dynamo in your city's electric power plant.

2. In the spark plug of your car, electrons jump because of the chemical energy in the battery.

3. Electrons jump out from the sun because intense heat strips them loose from their atoms and hurls them into space.

4. Electrons jump when you run a comb through your hair because of friction. The term "static electricity" refers to the stationary charges of electricity that are produced by friction or rubbing. When opposite charges on nearby objects are very strong, the air no longer separates them and they "jump" from one object to the other.

Summary

When electrons are in motion, they "broadcast" the fact by sending out electromagnetic waves (radio waves). Thus, we can "listen" to the sun on our radios because electrons pushed into motion by the sun's heat give out electromagnetic disturbances. Radio noise from the sun is most intense during solar flares because more electrons are thrown into motion. In fact, the sun is "blowing" solar winds our way. These "winds" consist of positively charged hydrogen nuclei and free electrons speeding toward us at some 900 miles per second. They broadcast the fact that they move.

Of tremendous practical importance is the fact that high voltage distributes itself over the outside of a metal conductor, as illustrated by various newspaper clippings:

"When Louis Orlandi slammed his car into a utility pole at Lake Ronkonkoma, N.Y., the impact knocked down a set of high-tension wires, caging him in a deadly tangle. Had he stepped from the car, he would have been electrocuted. Police had to shut off the current before he could get out."

"When a high-voltage wire snapped loose from its support and draped itself over the car of Alwyn Barnett of Brooklyn, N.Y., Mr. Barnett escaped electrocution by remaining in his car until emergency crews shut off the power."

In grim contrast is the tragic account in the *Dubuque Telegraph-Herald* of two young men who hit a power pole and their car became entangled in the 4000-volt wires. Both youths were electrocuted as they attempted to step from the car. (Please note: both boys would have been *perfectly all right had they stayed in the car*. They were killed when they attempted to step out.)

16

The previous chapter was so important it could save your life. (You know that you are safe from lightning and from the danger of fallen wires as long as you are inside an automobile.)

Exploring the Mystery of Electricity from Chemical Changes

Photo courtesy of Westinghouse Electric Corporation

Photo 16. Zap! An electric eel lights up his tank and takes his own picture with a 600-volt strike. The eel is attacking the rod waved in front of him by engineer Cedric R. Bastiaans at the Research Laboratories of the Westinghouse Electric Corporation. The electricity shoots through the water to electrodes at the ends of the tank. It turns on all the lights of the voltmeter at the top of the picture, flashes the strobe light just below the meter, creates the pattern on the oscilloscope screen, and sets off flash lamps to take the picture. Mr. Bastiaans wears big rubber gloves to insulate himself against the lethal voltage.

EXPLORING THE MYSTERY OF ELECTRICITY FROM CHEMICAL CHANGES

This chapter is so important it may be said to be part of life itself. According to Dr. William Likoff, President of the American College of Cardiology, "Death can no longer be related to heartbeat. Today, a person can be kept alive briefly with no heart at all. In the future, death must be defined as when the brain no longer sends electric impulses."

It is the watts in your life that keep you on the go! Your "homemade" electricity keeps you dynamic and makes you a member of the "Come-Alive" generation.

The phenomena of life and electricity are closely related. If our body were somehow to lose its electrical activity, we would no longer be alive. For over 100 years scientists have known that nerve and muscle tissues generate small but measurable voltages. In research labs instruments are used to measure and record these electrical potentials. These measurements are invaluable in medical diagnosis and in biological research.

DEMONSTRATIONS

Electricity for 2 cents

If you still have a zinc penny (left over from World War II) you can use it and a copper penny to make electricity for 2 cents.

Most likely you won't have a zinc penny, so simply get a strip of zinc and a strip of copper. Use alligator clips and wire to connect the metal strips to a sensitive milliammeter. Between the copper and zinc strips insert a cloth saturated with salt water. Note the amount of electricity that is being produced by the two unlike metals and the salt water.

16:1

Electricity from an orange!

A copper and zinc plate, each about 1 inch wide and 5 inches long, will do nicely for this demonstration. Clamp an alligator clip on one end of each plate and hook the wires into a milliammeter.

Insert the free ends of the copper and zinc strips into an orange and note the readings of the milliammeter. Push the strips into the orange to a depth of only 1 inch, then 3 inches. Does this make any difference in the reading? Note that

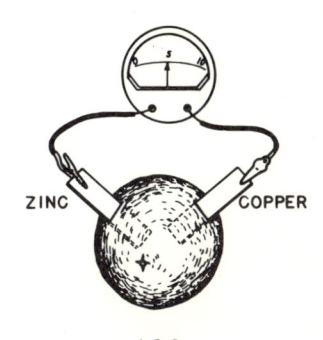

16:2

the more metal in contact with the acid, the greater the reading.

Now try the same experiment with a lemon. Do you get more or less electricity?

Electricity from Coke?

Use the same setup as in the previous experiment, only this time insert the zinc and copper strips into a glass of vinegar. Then try using Coke or 7-Up. Which gives the most electricity? Note that you are keeping the same electrodes (zinc and copper) but you are varying the *electrolyte* (the acid).

Try inserting the metals to various depths and notice how this affects the amount of current. Move the metals close together, then move them apart. Note what this does to the amount of the current.

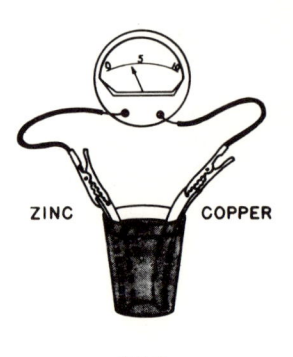

16:3

"Electrical tongue"

Use the same setup, but this time place the copper and zinc strips on your tongue. Do you get any reading on the milliammeter? Wash and clean the strips before the next student makes the test.

Wet cell in your head

Inform the students that the following experiment is personal in nature and may be performed by each student the next time he has a freshly filled tooth.

Gently bite down on a strip of tinfoil from the wrapper of chewing gum, etc. Or gently touch the filling with the prongs of a fork. The two dissimilar metals (the filling in the tooth and the tinfoil or fork) will act as electrodes. The saliva is the electrolyte. *Result*—a wet cell in your mouth! Electrons will be scampering around in your mouth! Too many for comfort!

16:4

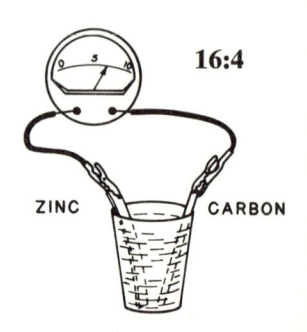

Use a dry cell to make a wet cell

If you have an old dry cell, take it apart. Immerse the carbon rod and strip of zinc in a glass of vinegar. Use wires and alligator clips to hook

EXPLORING THE MYSTERY OF ELECTRICITY FROM CHEMICAL CHANGES 221

Inside story

the wet cell to a milliammeter and note the reading.

Use a hacksaw to cut an old dry cell in half vertically so you can show the class the electrodes—the zinc container and the carbon rod. Show the dried-up paste, pitch seal, etc. Note where the ammonium chloride has dissolved the zinc and formed zinc chloride, a substance which is white and dry. The reason the cell is no good is that it is dry. The liquid left the cell. (Dry cells are misnamed. They are really non-spillable wet cells. The pitch seal is to hold in the liquid. When the acid eats holes in the zinc and escapes, the cell becomes truly "dry" and as such is no good. It has no electrolyte.)

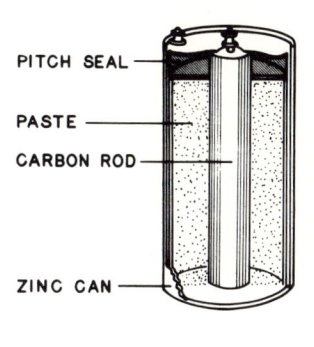

16:5

New life from old

To get "new life" from an old cell, punch holes in the zinc and place the cell in a container of solution made from 3 ounces of sal ammoniac dissolved in a pint of water. Or simply place it in a jar of vinegar, Coke, or lemonade. Connect the terminals of the cell to a milliammeter to see the results.

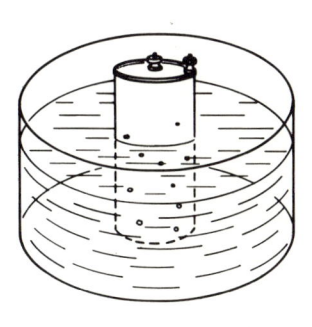

Heart waves

If you have a doctor friend with a portable electrocardiogram machine, perhaps he would consent to bring it to class for a demonstration on one of the boys.

16:6

If not, at least secure an electrocardiogram from a doctor to show your class how the tiny current from the heart "writes its picture" on a roll of paper. These waves look like an endless series of steeply waved lines, something like an outline of a mountain range or a series of church towers.

Since the earliest days of this science of the heart, these waves have been named P, Q, R, S, T. The "P" refers to the current given off when the heart's upper chambers contract, and the "Q,R,S,T" indicate contraction of the lower chambers.

Brain waves

If you have friends in the medical profession, perhaps they can arrange to have your class come to the hospital, where one of your lads can volunteer to demonstrate that the electrical activity of the brain can be picked up by metal electrodes pasted to the scalp.

Amplifiers boost these weak signals, and actuate a pen which records "brain waves." Recorded waveforms, called electroencephalograms, show whether the subject is asleep, alert, or dreaming. The basic frequency, known as the alpha rhythm, varies from 8 to 12 cycles per second.

Needless to say, this is a most fascinating demonstration.

Pacemaker

If you are as lucky as I am, you may be able to get a pacemaker (a used one) from a doctor friend, and show it to your class.

If you are like most people, you never give a thought as to why your heart beats. Most likely you take your heart for granted, and say, "My heart beats by itself. It is a sort of perpetual motion machine." Although the question, "What makes the heart beat?" was asked some 1700 years ago by the great scientist, Galen, it was not until comparatively modern times that investigators began to suspect electrical energy.

We now know that a kind of electrical timing apparatus called the pacemaker normally generates, 70 times a minute, a tiny charge of electricity which sweeps down and across the muscle fibers, causing them to contract.

The heart, then, is a kind of electric pump.

The electrical impulse, one for every heartbeat, comes from the pacemaker, a tiny area of specialized human tissue located in the wall of the heart's right side.

The squiggly lines of an electrocardiogram are recorded electrical signals transmitted by the pacemaker to all parts of the heart muscle.

Some people, however, have pacemakers that are faulty. What happens to these unfortunate people whose pacemakers slow down or quit?

Years ago, they died. Today, however, heartbeats come in an 8-ounce package that can be worn on a belt and attached to the heart by silver wires. These "cardiac pacemakers"—as they are called—send an electric current into hearts that lag or stop, and so restore their beat.

Many people who wear pacemakers on belts experience the difficulty of the cumbersome wiring. And they cannot take a bath except in piecemeal fashion. This was the experience of Mrs. Rose Cohen of Brooklyn only a few years ago when wires were placed in her heart and connected to a belt-worn pacemaker, which shot currents of electricity into her heart at the proper time to keep her alive.

But something new was coming up. Dr. Adrian Kantrowitz of Brooklyn's Maimonides Hospital, working with General Electric Electronics Laboratory, designed a new, small pacemaker, one compact and reliable enough to be implanted in the human body.

Using a modified soldering gun for the delicate task, Dr. Kantrowitz joined the wires leading from Mrs. Cohen's heart to those of the new, internal pacemaker placed inside Mrs. Cohen's chest.

The operation proved a success and Mrs. Cohen made medical history and the front pages of the newspapers.

There is only one drawback. Once every three to five years, Mrs. Cohen will need a new operation as the batteries inside her body wear out and must be replaced with new ones.

Today over 2000 American men, women, and children are kept alive by such pacemakers implanted inside their bodies. It is just such a pacemaker that did its work for three years and was taken from the body of a man, that I have to show my class. The students find it most interesting. Perhaps a doctor friend can secure one for your class.

Electric hands

Pierre Provencher made international headlines as being the first double amputee in North America to use a startling new device that gives him "electric hands."

Two years previously Pierre lost both his hands in an explosion. Today, with his electric hands, Pierre can mend his own clothes with needle and thread, play chess, and make model airplanes. Pierre's plastic hands each have a small electric motor that fits into the palm of each hand. The motor drives the fingers. But *what* turns the motor on and off? How can Pierre determine which hand he wants to bend? Just *how* do Pierre's "electric hands" work?

The answer—Pierre's hands work very much like yours do—by electricity!

"Wait," you object, "my hands don't

operate by electricity. My brain tells them what to do."

Is this objection of yours valid?

To find out, we will have to find out just *how* your brain "tells" your hands what to do. Your brain represents about 2 per cent of your total body weight, but this 2 per cent tells the other 98 per cent what to do and when to do it.

Your brain weighs only about 50 ounces and occupies a volume of only 1½ quarts. It consists of some 12 billion cells. Your brain functions as a control unit, analyzing, examining input information, making decisions, and issuing orders.

The force that keeps it working is electricity

Asleep or awake, sane or insane, an adult-size brain operates on tiny currents of electric energy. The source of this electrical energy is the individual nerve cells, each of which is in effect a wet cell! From a chemical fuel of glucose and oxygen, the cell generates within itself an electrical charge of "potential," and when this charge builds to a certain level the cell discharges. The "orders" that "tell" a muscle what to do are in the form of tiny electric currents that flow down through the cable of nerve fibers. When this current of electricity arrives at its destination, it causes a muscle to contract or move.

As you read this print, for example, your brain is sending out pulses of electricity that contract your eye muscles. When your eyes reach the last word on this page, an "end-of-page" signal causes your brain to dispatch electric impulses to your arm and hand muscles to turn the page.

The brain thus generates electric currents that travel down nerves to set muscles working. After an amputation, the nerve muscle system still works as far as the stump of the limb.

From the motors in Pierre's plastic hands run two wires that are attached by means of metal electrodes to muscles in the stumps of his arms—one for opening and one for closing his hands.

Since the amount of electricity coming from the contracting muscles is so tiny, the body's electric current must be magnified or made stronger many thousands of times, hence another wire leads to a battery and an amplifier. The 12-volt battery that Pierre has strapped to his back must be recharged at night.

Pierre's "electric hands" can do almost everything a real hand can do except feel. But even these "unfeeling hands" are still controlled by the brain. An amazing conquest of "mind over matter."

Conclusion

How fantastic to realize that electricity can be produced from two dissimilar metals and an acid, thus a copper strip and a zinc strip inserted into an orange or immersed in a glass of Coke or vinegar can produce that mysterious thing we call electricity.

Even more incredible is the realization that elements in the food we eat help our body to produce its own electricity. What we have between our ears is a "wet cell" whose electrical activity controls our body. If our body were somehow to lose its electrical activity, we would no longer be alive.

FOLLOW-UP EXERCISE

1. If you wish to relay a message via long-distance telephone, one essential condition for the message to get through is that the telephone wires be hooked up properly and are in working order.

   In normal life, the reason you can bend your leg or wiggle your little finger is that the brain generates electrical impulses that travel down the nervous system and set the muscles working.

   But suppose the nerves are "broken" and won't carry electrical impulses. Like broken telephone lines, no messages will get through.

A young man I knew had a garage door break loose from its overhead springs and fall on him. The impact shattered the nerves at the base of his spine. No "messages" from "'Mr. Big"—his brain—could get through to reach his legs. He was paralyzed from the waist down.

It was late in the eighteenth century that Luigi Galvani discovered that a frog's leg could be made to twitch by bringing it into contact with two dissimilar metals. We know now that the twitch resulted from electrical stimulation of the nerve and muscle tissue. This discovery established the basis for modern electrodiagnostic techniques. Now, when a man's brain can't tell his legs "Lift! Thrust! Pace!", a little electronic device packed in a box can do the trick.

Wires from an electronic gadget called a nerve stimulator go to the patient's legs. The paralyzed man is sitting in a wheelchair. The doctor turns the knobs on the stimulator. A current of electricity leaps into the "paralyzed" muscles, and *they obey the electronic command!*

The paralyzed man stands up!

Another twist of the dial, and the man sits down!

Summary

How amazing to realize that our body "works" because of a vast, complicated "Electrical System"! When you sense something, electric pulses travel up your nerves to your brain—the more pulses (up to hundreds per second), the more intense the sensation.

The brain also generates electric pulses that travel down nerves to set muscles working. To see all this for yourself, be sure to see the Bell Telephone 16-mm educational film entitled, "Gateway of the Senses." This beautiful and dynamic film brings out many of the facts mentioned in this chapter.

Here, now, is the most amazing thing of all. The brain is full of traveling messages—electrical currents. They must go somewhere—to some entity, a "mind"—and this, according to Lawrence Galton, "could explain how mere currents could lead to ideas."

Here is the core of the mystery. "The mind," continues Lawrence Galton, "has no spatial position." Or, in the words of Dr. Wilder Penfield, distinguished brain explorer, "We are beginning to learn where the brain action is, but we know no 'where' of mind."

Do you realize that life in our cities, as we know it today—our world of communications and entertainment via TV and radio —would come to a sudden, devastating standstill were it not for electromagnetic forces?

Just what is an electromagnetic effect?

Simply this—as Hans Christian

17

Developing an Understanding for Electromagnetic Forces

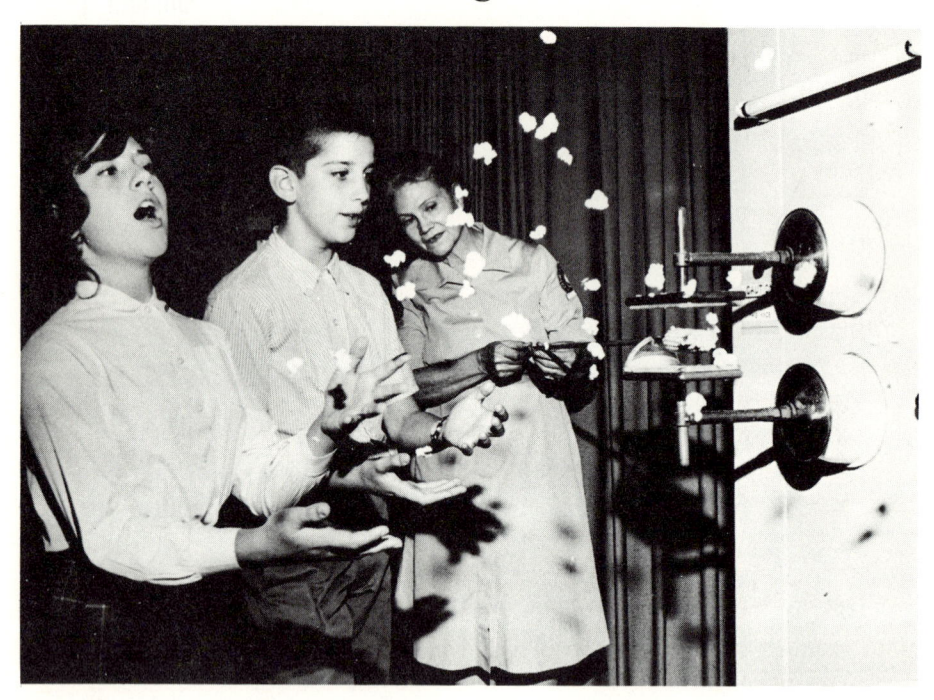

Photo courtesy of Chicago Museum of Science and Industry

Photo 17. *Youthful visitors to the Chicago Museum of Science and Industry's Electric Theater try to catch corn as it is popped with electromagnetic waves. An electric current, changing its direction thousands of times a second, produces a rapidly changing magnetic field. The energy from this electromagnetic field is focused on the kernels of corn. As the molecules of the corn rapidly rearrange themselves under the influence of the microwaves, the major result is friction. This friction causes the heat that pops the corn.*

DEVELOPING AN UNDERSTANDING FOR ELECTROMAGNETIC FORCES 229

Oersted discovered in 1820—a current of electricity moving through a wire creates a magnetic field.

A *current of electricity* is simply the motion of negative charges of electricity, called *electrons*. If you have 6.3 billion billion electrons flowing past one point in one second, you have 1 *ampere* of current.

The amazing thing is that when electrons are in motion they "create" or "produce" a magnetic field or magnetic effect.

Equally amazing is the opposite effect, discovered by Michael Faraday on August 29, 1831. If you move a wire through a magnetic field, you induce or "create" a current of electricity in the wire.

DEMONSTRATIONS

Invisible fingers

Place a compass needle mounted on a pivot stand on the table. About ½ inch above the compass needle and parallel with it, hold a wire which you touch momentarily to the terminals of a dry cell. The compass needle will swing around to line up at right angles with the wire, thus showing that a current of electricity through a wire produces a magnetic field and the direction of this field is at right angles to the motion of the current. (If your dry cell is old, you may have to connect two or three cells in series to get a dramatic effect, or simply try using a 6-volt battery.)

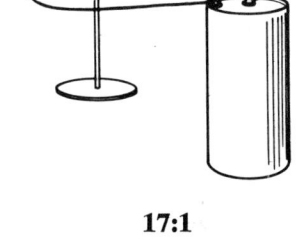

17:1

Electro-magnet

Wrap an insulated wire about five times around an empty oatmeal box, or simply twist it into a circular coil about 4 or 5 inches in diameter. Hold the coil in a vertical position near a compass needle. Touch the ends of the wires to a 1.5-volt dry cell (or 6-volt cell) and watch the compass needle swing around to line up perpendicular to the plane of the coil. You have an electromagnet.

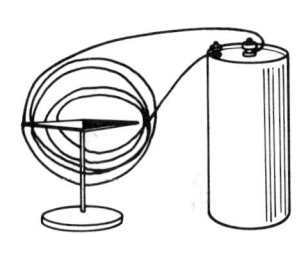

17:2

More power

Use the same apparatus as before, only this time make about 40 or 50 turns or loops of wire. Note the increase in the strength of the magnetic field, as shown by the increased speed and force with which the compass needle swings perpendicular to the plane of the coil. You have an air-core electromagnet.

Iron core

The air-core electromagnet mentioned in the above experiment will attract a compass needle, but it won't pick up paper clips or small nails.

To increase the strength of your electromagnet, wrap 50 turns of insulated wire around an iron core. A big nail or bolt will do nicely for the iron core. Switch on the current and the electromagnet will be so powerful, it will pull the needle around with a jerk. Reverse the wires at the terminals of the dry cell. The compass needle will reverse directions.

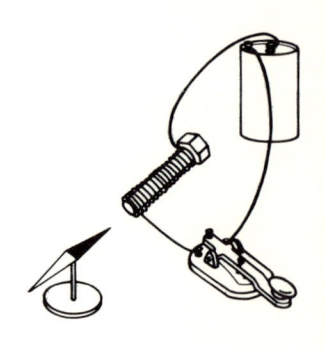

Now hold the nail or bolt of your electromagnet near a pile of paper clips or small nails. Switch on the current and see how many clips are attracted by your electromagnet. Turn off the current and watch what happens.

17:3

Still more power

Use the same setup as in the previous experiment, only this time use three dry cells hooked up in series to increase the voltage. The resulting increase of current will provide a still greater magnetic field, as can be demonstrated by the additional paper clips the electromagnet will now hold. You have demonstrated that one of the factors determining the strength of the electromagnet is the strength of the current going through the coil.

Telegraph

Wrap about 200 or 300 turns of #24 insulated copper wire around a big bolt or piece of iron to serve as the core. Connect the coil in series with a key switch to a 1.5-

DEVELOPING AN UNDERSTANDING FOR ELECTROMAGNETIC FORCES 231

or 6-volt dry cell or battery.

Hold the coil in your left hand in a vertical position with the bottom of the bolt about ½ inch above a nail resting on the table. Turn on the current. The nail will be pulled up against the iron core. Switch off the current. The nail falls back to the table. By working the key switch at the proper intervals, you can make the nail act like the sounder of a telegraph instrument. Each time the nail jumps up to hit the iron core is a "click." Each time it hits the table is a "clack." You have a simple, homemade telegraph!

17:4

Junkyard helper

The above apparatus will also demonstrate the advantages of a temporary magnet over a permanent magnet for use in junkyards where freight cars are to be loaded with scrap iron.

As you can demonstrate with your electromagnet, when the current flows through the coil the nail is held in place against the iron core. When the current is turned off, the iron core loses its magnetic qualities, and the nail falls off.

Doorbell

As the students will see from the previous demonstration, the effect of a direct current is to create a steady, unchanging magnetic field, as evidenced by the fact that the electromagnet holds on to the nail until the current is turned off.

How, then, can we use direct current to ring a doorbell?

Show the students the "insides" of a doorbell. Explain how current flowing through the coils makes the U-shaped iron a temporary magnet to pull over the soft-iron armature, thus causing the gong to hit the bell.

As soon as the armature swings

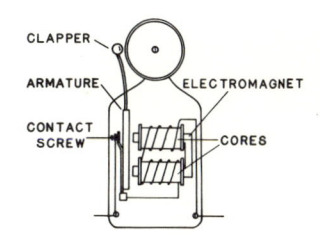

17:5

over, it cuts off the current at the contact screw. Now, with no current flowing through the coils, the U-shaped iron loses its magnetism. The spring can now pull the armature back to its original position, thereby closing the circuit and starting the cycle all over again.

Buzzer

Here is an excellent way to demonstrate one difference between A.C. (alternating current) and D.C. (direct current).

We have already shown that D.C. produces a steady, unchanging magnetic field; hence, in order to ring a doorbell a mechanical device had to be used to switch the current on and off.

With A.C., however, you can have a "buzzer" without the "breaker system" needed in a D.C. doorbell.

Simply hook up your electromagnet in series with a 60- or 120-watt lamp and a switch. The only thing you need now is a metal box, such as a candy or cake container or simply an empty coffee can.

Depress the key switch with your left hand to send the current through the coil. With your right hand, bring the metal box over the top of the iron core. The metal can will begin to vibrate while you are still 2 or 3 inches away. It will be most loud when you hold the metal can about 1 centimeter above the iron core.

For the second part of the demonstration, simply rest the metal container on top of the iron core. Close the switch and you have a buzzer. When the current flows through the coil, the coil becomes an electromagnet. When the A.C. falls off to zero, the iron core quickly loses its magnetic qualities. The elasticity of the metal pulls the metal container back into its original shape. But

60 WATTS

17:6

only for a tiny fraction of a second. The incoming surge of A.C. builds up to another maximum. The rapidly changing current produces a changing magnetic field, which causes the metal container to vibrate or "buzz."

"Jumping" ring

To show that aluminum is repelled by a magnetic field use the same apparatus as before, only this time instead of a steel candy box place an aluminum ring around the top of the iron core. So as to produce a more intense magnetic field, use a 200-watt lamp in series with the coil. Depress the key switch and watch what happens.

Cook with a magnet!

Keep the current flowing through the above apparatus for a few minutes, then turn off the power. With extreme caution, pick up the iron core. If it is not too hot to handle, pass it around so that the class may experience firsthand the heating effects of a changing magnetic field.

Why did the iron core get hot?

For a tiny fraction of a second, as current was flowing through the coil, a magnetic field was created that forced the molecules in the iron to turn around like small compass needles and face in a certain direction.

As soon as the current changed direction, the magnetic field also changed direction. This changing magnetic field made the molecules in the iron swing around and face in the opposite direction. This "turning around" made the molecules "rub shoulders", so to speak, with their neighbors. This friction caused heat. The A.C. current supplied to your home is 60 cycle, which means that it "turns around" or "reverses itself" that many times in one sec-

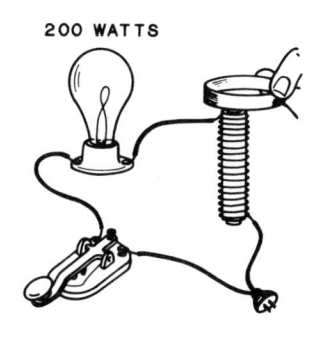

200 WATTS

17:7

ond. This, in turn, made the molecules of iron inside the core turn around 60 times a second. The friction caused the heat you experience.

But imagine what would happen if the molecules in the iron had to turn around, not 60 times per second, but thousands upon thousands of times per second!

Radio frequency heating, as it is called, puts this fact to work by alternating the current at frequencies of 200,000 cycles a second to hundreds of millions of cycles per second.

Induction furnaces, as they are called, consist of a copper coil surrounding a container with the metal to be melted. The current in these new oven coils may run from 4000 to 35,000 amperes. The temperature can be raised at the rate of 125° a minute. The high concentration of energy within the coil will melt 1000 pounds of ingots four times as fast as the old methods.

Cupcakes in 20 seconds

Something similar to this is at work today in modern electronic ranges that grill a hot dog in ten seconds, bake a cupcake in 20 seconds, and a cake in five minutes.

Special electronic tubes step up 60-cycle A.C. to super-high frequencies of some 3 billion cycles a second. The resulting electromagnetic field causes the molecules in the food to move back and forth rapidly. Resulting friction generates heat inside the food. The food literally cooks by its own "heat"—but only the food gets hot. The dish (which cannot be magnetized) stays cool! Naturally, you don't cook with metal pots and pans in this electronic range. Steel pans might get hot enough to melt. You cook on paper dishes, glass, or ceramics, which are not magnetic and therefore are not affected by the rapidly changing magnetic field.

With the use of china or glass or paper there is no danger of burned fingers from this range. The magnetic waves pass through them without heating them. Thus, your serving dishes can double as your cooking utensils.

In many cities the local electric company has electronic ovens on display, and will be happy to have your class come down for a demonstration.

Popcorn on the cob

When I took my class down to the electric power company for a demonstration of the electronic oven, the attendant placed an ear of popcorn in the oven. Through the glass door of the oven we watched corn pop, as we never saw it pop before.

In the Museum of Science in Chicago, the cob of popcorn is placed out in the open between the jaws of the powerful electromagnet. When the rapidly alternating magnetic field goes through the corn, it heats so fast it truly *"pops"* and goes flying all over the stage and out into the audience.

Warm me with a magnet!

If you have a doctor friend with a portable diathermy machine, perhaps he will bring it to class for a demonstration. It operates on much the same principle as the electronic oven, but instead of cooking you it will only warm you. To avoid the danger of "cooking" you, only a trained operator is permitted to use the machine.

The doctor may wrap a cable or coil of insulated wire around your arm or waist. As high-frequency current goes back and forth through the wires, it sends out magnetic waves that go through your body or, in this case, your arm. The temperature of deep muscles may rise as high as 105° or 106° even though the skin temperature is not above 99°.

This heating of tissues beneath the skin by means of high-frequency electrical oscillations is called diathermy, or short-wave therapy. Diathermy comes from two Greek words, "dia" meaning through and "thermos" meaning heat.

Glowing lights

For a most dramatic demonstration, have the doctor place the coils of the diathermy machine on the table and turn on the current. Now pick up fluorescent lamps and bring them near the coils. Watch them glow when they are in the electromagnetic field. You can also place neon wands in the high-frequency field and they too will glow beautifully.

Vibrating filament

Here is a uniquely beautiful and fascinating demonstration. All you need is an old-fashioned carbon filament lamp that has the filament wound in a coil, plus a bar magnet. Hold the north pole of the bar magnet next to the glass bulb. As the A.C. current flows through the filament, it sets up a magnetic field. For a split second the side of the coil next to the bar magnet is a north pole, and thus is repelled. A fraction of a second later, as the current through the coil changes direction, this same side of the coil becomes a south pole and is attracted to the magnet.

This alternating repulsion and attraction causes the filament to vibrate in a most pleasing pattern. But be careful—these vibrations

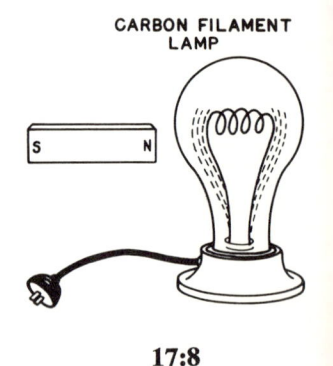

CARBON FILAMENT LAMP

17:8

may increase and build up enough violence to tear the filament loose from its moorings!

Listen to the difference

Here is another demonstration that helps show the difference between D.C. and A.C.

Take an old telephone receiver and touch the end wires to the terminals of a dry cell. All you get is one click as the diaphragm is pulled over by the electromagnet and then held in place by the steady flow of current from the dry cell. (If you don't have an old telephone receiver, a pair of headphones will do equally as well.)

Now hook the receiver up in series with a 40-watt lamp and plug into a 110-volt line. You get a 60-cycle A.C. hum as the alternating current pulls the diaphragm back—then, when the current falls off, the elasticity of the metal makes the diaphragm spring back to its original position. A fraction of a second later the diaphragm is again pulled back when the next surge of current flows through the coils. And thus it goes—the diaphragm moving back and forth 60 times a second under the influence of the changing magnetic field set up by the changing current.

40 WATTS

17:9

Make a galvanometer

To show how a galvanometer works, hold a coil of wire between the jaws of an alnico horseshoe magnet. (Alnico magnets are generally stronger than the old iron type.)

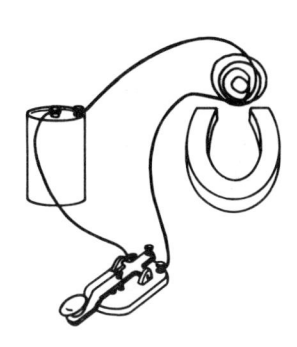

Hook the wire to a dry cell and switch. Hold the coil so that its plane is perpendicular to the magnetic field or at right angles to the ends of the magnet.

Depress the switch and note how the north pole of the coil swings around to face the south pole of

17:10

the magnet. Now change the leads of the coil to the opposite terminals on the dry cell and notice how the coil changes direction.

Now use two dry cells in series and note the difference in the speed with which the coil turns, and also the amount of turning. If your first dry cell is weak, the coil may turn only about ½ turn. With two cells, and more current flowing through it, the response of the coil will be more energetic. Thus, the amount of the turning of the coil is an indication of the amount of electricity flowing through the wires.

Swinging wire

To show the magnetic field surrounding a wire carrying a current of electricity, use two support stands to suspend an insulated copper wire between the poles of a strong alnico magnet. Hook the wire to a 6-volt battery and a switch. Momentarily depress the key switch and notice the result. (*Don't* keep the key pressed down or you will drain the battery.)

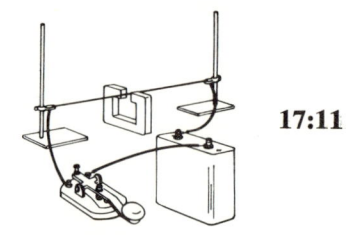

17:11

Now change the ends of the wires to the opposite terminals of the battery and repeat the experiment.

Make electricity with a wire and a magnet

All you need to make electricity by electromagnetic induction is a strand of wire and a magnet. Connect the copper wire to a galvanometer, move the wire between the jaws of a magnet, and watch the result. I find it convenient to use a piece

17:12

of heavy copper wire hooked up to the galvanometer with thinner copper wires. Move the copper wire down between the poles of the magnet and the needle of the galvanometer moves in one direction.

Move the copper wire up and the needle goes in the opposite direction. You have alternating current. Hold the copper wire stationary between the poles. You get no current.

Move the copper wire back and forth between the poles, but not across the lines of force, and again, no current.

This shows that current is generated *only* when there is *motion* of a conductor *across* the *magnetic field*.

And as the needle of the galvanometer shows, when you *change* the *direction* of the motion of the *conductor* (or wire) through the field, you *change* the *direction* of the motion of the *current* through the wire.

More electricity

This time instead of using a single strand of wire or a big thick wire, use a small coil of many turns of insulated wire.

Now each time you swing the coil through the magnetic field you get much more current. And the faster you move the coil across the magnetic field, the greater the current. Thus you demonstrate that the *amount of current* generated *depends* upon the *number of wires* (conductors) that *cut* the magnetic field and their *speed* through the magnetic field.

As in the previous experiment, hold the coil stationary between the poles to show that when there is no motion there is no current.

Then move the coil back and forth

17:13

between the poles, but *not* cutting the lines of force, to show that when you do not cut lines of force you get *no* current.

Move the magnet

In the two previous demonstrations, we made electricity by using a stationary magnet, and moving a wire. Now demonstrate that you may use a stationary coil of wire and make electricity by moving the magnet. Connect a galvanometer to a big coil of insulated copper wire. Insert a powerful alnico bar magnet into the coil.

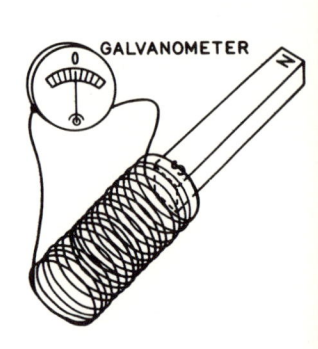

Note that the current through the galvanometer flows one way until the middle of the magnet enters the coil. Then, as shown by the needle, the current through the galvanometer changes direction, since a different magnetic pole is approaching the coil, and according to *Lenz's law,* "the direction of an induced current is such as to oppose by its magnetic field the motion that produced it."

Let the bar magnet rest inside the coil. There is no current, even though we have a conductor (the wire) and a magnetic field. There is *no motion*.

Now, gently move the magnet up and down inside the coil, but not through it. Again, no current. The motion was not cutting lines of force.

We obtain current only when there is motion at right angles or across a magnetic field. To have a generator, therefore, that is furnishing electricity, you need: (1) a magnet, (2) a conductor [a wire], (3) motion *across* the magnetic field.

17:14

Generator principles

To demonstrate how to generate electricity, place a large horseshoe magnet on its side. Bend a stiff wire

DEVELOPING AN UNDERSTANDING FOR ELECTROMAGNETIC FORCES

into a rectangular loop to fit inside the magnet and serve as your armature.

To show the magnetic field, I tape a number of red threads to the north pole and let them hang straight down to the south pole.

Hold the armature inside the magnet as in position 1, with its plane in a horizontal position. In this position, the armature is not cutting lines of force. There is no current.

Now turn the armature until it is vertical and begins to "cut" across the lines of force, as shown by the wire pushing the red threads. The current leaps to a maximum, position 2.

In position 3, the armature is again in a horizontal position. As shown by the red strings or threads, no lines of force are being cut. There is no current.

As the armature moves into position 4, the current mounts once again, but since the armature's sides or "arms" are moving in an opposite direction to what they were in position 2, the current likewise changed direction.

> **Note.** *In position 2 the "white" side of the armature is moving towards you, while the "black" side moves away from you. In position 4, things are reversed. The "white" side is moving away from you, while the "black" side moves towards you.*

By the time the armature swings into position 5, we are back where we started. No lines of force are being cut.

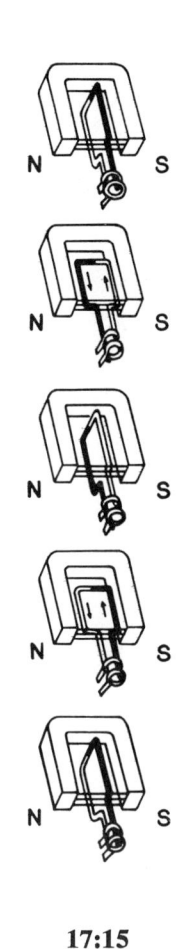

17:15

242 DEVELOPING AN UNDERSTANDING FOR ELECTROMAGNETIC FORCES

During the entire cycle or "turning" of the armature, we generated electricity but twice; i.e., when the armature was cutting across the magnetic field in positions 2 and 4.

Plot the curve

We may plot the current on a curve, using the same number system as previously to designate the various positions of the armature.

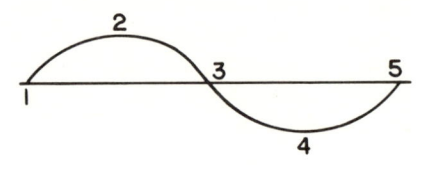

17:16

1. Represents armature in horizontal position #1. No electricity.
2. Represents armature in vertical position #2. Maximum current of electricity.
3. Represents armature in horizontal position #3. No electricity.
4. Represents armature in vertical position #4. Maximum current, but now flowing in opposite direction, as indicated by curve beneath the straight line.
5. Represents armature in horizontal position #5. No electricity.

Big tangle

Now connect the armature to a galvanometer and go through all the steps once again, so that the students may see for themselves that all the above is true. Point out that each time the armature makes one complete revolution, there are but two surges of current, each opposite in direction. You are generating A.C.

Students will be quick to see that the above hookup is not practical. A few turns of the armature and

17:17

DEVELOPING AN UNDERSTANDING FOR ELECTROMAGNETIC FORCES

the connecting wires are in a frightful tangle.

Slip rings and commutators

This introduces the need for a device to take electricity from the armature without tangling the wires. One of the most convenient ways to show how commutators and slip rings work is with the old, familiar "St. Louis Motor" or with the Cambosco "Genamotor."

Shocking

The generators we have used thus far give only small currents which may be detected only with galvanometers. For a jolt that will tingle from scalp to toes, and at the same time throw light on the subject, get a generator from an old telephone or get an Army surplus field telephone and take the generator out of it.

Point out to students the two reasons for the "punch" of these generators.

The armature is made of hundreds upon hundreds of turns of fine wire, and a gear system is used to turn the armature at a dizzy speed. You cut more lines of force and you cut them more often.

Connect the generator to a neon light and turn the armature. The only time current flows is when the armature cuts the magnetic field. The faster you spin the armature, the faster the light blinks. If you can spin fast enough, the neon light will appear to be almost a steady light.

Electric motor

Here is a beautiful demonstration to show how to produce continuous motion with a changing magnetic field.

Suspend a bar magnet from a string tied to a convenient support rod. About an inch from the bar magnet place a coil of wire of many turns, into which you insert an iron core (a bolt or piece of steel).

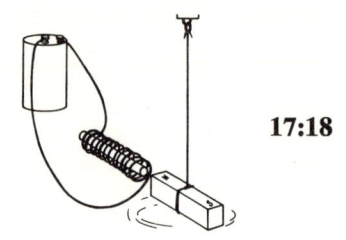

17:18

Now touch the ends of the wires leading from the coil to a dry cell. As soon as the bar magnet swings around half a turn, immediately switch the wires to the opposite terminals of the dry cell and thereby reverse the magnetic field. If your timing is good, you can make the bar magnet continue to swing round and round in a circle. And thus you show that an electric motor is the result of one magnetic field "chasing" or "repelling" another.

"Electric swing"

Wrap about 100 turns of fine, insulated copper wire around your pen or pencil, and connect the wires to a dry cell or battery through a key switch.

Use both hands to hold the coil-wrapped pencil between the jaws of a strong horseshoe magnet. Have a student push down on the key to complete the circuit. The electromagnetic field set up by the current flowing through the coil will interact with the permanent field of the horseshoe magnet. The pencil will swing.

Reverse the wires at the terminals of the battery and the coil will reverse the direction of its swing.

By depressing the key at just the proper intervals, you can get the coil into a delightful swinging motion.

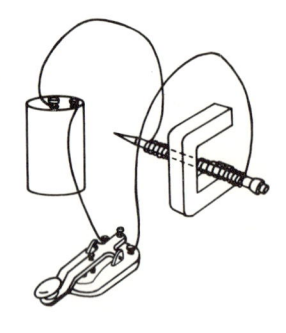

17:19

DEVELOPING AN UNDERSTANDING FOR ELECTROMAGNETIC FORCES

Fly-apart nails

Hook up a coil of copper wire (insulated) in series with a 120-watt lamp and key switch. Tie about 4 inches of string to each of two big nails. Hold the free ends of the string together between thumb and forefinger and suspend the two nails in the center of the coil. The nails rest against each other comfortably. Now press the contact switch. The nails immediately fly apart and "stand" at opposite sides of the coil. Current flowing through the coil sets up a magnetic force that makes magnets of both nails. Their like poles repel each other.

As the alternating current changes, so do the poles. The nail heads, for example, are both north poles for a fraction of a second, then south poles. But since they are both always poles of the same kind, they repel each other.

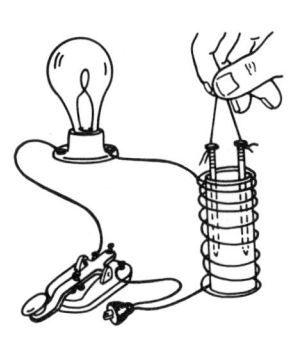

17:20

Little light from big light

To demonstrate the principle of the transformer, connect a large coil of insulated wire in series with a 120-watt lamp and plug into a 110-volt line.

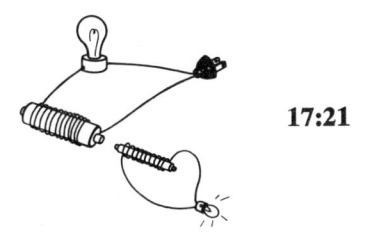

17:21

Connect a smaller coil to a flashlight lamp. Move the small coil towards the big coil. You may get a dim light glowing in the flashlight lamp. You have an air-core, step-down transformer.

Now insert a big iron bolt in each coil to serve as an iron core. Note how much more effective is the iron-core transformer than the air-core transformer. In fact, you had better separate the coils several inches before inserting the iron cores, then slowly move the smaller coil towards the big coil. If you get too close, you may burn out the flashlight bulb.

Current going through the big coil is sending out electromagnetic waves. These electromagnetic waves cut across the wires of the smaller coil, inducing or "creating" a current in it.

Would you believe it?

Use the same apparatus as before, but this time connect the small coil to a set of headphones or to an old telephone receiver. You will get a 60-cycle hum, which will get louder the closer you bring the coils.

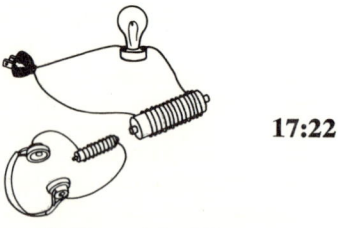

17:22

Would you believe it? What you have here is a "broadcast station" and a "receiving station" or the essence of radio.

Electricity running through the big coil makes it a "broadcasting station" that sends out electromagnetic or radio waves. These waves cut across the wires in the small coil and induce or "create" electricity, which operates the headphones.

You get a 60-cycle A.C. hum on your headphones because an A.C. current is moving back and forth through the big coil 60 times each way per second.

Buzz me

Use the same apparatus as before, only this time simply tie the end wires of the small coil together. Place a metal candy box next to

DEVELOPING AN UNDERSTANDING FOR ELECTROMAGNETIC FORCES

the iron core of the small coil and listen to it vibrate. All the transformers we have been using so far have been step-down transformers. Since there were fewer turns of wire in the second coil (the secondary) the voltage was reduced.

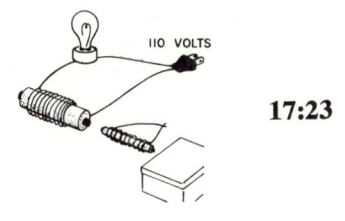

17:23

Iron whiskers

A simple way to demonstrate that a current flowing through a wire creates a magnetic field is to place a heavy piece of straight, bare copper wire on top of some iron filings.

Lift the wire up out of the filings to show the class that the wire, itself, does not attract or hold on to the iron filings.

Now connect the wire to a 6-volt battery and momentarily depress the key switch. Lift up the wire to show the students that it suddenly has "grown whiskers." (Be careful—don't burn your fingers on the wire when current goes through it.) Quickly turn off the current, so as not to drain the battery. The wire gets a "quick shave" and suddenly loses its "whiskers." As soon as the current stops the wire loses its magnetism, and hence the iron filings drop off.

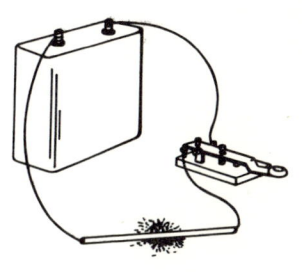

17:24

A.C. on the swing

By means of a string, suspend an alnico horseshoe magnet from a support rod so that one of its poles is directly above a big coil of insulated wire that is connected to a galvanometer.

Twist the string, then release it. As the north pole of the magnet spins

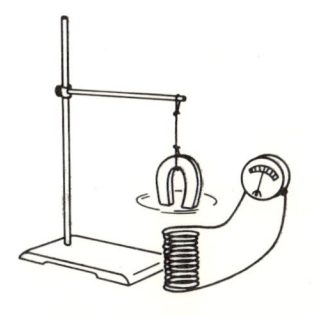

17:25

Electricity on time

over the coil, the needle of the galvanometer is deflected in one direction. Then, as the south pole sweeps over, the needle changes direction.

As an interesting variation of the above experiment, tie a string to an alnico bar magnet and suspend it from the support rod.
Draw the magnet to one side of the coil, then release it so that it will swing back and forth over the coil. Note the action of the galvanometer each time the bar magnet swings over the coil.
Finally, place an iron core in the coil. Note the results as shown by the galvanometer.

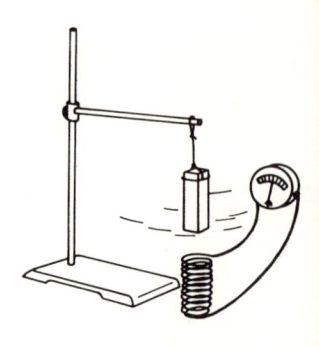

17:26

Homemade galvanometer

In case some student would like to construct a galvanometer, here is a simple way to make one.
Wrap about 50 or 100 turns of insulated wire around an empty Morton Salt container. By means of a thread, suspend a magnetized needle inside the cylinder. Place the unit on the table so that the open end of the coil and the needle inside face towards the north. Now switch on the current and watch the results.
Instead of using a magnetized needle, it is even more simple to merely place a small compass inside the coil.

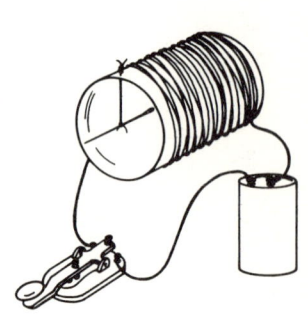

17:27

Wrap-around radio

Here is a fascinating demonstration to show students why radio reception is poor in many modern steel-frame buildings, and why radio reception fades away when you drive in a car across a steel bridge with steel girders encircling your car.
Place a pocket-size transistor radio on the table, and tune in some music. Now, while the radio is playing, pick it up and place it in an empty

17:28

coffee can or wrap a sheet of aluminum around it. The music stops. The covering of aluminum foil prevents the electromagnetic waves from reaching the aerial of the radio. As the electromagnetic waves bump into the aluminum foil (or into the metal can), they generate a current of electricity in the foil rather than in the aerial.

This principle is made use of in "shielding" delicate electronic equipment from outside magnetic influences. The equipment is surrounded by a metal grill or wire mesh or a piece of solid metal.

Wrap-around cable

Sometimes it is necessary to run an A.C. power line parallel to a telephone line. Unfortunately, the A.C. power line sends out electromagnetic waves that cut across the telephone wire, inducing a current in it, and thus creating a 60-cycle A.C. hum that is most distressing when you are trying to listen to someone speak.

To prevent this hum, the telephone cable can be wrapped around with an outside layer of metal that looks like a small pipe. The combination is called a coaxial cable. Perhaps you can obtain a sample from your local telephone company.

Watch the difference

A galvanometer that can reverse directions is a handy demonstration unit to help show how direct current differs from alternating current. By means of wires and alligator clips connect the galvanometer to copper and zinc strips inserted in an orange. The movement of the needle will indicate two things: the current flows in one direction only and the current is steady.

Now connect the galvanometer to a big coil of insulated copper wire

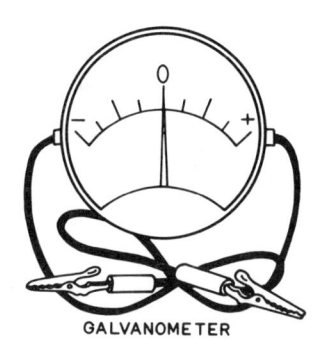

GALVANOMETER

17:29

through which you shove a bar magnet, or simply move the magnet back and forth. Note that each time the bar magnet goes through the coil, the needle rises to a maximum, then dips to zero, then reverses direction. And each time the bar magnet is shoved in a different direction through the coil, the needle changes direction, thus indicating that the current goes first one way, then another. It alternates.

Red-hot wire

Copper is ordinarily a good conductor of electricity, but if the wire is too thin its resistance increases to the point where the current will melt the wire. To prove it, secure a very thin strand of copper wire, and with the aid of two wooden matchsticks, shove the thin wire against the terminals of a standard dry cell. (*Caution*: Use the matchsticks or you may burn your fingers.)

17:30

Ohm's Law in action

Connect a 3-volt flashlight lamp to one dry cell of 1.5 volts. The filament will glow but dimly. The resistance is too great.

Now connect the 3-volt lamp to two dry cells in series. You now have a total voltage of 3 volts and the lamp glows brightly. By increasing the voltage, you increased the current.

Don't continue this line of reasoning by deciding to connect three or four cells in series to get still higher voltage. You will get the voltage to be sure, but the resulting current will be too much for the filament and will burn out your lamps in a flash.

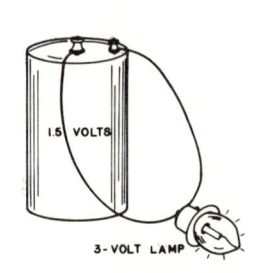

17:31

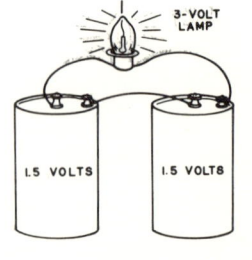

Hot-plate

Turn a hot plate on its edge so that

17:32

DEVELOPING AN UNDERSTANDING FOR ELECTROMAGNETIC FORCES 251

lesson

the students may see the coils glow cherry red. Point out that the copper wires in the extension cord carry the same amount of electricity that is in the coils, yet the copper wires stay cool while the nichrome coil glows red. This demonstrates that resistance depends upon the material.

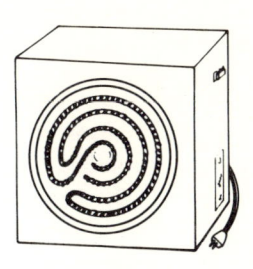

17:33

Throttle the doorbell

To show how resistance varies with the length of the conductor, perhaps you may secure a discarded radio and remove the volume control. It will most likely consist of a long piece of wire wound into a circle with a sliding contact that permits you to cut the volume to any desired level by making contact with various lengths of wire. Connect the volume control to a doorbell in series with a dry cell or a 6-volt battery. Note how easy it is to regulate the volume of the sound by simply turning the control knob. The greater the length of the wire, the greater the resistance, and you "throttle" the doorbell.

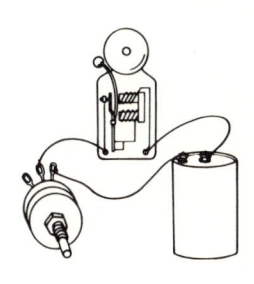

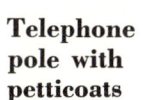

17:34

Telephone pole with petticoats

It is always a source of amazement for many students to learn the construction of the glass or ceramic insulators used on telephone poles and power lines. Perhaps your local telephone office will give you an insulator with which you can demonstrate that the resistance to the flow of electricity depends upon both length and dryness.

The petticoat insulator is built in the form of superposed inverted cups. This surface enlargement increases the insulation. The petticoats also keep the undersurface of the glass dry, thereby adding to the insulating qualities.

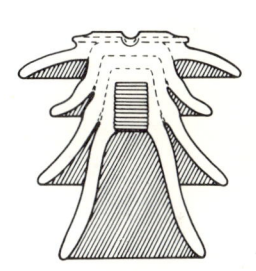

17:35

> **Conclusion**
>
> How fantastic it is! A current of electricity moving through a wire creates a magnetic field. And a wire cutting across a magnetic field produces a current of electricity.
>
> Our modern electrical world of instant communications, radio, TV, telephone, telegraph, plus doorbells and buzzers depend upon these amazing discoveries by Oersted and Faraday. From the giant dynamos that furnish lights to a great city to the small motors that spin a dentist's drill, we are forever applying the dynamic findings of Oersted and Faraday. We may say that these two men laid the foundation for the modern world of electricity we use on practically every side.

FOLLOW-UP EXERCISE

1. Can you "light a lamp with salt"? Fill a drinking glass with ordinary tap water. On the opposite side of the glass run in wires that are hooked up in series with a 40-watt lamp. Most likely the water will offer so much resistance to the flow of the electricity that the lamp lights up only dimly, if at all.

   17:36

   Now pour salt into the water and watch the lamp glow with full brilliance. You have thrown light on the fact that salt water is a good conductor of electricity.

Summary

What a marvelous world! The air around us is filled with electromagnetic waves which can bring us delightful melodies or TV pictures of Apollo astronauts walking on the moon. But these waves cannot be detected directly by our senses. The only way we have to "capture" the energy of these "action-packed," invisible silent waves that vibrate all around us, is to let them cut across a conductor (a TV antenna or aerial). By so doing, the energy of the electromagnetic waves is converted into a current of electricity that can be amplified to give us "the sweetest music this side of heaven" or pictures on our TV screen. Thanks to the discovery of Faraday—that an electromagnetic field cutting across a wire creates a current in it—we can literally "snatch" music and pictures "out of the air." Next time you flick on your radio or TV set, remember you are making use of electromagnetic induction to provide the program.

And remember also, that back at the broadcasting towers the discovery of Oersted is being applied. A current of electricity running through a wire puts out an electromagnetic field. The air is filled with radio waves, thanks to his discovery. (Developed and applied by others who came after him, of course.)

How surprised Oersted and Faraday would be to realize the world of communications, entertainment, and satisfaction based on their discoveries!

The importance of this chapter is evident when we consider that without light we would remain forever in total blackness—unable to see the wonders of the beautiful world around us.

Your objective in this chapter is to introduce your students to some of the wonders of light. You will show them how to bend it, bounce it, and send it through objects of varying density. Then the students should be asked to observe the results and try to explain them.

18

Increasing Our Knowledge of Light

Photo courtesy of Railway Express Agency

Photo 18. *Light beams weave a magic pattern in the night.*

INCREASING OUR KNOWLEDGE OF LIGHT

DEMONSTRATIONS

"Bounced light"

If the sun is shining through the classroom window, hold a flat mirror in the path of the incoming beam of light and reflect it on the opposite wall or ceiling. Point out that the angle of reflection (R), is equal to the angle of incidence (i). Young people are fascinated when allowed to do this experiment. They can continue with this experiment at home.

If the sun is not shining, use the beam from a spotlight.

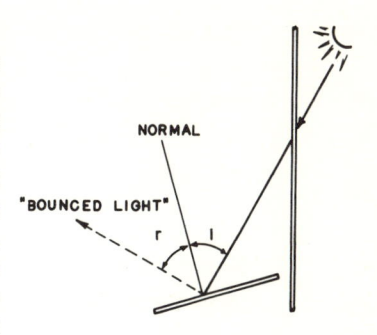

18:1

Can you see Joan?

Hold a good-size mirror up in front of the class. Ask a student in the front row, on your extreme left-hand side, whether he can see himself in the mirror. Most likely his answer will be "No." Likewise, a student on your extreme right-hand side won't be able to see himself. But, they may be able to see each other!

Only students directly in front of the mirror will be able to see themselves. Indicate how this illustrates that the angle of reflection is equal to the angle of incidence.

18:2

Periscope

To demonstrate the working principles of a periscope, place one mirror flat on the lecture table. Now hold a second mirror about 3 feet above it and tilted at such an angle that by looking down into mirror #1 on the table you can see the class.

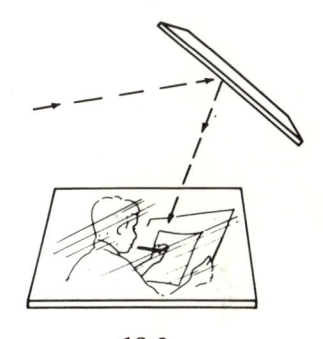

18:3

Double your money

Hold two mirrors straight up with their bases resting on the table and the edge of one mirror touching the edge of the other to form a corner.

Place a half-dollar in the "corner" formed by the two mirrors, and see how your money multiplies as you decrease the angle between the mirrors.

For an even more dramatic demonstration, place a 40-watt lamp in the "corner" and count the images as you vary the angle between the mirrors.

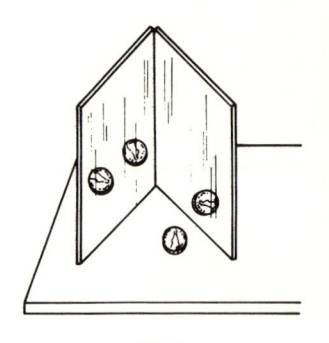

Watch the "big parade"

Hold a mirror with its edge resting on the table. In front of this mirror place a 40-watt lamp. On the other side of the lamp place a second mirror parallel to the first mirror.

Lower your eyes until you glance just over the edge of mirror #2 and look into mirror #1. You will see a shimmering "parade" of gleaming lights that seem to march forever. So that the students may enjoy this demonstration for themselves, leave the unit on the table for them to perform at their leisure, and thus treat themselves to the fascinating "parade."

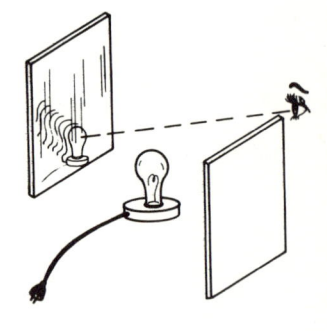

18:4

18:5

Star = rats

To show students how a plane mirror reverses an image, write the word STAR in big letters on a piece of paper, and hold it in front of a mirror. Ask a student to read the word as it appears in the mirror.

18:6

Make a kaleidoscope

Get three plane mirrors, each about 6 inches or more long and 3 or 4 inches wide. Arrange the mirrors with their bases resting on the table and their sides touching so that they form a triangle.

Place a few coins down inside the bottom of your tall triangle. Enjoy the multiple reflections in the mirrors.

Better yet, use a 40-watt lamp with a clear bulb for your "centerpiece" in the middle of the triangle. This demonstration cannot be enjoyed by the class as a unit, but may be left

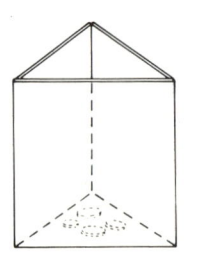

18:7

on the table for individual inspection.

Shaving mirror

With a concave shaving mirror and a carbon filament lamp with a clear bulb, you demonstrate the object and image relations for a concave mirror. I find a carbon filament lamp most convenient. If you don't have a carbon filament lamp, use a tungsten filament.

For a screen, on which to throw the image, I use a big piece of white cardboard, about 3 X 4 feet, which I fasten to the blackboard.

Hold the lamp in your left hand and the mirror in your right hand, and try the following demonstrations:

Hold the lamp as far away as possible from the mirror. The image will be real, inverted, and diminished.

Bring the mirror closer to the lamp so that it is still beyond the center of curvature of the mirror. The image is larger than it was before, but is still inverted and diminished.

Bring the mirror closer so that the lamp is at the center of curvature of the mirror. Now the image is the same size as the filament itself, though inverted.

Bring the mirror still closer so that the lamp is now between the center of curvature and the focus of the mirror. The image is enlarged and inverted.

Bring the mirror closer still so that the lamp is at the focus of the mirror. No image is visible, instead, you have a blob of light that illuminates the screen.

Now put the mirror on the opposite side of the lamp and bring it inside the focal point. The students will see in the mirror itself an enlarged, erect image of the filament. Try to

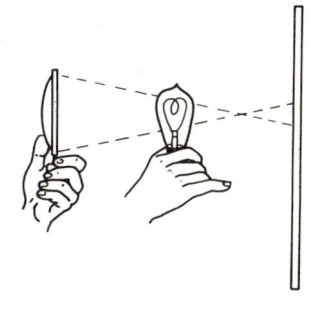

18:8

throw this image on the screen. You can't. It is a virtual image.

Draw via mirror

Students are so accustomed to looking into a plane mirror they often fail to realize that the image is reversed.

To prove that a mirror reverses an image, try this demonstration.

Place a plane mirror upright on the table. In front of it place a sheet of paper. Take a pencil and attempt to draw a triangle or rectangle by watching *only* the *image* in the *mirror*. To keep from seeing the paper directly, have someone hold a large cardboard over your right hand.

Invite students to try this demonstration for themselves.

18:9

Burning mirror

Find the focal length of a concave shaving mirror by focusing the sun's rays on a piece of paper. The distance from the center of the mirror to the intensely bright spot of light on the paper is the *focal length*.

Try to start a fire by focusing the sun's rays on a white, smooth, glossy paper. Then use a black paper with a rough surface. Notice how much faster the black paper bursts into flame. Black is a good absorber of heat, while white reflects heat.

18:10

Now I don't see me

Ask a student to hold a concave shaving mirror in front of his face and slowly move the mirror back and forth. Have him explain why the change of images. Why does the image vanish at one place, then turn upside down? When is the image enlarged?

Bend light

To show how light is bent in going from one medium to another, place a pencil in a glass half-full of water. Hold the glass at eye level, and the pencil appears to be "bent" or "broken."

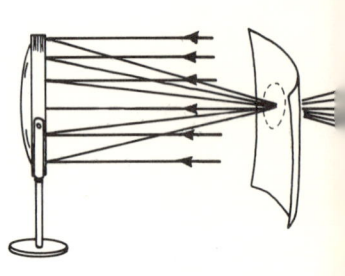

18:11

INCREASING OUR KNOWLEDGE OF LIGHT

As a variation of this, put a 1-foot ruler in a gallon jar of water.

Giant filament

Put a gallon jar of water on the table. Behind the jar place a 40-watt lamp with clear bulb. Students will be amazed to see the filaments enlarged to giant size.

Now put a red or green light behind the gallon jar and notice how it appears from the other side.

Finally, stick your fist into the jar of water. Your hand will appear Paul Bunyan size. You can also tie an apple to a string and lower the apple into the water. The "bent" rays of light will give you a "giant" apple.

18:12

Water mirror

Some students know that the top surface of a quiet pool of water acts like a mirror, but few know that the underside of the water surface does likewise.

To demonstrate this I place an aquarium on top of a wooden box 1 foot high. I fill the aquarium almost to the top. On one side of the wooden box I place a 40-watt lamp. On the other side, a mirror which I adjust until I see a reflection of the lamp in the mirror. The black bent line indicates the path of the beam of light from the lamp.

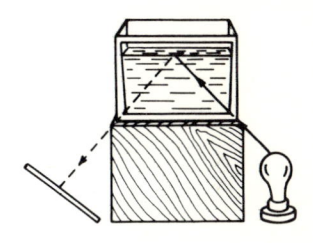

18:13

Look up to see down

As an interesting variation of the above experiment, remove the mirror and tell the student to rest his head on the table and look up from the position previously occupied by the mirror.

Then, have another student place the tips of his fingers into the water. They will look like "disembodied fingers without a hand" wandering around in a sea of shining mercury. (Sounds incredible? Try it yourself!)

Regular versus diffuse

Put some water in a pan or dish. Call attention to the fact that the smooth surface of the water acts like a mirror, making it possible to see yourself. You have *regular reflection.*

Now wiggle your finger in the water. The rippled surface makes it impossible to obtain a clear picture of yourself. You have *diffuse reflection.* Let students try this demonstration for themselves.

18:14

Smoke and incense

My students tell me this is one of the best demonstrations of the year. On a piece of burning charcoal, I heap a generous supply of incense until the lecture table and environs are "fogged in" under a heavy cloud cover. Now I'm ready for the "magic." I close the shutters on the windows and turn off the overhead lights.

Now I turn on a projector. (A 35-mm projector is excellent.) The dramatic moment approaches. I pick up a big convex lens and place it in the path of the beam of light. Thanks to the smoke, the students can see how the lens bends the beam of light.

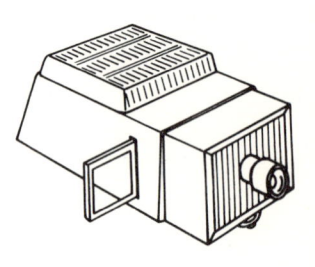

18:15

I use a variety of convex lenses, big and small, and show that the greater the curvature of the lens, the greater is the converging power.

Next I use concave lenses, and, finally, the greatest moment of all. I insert a big prism in the beam, and the students are amazed to see the light bent through 90°!

Then I take a plane mirror and reflect the light. With the smoke making the path of the light beam easy to follow, students can see quite vividly that the angle of reflection equals the angle of incidence.

I also place a water-filled, ball-shaped goldfish bowl in the beam. It acts like a convex lens.

Then I slip a 35-mm color slide into the projector. The picture is thrown on to the opposite wall. Then I insert the big prism in the beam coming from the projector, and behold, the picture is thrown to the ceiling. By turning the prism just right, you can have a picture both on the wall and on the ceiling!

Camera—microscope—or what?

I hold up a double convex lens and ask the class, "What can a lens like this be used for—a camera, a microscope, or what?"

To show the variety of uses to which the lens may be put, I do the following.

On the blackboard I mount a big, white cardboard to serve as a screen. I mount a carbon filament lamp with clear bulb on a convenient stand. (I use a carbon filament because it is so big, and so easy to see. Also, students may see at a glance whether the image is right side up or upside down.)

Now, with the convex lens in my right hand, I'm ready for the demonstrations. I place the lamp on the far side of the room, and hold the convex lens at the distance of its focal length from the cardboard screen. The image is real, inverted, and diminished. I'm using the lens as a *camera* to take a picture of a distant object.

If the sun is shining through the window, I use the convex lens to throw a picture of the sun on a piece of paper. The "picture" is so hot, it starts a fire. I'm using the lens as a *burning glass*.

Now I bring the lamp closer to the convex lens. Although the image is bigger than it was before, it is still inverted and diminished. I'm using the lens as a *camera* to take a picture of a not-too-distant object. (In this case, the object is a distance

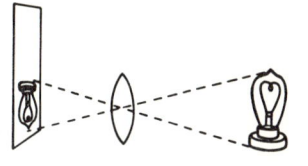

18:16

of more than twice the focal length from the lens. The image is on the opposite side of the lens at a distance between the focus and twice the focal length.)

Now I place the lamp so it is a distance of twice the focal length from the lens. The image on the opposite side of the lens is likewise at twice the focal length. I'm using the lens as a *copying camera*. The *image*, though inverted, is the *same size* as the *object*.

The lamp is now placed between twice the focal length and the focal length from the lens. The image is on the opposite side of the lens beyond twice the focal length. I'm using the lens as a *projector*. The *image* is inverted and *enlarged*.

If the lamp is placed at the focal length from the lens, there is *no image*. Instead, we have a blob of light. This represents the setup in your automobile headlights. They are so arranged to throw a circle of light down the highway, not an image of the filament on the pavement!

Now I place the lamp between the focal length and the lens. For the first time the image is virtual, and on the same side of the lens as the object. I'm using the lens as a *microscope*. The *image* is *enlarged*, but this image cannot be thrown on the screen.

Dangerous jug!

Newspapers sometimes carry accounts of houses being set on fire by jugs of water and goldfish bowls.

To show how this is possible, I place a glass gallon jar filled with water and a ball-shaped goldfish bowl in the window. If the sun is in the right position, the goldfish bowl, especially, becomes a "burning

18:17

INCREASING OUR KNOWLEDGE OF LIGHT

263

glass" that concentrates the light into an intensely hot focal point, which may set a piece of paper or cloth on fire.

Goldfish bowl is a lens

A bowl-shaped goldfish bowl makes a beautiful double convex lens. To prove it, place a lamp with clear bulb on one side of the bowl. Now look at the lamp through the opposite side of the bowl. It will give you a giant-size image of the gleaming filament.

18:18

Take picture with goldfish bowl

A goldfish bowl that is a sphere is a convex lens, and will throw a picture on a piece of paper or on the wall. Students are quite amazed to find they can "take a picture" with a goldfish bowl!

18:19

Drive-in theater

How does a drive-in theater get bigger pictures than the local neighborhood theater?
It is because they use the formula:

$$\frac{\text{Image Size}}{\text{Object Size}} = \frac{\text{Image Distance}}{\text{Object Distance}}$$

To prove this ratio to your students, get a filament lamp with clear bulb and hold it between one and two focal lengths from a convex lens. Throw the image on a nearby wall.

18:20

Now throw the image on a more distant wall. Call attention to the fact that you now have a *bigger image* because the *image distance* is greater.

Head-shrinker

You may also use the above formula to "shrink" a head!
If you have a 35-mm projector, throw a picture of a person on a cardboard screen. Now have a student take the cardboard and walk very slowly towards the projector. As he walks towards you, keep the picture in focus, and call attention

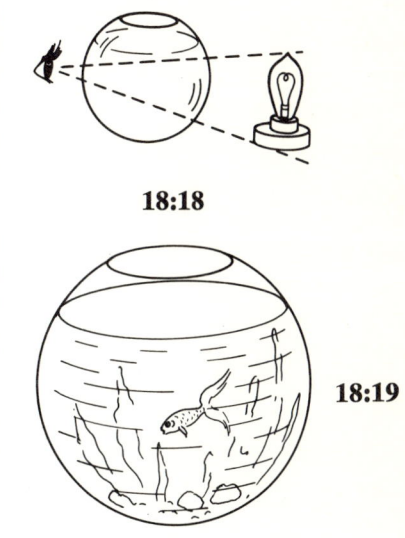

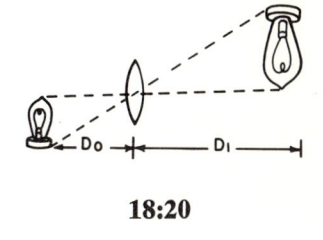

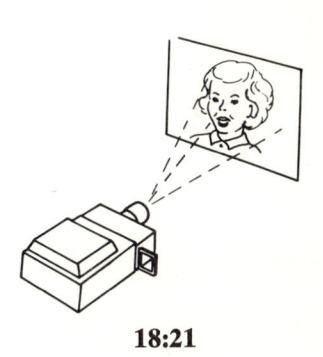

18:21

Daddy long legs

to the fact that the closer the image is to the projector, the smaller the size of the image. You "shrink" the image by decreasing the image distance, according to the formula in the previous demonstration.

I pass some concave lenses around the class, and ask students to look at print in their books, and then at their feet. They are amazed to find that the lens makes things look so small, and therefore so far away.

Stereoscopic vision

Here is a demonstration to help students acquire an appreciation of binocular vision in depth and distance perception.
Ask for a volunteer to step forward. He is to stand facing the class and stretch out his arms in T formation. Now, keeping his left eye closed, he is to rapidly bring the tips of his index fingers together. Why the results?

18:22

Hot dog for everyone

Everyone can try this. Hold your index fingers together at arm's length in front of your face. Make your eyes look past your fingers, and focus on the distant sky or on the opposite wall. You will see a tiny "hot dog" stuck between your fingertips.

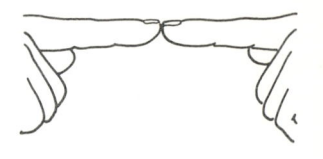

18:23

Floating sausage

Do the same experiment as before, only this time, while keeping your eyes focused on the sky or distant wall, slowly pull your index fingers apart. A tiny "sausage" will appear to float in the space between the tips of your fingers.

Blind spot

Tell students to draw an X and a circle about 3 or 4 inches apart on a piece of paper. Hold the paper about 16 inches away. Close the left eye and look with the right eye at the X. Naturally, you will also see the circle.

INCREASING OUR KNOWLEDGE OF LIGHT

18:24

Now, slowly bring the paper closer. At a certain distance the circle vanishes. If the paper is brought still closer, it will reappear.

The circle disappears when its image falls on the blind spot of the eye, a region where all the nerves on the retina come together and continue on to the brain through the large bundle called the optic nerve.

Hole in your hand?

Get a long mailing tube, such as calendars come in. Hold the tube in front of your face so that you can look through it with both eyes. Place your left hand, palm up, against the side of the tube and at a distance of about 20 inches from your face.

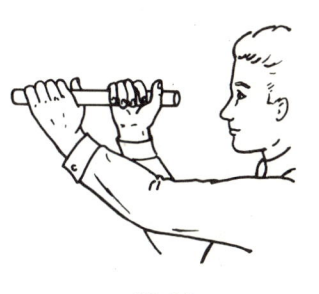

Now look through the tube at some distant object. Behold! You will find you are looking through a hole in your left hand!

I tell the students how to work this demonstration during class, then let them work the demonstration for themselves with the tube after class.

18:25

Jumping thumb

Tell students to hold their right arm out in front of their face and stick up their thumb. Now close the left eye and line their right thumb up with a distant pole, tree, doorjamb, etc. Rapidly close the right eye and open the left eye. The thumb appears to "jump" back and forth.

Which makes the best microscope?

I place a number of convex lenses on the table. The biggest is 6 inches in diameter. The smallest only ½ inch. I ask the students to tell me which lens will make the best microscope. Let students look through the lenses to determine the answer for themselves.

Marbles = microscopes?

A clear glass marble makes an excellent simple microscope. Ask students to bring various-size marbles of clear glass to class. Examine this print. Note that the greater the radius of curvature of the marble, the greater is the magnifying power. Students are quite fascinated in doing these experiments for themselves.

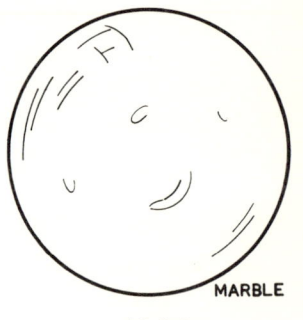

18:26

Color parade

If your classroom faces the sun, by all means try to get a big glass prism to throw the spectrum on the wall or ceiling. This breaking up a beam of sunlight by means of a prism into its colors is a truly beautiful demonstration.

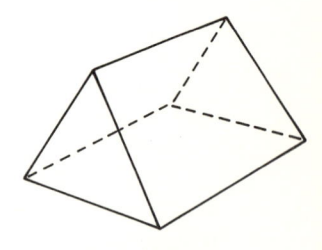

18:27

Funny paper

The color an object reflects to our eye depends in part upon the color of the light that falls upon it. Thus, an apple looks red because it reflects red light.

But suppose there is no red light to reflect?

To show students what happens, I put a red apple on the table, close the shutters, turn off the overhead lights, then shine a green light on the apple, and then a blue light. The results are dramatic.

Next I post the Sunday comic page to the blackboard and look at them under various colored lights. Students are amazed to see the "colors" of the comic strip as they never saw them before.

45 r.p.m.

If you have any old 45 r.p.m. Red Seal records put out by RCA Victor, they make wonderful color filters. Hold the record close to your eyes, so that you are looking through the clear portion of the record next to the label.

Use a red, blue, and green "filter" to examine the grass, sweaters of students, makeup, etc. The results will amaze you. Look at a red sweater, for example, or red lipstick through a red filter.

I hold a Red Seal record over some of the colors on a paint chart and ask the students to guess the true color of the samples.

Blue and green = black?

You may use either pieces of colored glass or the above-mentioned records for this experiment. Hold a blue glass on top of a green glass. Everything is black! The blue transmits blue only, not green which is blocked. The green transmits green only, not blue which is blocked. The result, you "subtract" colors and wind up with a "blackout"! Try various colors and watch the results.

White from colored lights

Darken the classroom, then put a large piece of white paper on the table between a yellow and blue lamp. Note that the paper near the yellow lamp is yellow. The portion of the paper near the blue lamp is blue. The middle part of the paper is nearly white. Have students check Newton's color wheel to see whether or not the results tally.

18:28

Christmas tree

Remind students to make this demonstration next December when the Christmas tree lights are turned on. (No other lights should be on in the room for this demonstration.) Hold a white card near a red bulb. It will appear red. Now hold the card some distance from the tree so that the combined light from all the colored bulbs fall upon it.

Prisms in the sky

Remind students to be on the lookout for the grandest prism demonstration in the world. After rain-

18:29

storms, nature supplies her own prisms in the shape of tiny drops of water, each of which acts like a prism dispersing sunlight into all the flaming glory of the rainbow.

Color tops

Dime stores and toy shops frequently stock huge, multicolored tops. When they spin, the colors change with the speed of rotation. Be sure to demonstrate one of these unusual tops.

Do you "see heat waves"?

On cold winter days, when the radiator is turned on, students may remark that they see heat waves rising from the top of the radiator. Indicate that they don't see the heat itself, but the result of a beam of light passing through moving air of varied density. This bends or refracts the light.

If you are lucky, the shadow of one of these moving air columns interacting with the light beam will cast a shadow on the opposite wall. The effect is truly captivating.

Twinkle, twinkle little star

Be sure to mention one of the most dramatic examples of refraction—the twinkling of the stars. In passing through the atmosphere, the beam of starlight is bent back and forth by layers of air of different densities—and thus the "twinkling" effect.

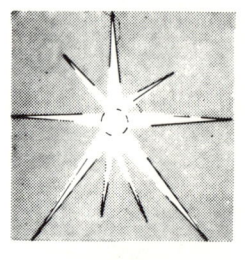

Circle around the moon

And remind students that the circle around the moon is still another example of refraction. Moonlight coming through the upper atmosphere is bent by tiny ice crystals which sometimes form high in the sky.

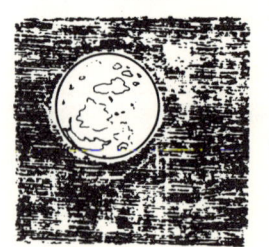

Polarized light

All you need for this demonstration are two pair of polarizing sunglasses. Place one lens on top of the other and rotate it. As you rotate the second lens, note how you cut off the intensity of light until, at last, no light comes through.

Cellophane magic

With the above-mentioned Polariod sunglasses, plus some cellophane, you can "make colors." Cover one lens with several layers of crumpled cellophane. Hold this cellophane-covered lens up to the light. Now place the lens of the second pair on top of the cellophane-covered lens and rotate it. Students are always amazed at the pastels that continually change as you turn the second lens.

Scotch magic

Stick two lengths of Scotch tape at right angles to each other across the lens of one pair of Polaroid sunglasses. Hold the taped lens up to the light, and place a second lens on top of it. Rotate the second lens and notice the colorful results. Apply more Scotch tape at various angles and look again.

Floating rainbows

In the dime store you can buy soap bubble liquid and a wire "dipper" that will enable you to fill the air with delicate pastel colors—all a result of interference.

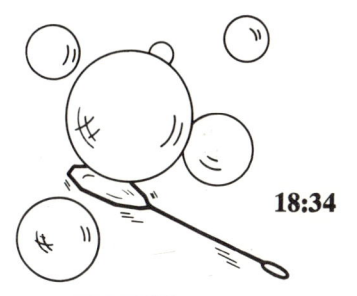

18:34

Conclusion

How strange the world of light in which we live. We do not see light itself directly. We see things that give off light (the sun, a lamp) or things that reflect light (an apple, a rose).

And we say that ordinary light is white because it shows no color. This "colorless" or "white" sunbeam hits a rose. The rose absorbs the blue and green light. The red light it cannot absorb, and so it "bounces" this light back into our eyes; therefore, we call the rose red, when actually it is not red at all. Red is the one color the rose "rejects" and "throws away" and this is the light that "bounces" into our eye. The blue and green light was absorbed. Should we call a "red" rose a "blue-green" rose?

FOLLOW-UP EXERCISES

1. Hub caps on some cars have curved surfaces that make beautiful convex or concave mirrors. Perhaps a local car dealer will give you some hub caps so that you can show students the various images.
2. Some gardens have an an ornament, a large, highly polished, silver-looking sphere. Next time you pass one, take a look at a wonderful convex mirror and note the view.
3. How is a young student pilot instructed in the art of "Blind Flying"? In cooperation with the Bureau of Aeronautics of the U.S. Navy engineers, the Polaroid Corporation developed a red plastic for aviator's goggles for blind flying. The student pilot wears these blind-flying red lenses in goggles that fit snugly over his eyes.
The cockpit windows are made of green plastic, transmitting only green light. The student can thus see only the instrument panel, and the inside of the cockpit.
The instructor wears no goggles. He can see not only everything inside the plane, but also the clouds and the scenery outside. In this way the instructor can spot other aircraft, check the plane's course against landmarks, estimate the altitude of the plane, and at the same time study the student pilot's reactions and technique. Should there be any danger of mishandling, the instructor can take over instantly.
4. The first historic photos taken of man on the moon show a "black" sky. Light coming from the sun illuminates the surface of the moon, but above the surface there is no atmosphere to break up and scatter the sunlight. With nothing to reflect the light, the area above the surface of the moon appears black, even though it is "drenched" with sunlight.
5. Next time you are on the playground, take a rubber ball and bounce it. If you throw it straight down, it bounces straight back. Throw it at an angle, it bounces away at the same angle, and thereby gives a good example of how a light beam "bounces."
6. From a junkyard you may obtain some old automobile headlights. They are gleaming concave mirrors, whose job is to reflect light from the filament to the highway.
7. Next time you are in a supermarket or drugstore you may find yourself being "watched" by a convex mirror!
8. Newspaper clippings often bring home lessons learned in class. Here is one from Lewiston, Maine: "Two buildings were set on fire within two weeks here when the sun's rays shone through two different jugs of water igniting the sides of the structures."

INCREASING OUR KNOWLEDGE OF LIGHT 271

9. On a dark, cloudless night when there is no moon, shine a flashlight directly up into the sky. If the air is clear and free of dust, you will not be able to trace the outline of the beam of light. Try the experiment again when there is a dense fog. What are the results and how do you explain the results?

10. Look at your image in a shiny tablespoon. If you hold it vertically, you will look tall as a bean pole on the convex side. Turn the spoon to a horizontal position and describe your image. How does the shape of the image on the concave side differ from that on the convex side?

11. Do you ever see things that aren't so? Yes, every morning you watch the sun "rise" over the horizon. You think you see the sun "rising" when actually it is still below the horizon!

The earth's atmosphere bends the sun's rays and thus provides an optical illusion. You think the sun is where it isn't!

And for the same reason, you see the sun for some eight minutes after it sinks below the western horizon!

Mirages seen by a thirst-maddened desert nomad are caused by refraction. But you don't have to ride a camel across the sands of the Sahara to see a mirage.

The next time you are cruising down a highway, you may see "wet" spots or "pools of water" that mysteriously disappear when you approach closer.

This optical illusion is caused by the fact that the air in contact with the highway is heated, and therefore becomes less dense than the air above it. Rays of light coming from the sky are refracted or "bent" and you see "pools" that may be called "patches of sky fallen down from on high."

Or, to be less poetic, they are simply beams of light from the sky that have been bent.

One of the most amazing mirages took place during the last year of World War II. An American sub was on routine daytime patrol in the South Pacific. Intelligence had reported that there were no Japanese ships closer than Formosa Strait several hundred miles to the north, and so the crew was given the day to relax.

The men were on the deck of the sub, enjoying the sunlight and acquiring a tan. Suddenly a sailor jumped up, excitement almost choking him. "Look," he exclaimed. "The Jap fleet is coming at us!"

The officers stared in amazement as the convoy steamed into view. Quickly all hands were ordered below. The sub submerged, and moved in toward the target. For two hours the sub tried to gain on the convoy. At last, in mad desperation, the captain gave the command to surface.

The phantom convoy had vanished into thin air!

That night Intelligence reported that there had been a convoy: "It was our convoy, but you couldn't have seen it. It was 100 miles away from your sector."

The officers and crew had been victims of nature's light bending. Beams of light, bouncing off ships far over the horizon, had been bent so that a "picture" or "image" of the fleet was projected on the surface of the water in line of vision with the sub.

One of the most expensive mirages in history cost the American Museum of Natural History $300,000.

In 1818 Sir John Ross reported a new range of mountains to the north of Baffin Land, but unfortunately he could not penetrate the vast stretches of ice to explore them.

Almost a century later, in 1906, Admiral Robert Peary spotted a similar range of lofty peaks and called them Crocker Land. In 1914 Commander Donald B. MacMillan headed an expedition, outfitted at great cost by the Museum of Natural History to map Crocker Land.

The task proved as futile as trying to catch up with your shadow. The farther they traveled, the farther the mountains retreated before them. At last, after long days of useless chase, the defeated expedition turned back, consoled however, by the cold fact that their observations proved conclusively that Crocker Land did not exist. Light beams, reflected off some distant, faraway, unknown mountains, were being bent by the atmosphere so that the massive mountains appeared to be sitting on the horizon. Another case of "seeing things that aren't so."

You don't have to go to Crocker Land to see mountains that really aren't there. Simply turn to page 533 of the *National Geographic* for October 1959 and see one of the most unusual and fascinating mirages.

The beautiful, lofty, inspiring mountains photographed on the horizon are a mirage. "Cold, dense pockets of atmosphere in Antarctica bend light rays like a prism," says *National Geographic,* "or reflect them like a mirror. Observers have reported seeing mountains upside down in the sky. Whether in desert or across water or ice, visual hoaxes may waver and beckon wherever sharp temperature variations lie near the surface."

Refraction may explain some of the so-called flying saucers. If the thing you see is not actually a weather balloon or shooting star, it may be a beam of light reflected from some distant airplane or refracted from some object over the horizon. Approximately 4000 balloons are released in the United States each day; some are weather balloons, others are used for upper air research. Ranging from 4 to 200 feet in diameter, they usually carry running lights at night, and travel in jet streams at 200 miles per hour. Their appearance can be deceiving even to experienced pilots.

Aircraft observed at high altitude, when the sun is reflected on their wings, often appear to be disk-shaped or rocket-shaped vehicles. Vapor trails often reflect sunlight and sometimes are circular in shape. Planets observed through fog or haze often seem to move at high speed on erratic courses. Venus is credited with initiating many saucer sightings, sometimes appearing to be fast moving with an intense blue light, again, as low-flying aircraft with sweptback wings. According to Dr. Donald H. Menzel, noted astronomer, "Some of the things reported as flying saucers have been reflections from all kinds of balloons and airplanes. As a plane changes course, it may suddenly reflect sunlight brightly. When it dims a moment later, a person may think that a saucer has come in close and disappeared."

Dr. William Markowitz, nationally known physicist, says the reported motions of UFO's break the laws of Physics.

Just *why* and *how* do UFO's break laws of science?

No doubt you have read accounts in the newspapers of people who claim that flying saucers travel at "unheard of" speeds, many times faster than a Boeing 707 or Douglas DC-8.

Most amazing of all, these flying saucers can make a *right-angle turn, stop, and go backwards instantly!*

If these accounts are true, we will have to throw away our Physics books, and start all over again to find out just what the laws of nature are.

You can demonstrate Newton's First Law of Motion for yourself. Run through an open doorway as fast as you can or dash down the sidewalk or driveway. Then, without slackening your speed, make a sudden right-hand turn.

You will find you can't make such a right-hand turn. Newton's First Law of Motion informs us that "a body in motion tends to stay in motion in a straight line."

When a Boeing 707 lands at an airport, the plane doesn't come to a sudden stop as soon as the wheels touch down. Nor does the pilot attempt a sudden right-hand turn immediately upon landing. He knows that Newton's First Law will keep the plane moving forward in a straight line.

If an automobile is speeding at 80 miles an hour along a mountain road, it won't be able to make a sharp turn. Newton's First Law of Motion will carry it forward and out over the edge of a cliff, into the wide, blue yonder—to decorate the tree tops a thousand feet below, when it falls.

Likewise, the bigger and more massive a thing is, the more time it takes to get moving, or, as Newton's Second Law of Motion says,

"The force and time required to get an object moving depend on its mass."

A freight train can't leap from a standstill position to 60 miles per hour. A Saturn rocket blasting off from Cape Kennedy doesn't leap up at 25,000 m.p.h. As you know from watching TV, it "lifts" off the pad, quite slowly at first, and gradually picks up speed.

A Boeing 707 can't jump up into the sky like a jackrabbit. It has to taxi down a long runway to pick up enough speed to lift off the ground.

By now you may realize why Dr. Markowitz says that certain laws of Physics limit what can be done by a flying machine.

Dr. Edward U. Condon recently wrote to Prof. Gerald Holton calling his attention to the classroom use of popular writings on UFO's. Dr. Condon's strong comments on the subject are contained in the new book *Scientific Study of Unidentified Flying Objects* (Bantam Extra, $1.95) and are quoted here:

"The subject of UFO's has been widely misrepresented to the public by a small number of individuals who have given sensationalized presentations in writings and public lectures. So far as we can judge, not many people have been misled by such irresponsible behavior, but whatever effect there has been has been bad.

"A related problem to which we wish to direct public attention is the miseducation in our schools which arises from the fact that many children are being allowed, if not actively encouraged, to devote their science study time to the reading of UFO books and magazine articles of the type referred to in the preceding paragraph. We feel that children are educationally harmed by absorbing unsound and erroneous material as if it were scientifically well founded. Such study is harmful not merely because of the erroneous nature of the material itself, but also because such study retards the development of a critical faculty with regard to scientific evidence, which to some degree ought to be part of the education of every American.

"Therefore we strongly recommend that teachers refrain from giving students credit for schoolwork based on their reading of the presently available UFO books and magazine articles. Teachers who find their students strongly motivated in this direction should attempt to channel their interests in the direction of serious study of astronomy and meteorology, and in the direction of critical analysis of arguments for fantastic propositions that are being supported by appeals to fallacious reasoning or false data."

My hat is off to Dr. Condon for "putting it on the line."

And may I suggest that if a student asks for a book on UFO's, you advise him to read Dr. Condon's report, the *Scientific Study of Unidentified Flying Objects*.

It is interesting to note that the "Soaring Sixties" or the "Decade of Man in Space"—as the Sixties were called—climaxed their final year with two fascinating "Science Specials."

On Sunday, July 20, 1969, man first set foot upon the moon. Then, in the last month of 1969, the Air Force concluded its study of Unidentified Flying Objects.

During the past 22 years, the U.S. Air Force has carefully logged every unidentified flying object that has been reported in the American skies.

During that time, Project Blue Book, as the operation was called, looked into a total of 12,618 UFO sightings. "Yet lately," says *Time* magazine for December 26, 1969, "the flying-saucer business has fallen on hard times. Only 146 UFO sightings have been reported to the Air Force so far this year vs. a peak of 1501 in 1952.

"The decline is due partly to the Condon report, which last January decisively debunked flying saucers, and urged the Air Force to call off all UFO investigations."

As a result, the Air Force wrote the final chapter to Project Blue Book. "The continuation of the study," said Air Force Secretary Dr. Robert C. Seamans Jr., "no longer can be justified either on the ground of national security or in the interest of science."

The final sentence of the *Time* article is most interesting, "In a year man has assured himself that there are no moon men or Martians, UFOs seem more than ever to be a product of terrestrial imaginations."

Summary

Light is truly a "dark subject" as is proven when you look up and see the golden moon high in the sky. Light from the sun is cascading through space on all sides of the moon, but the moon is the only thing you see, for it is the only thing "hanging" in the sky that "bounces" or reflects the light from the sun back to us. And when there is no moon, the sky is dark.

Likewise, the first photos of the American astronauts on the moon show its "sky" as black, for there is no air to scatter and reflect the light.

Although we are not quite sure just what light is, we can "bounce" it, "bend" it, and "disperse" it into rainbow colors.

Light is truly our "invisible servant" bringing us the faces of those we love and the pictures of footprints on the moon.

INDEX

A

Acceleration due to gravity:
  arc, 135
  conclusion, 140
  demonstrations, 134-135
  final velocity, 138
  follow-up exercises, 140-143
  introductory discussion, 134
  invisible brakes, 139
  length of pendulum, 136
  "negative" acceleration, 140
  period of the pendulum, 135
  "positive" acceleration, 139
  "pulsebeat" of earth, 134
  reaction time, 138
  summary, 143
  weight of bob, 135-136
Adhesion, 121
Air:
  beginning first class, 57-59
    atmosphere pushes in, 59
    earth from the moon, 59
    inside body, 59
    meteorite, 58
    meteors, 57, 58
    micrometeors, 58
    moon, 57-59
      (*see also* Moon)

Air (*cont.*)
    space suit, 58
    we breathe, 59
  conclusion, 67
  demonstrations, 60-66
    balloon you can't blow up, 64
    basketball pump, 63
    basting tube and Boyle's Law, 61
    compressed air and water fountain, 63
    do you really inhale?, 62
    do you smoke?, 65
    float cork under water, 60-61
    honk your horn, 66
    paper submerged in water, 60
    popgun and cork, 62
    resists being squeezed, 60
    rubber pistol and ball, 62
    snow in classroom, 66
    soda pop, 64-65
    squeeze-me tube, 65-66
    what balloon says, 64
  follow-up exercises, 67-68
  gravity "holds on to it," 57
  masses, 85-86
  "resists" being "dented," 57
  summary, 68
  thermometer, 167
  weight, 69-83
    (*see also* Weight, air)

Aluminum, conductivity, 172
Ampere, 229
Archimedes' Principle, 97

B

Bends, avoiding, 99-100
Bernoulli's Principle:
  conclusion, 149
  demonstrations, 146-149
    airplane "lift," 146
    apples together, 146
    atomizer, 148
    balloon in air, 146
    Bernoulli on your chin, 148
    floating ping-pong ball, 147
    flying puffed rice, 148
    friendly papers, 149
    hugging cardboard, 147
    ping-pong ball in funnel, 148-149
    spool and cardboard, 147-148
  follow-up exercises, 149-150
  stated, 145
  summary, 150
Boyle's Law, 98
Brain waves, 222, 225-226
Brass, expansion, 179
Brownian movement, 129
Buoyancy, 97

C

Capillary action, 126
Centripetal force, 32-33
Chemical energy, 152
Cohesion, 120, 121
Color, 266-269
Conduction, 175
Conductivity, 170-172, 175
  (see also Heat)
Continental air mass, 85, 86
Convection, 172-175
Copper, conductivity, 171, 172

D

Density of matter, 116, 117
Dew point, 88
"Dry liquid," 121

E

Elasticity, 129
"Electric hands," 224-225

Electricity from chemical changes:
  conclusion, 226
  demonstrations, 219-226
    brain waves, 222, 225-226
    Coke, 220
    electric hands, 224-225
    "electrical tongue," 220
    heart waves, 221-222
    inside a dry cell, 221
    "new life" from old cell, 221
    orange, 219-220
    pacemaker, 222-224
    wet cell from dry cell, 220-221
    wet cell in your head, 220
    zinc penny, 219
  follow-up exercises, 226-227
  summary, 227
Electricity, static:
  conclusion, 215
  demonstrations, 207-215
    lightning, 212-214
    making electroscope, 207-211
    radio waves, 211-213
    safety during storm, 214-215
  follow-up exercises, 215-216
  summary, 216
Electrocardiogram, 221-222
Electroencephalogram, 222
Electromagnetic forces:
  ampere, 229
  conclusion, 252
  current of electricity, 229
  demonstrations, 229-251
    A.C. and D.C., 232-233, 237
    A.C. on swing, 247-248
    aluminum repelled by magnetic field, 233
    "broadcast station" and "receiving station," 246
    coaxial cable, 249
    cook with magnet, 233-234
    diathermy machine, 235-236
    doorbell, 231-232, 251
    electric motor, 243
    electromagnet, make, 229-230
    electronic ovens, 234-235
    galvanometer, make, 237-238, 248
    galvanometer reverses directions, 249-250
    generator pinciples, 240-242
    hot-plate, 250-251
    invisible fingers, 229

INDEX

Electromagnetic forces (*cont.*)
    iron whiskers, 247
    make electricity, 238-240
    Ohm's Law, 250
    plot current on curve, 242
    poor radio reception, 248-249
    red-hot copper wire, 250
    slip rings and commutators, 243
    telegraph, homemade, 230-231
    telephone pole with petticoats, 251
    temporary or permanent magnet, 231
    throttle the doorbell, 251
    vibrating filament, 236-237
  electrons, 229
  follow-up exercises, 252
  summary, 252-253
Electrons, 229
Electroscopes, making, 207-211
Energy:
  conclusion, 156-157
  defined, 152
  demonstrations, 152-156
    bow and arrow, 153
    coal is "buried sunshine," 155-156
    foot-pound, 152-153
    gram-centimeter, 154
    gun, 153
    hammer with potential energy, 153
    horsepower, 156
    hourglass, 154
    matchstick magic, 155
    mixing bowl and marble, 154
    mousetrap, 155
    pendulum, 154
    radiometer, 154-155
    solar powered wristwatch, 155
    yo-yo, 154
  follow-up exercises, 157-159
  kinetic, 152
    doing work, 152
    energy of motion, 152
  potential, 152
    ability to do work, 152
    chemical, 152
    magnetic, 152
    mechanical, 152
    when it becomes kinetic, 152
  summary, 159-160
  work, 152
Equilibrium:
  neutral, 21
  stable, 20-21
  unstable, 19-20

F

Friction:
  amount, 188
  coefficient, 190
  conclusion, 191
  defined, 188
  demonstrations, 188-191
  follow-up exercises, 191-192
  "rolling," 191
  "sliding," 191
  summary, 193

G

Gas expands, 164-166
Glass, conductivity, 174-175
Gravity:
  acceleration of objects, 133-143
    (*see also* Acceleration due to gravity)
  beginning first class, 16-19
  cannot increase, diminish or bend, 16
  center of gravity, definition, 17
  conclusion, 25
  demonstrations, 19-25
    bending over, 22
    broom, 24
    hammer, 24-25
    leaning towers, 21-22
    marble in balloon, 23
    neutral equilibrium, 21
    pencil, 24
    rockabye, 23
    rolling uphill, 23
    roly-poly, 23-24
    sand in vase, 23
    sharp pencil, 25
    stable equilibrium, 20-21
    stable students, 22
    tipping flask, 24
    unstable equilibrium, 19-20
  establishing importance, 14-28
  follow-up exercises, 25-28
  introduce students, 14
  mass, definition, 17
  Newton's Law of Universal Gravitation, 17, 18, 19
  pervades and permeates everything, 16
  summary, 28
  universal and unique, 16
  weight, definition, 18

INDEX

H

Heart waves, 221-222
  air thermometer, 167
  body as temperature gauge, 166
  brass expands, 179
  burn steel, 167-168
  CO_2 puts out fire, 169
  conclusion, 184-185
  conduction, 175
  conductivity, 170-172, 175
    aluminum, 172
    cooking, 172
    copper, 171, 172
    glass, 174-175
    iron, 172
    silver, 171-172
    wood, 170, 172
  convection, 172-175
  converting into work, 167
  demonstrations, 162-184
  different from temperature, 169-170
  doesn't expand molecules, 162
  drives out air in water, 182-183
  ether or rubbing alcohol, 183-184
  expands gas, 164-166
  flash bulb, 168
  follow-up exercises, 185
  light bulb, 168-169
  liquid expands, 179-180
  metal combining with oxygen, 169
  metal expands, 180, 184
  oxidation, 168, 169
  produced by kinetic energy, 163-164
  radiation, 175-178
  regelation, 180-181
  speeds molecules, 162-164
  sublimation, 181-182
  summary, 186
  thermal currents, 179
Hooke's Law, 130
Humidity, *absolute* and *relative,* 87

I

Incidence, angle, 255
Inertia, 43, 47
Iron, conductivity, 172

K

Kaleidoscope, 256-257
Kinetic energy, 152

L

Light:
  conclusion, 269
  demonstrations, 255-269
    bent light, 258-259
    binocular vision, 264-265
    colors, 266-269
    concave lens, 260, 264
    concave mirror, 257-258
    convex lens, 260, 261-262, 263, 265-266
    heat waves, 268
    marbles = microscopes?, 266
    periscope, 255
    plane mirror reverses image, 256-258
    polarized light, 268-269
    reflection and incidence, angles, 255-256
    refraction, 268
    regular or diffuse reflection, 260
    water mirror, 259
  follow-up exercises, 270-275
  summary, 275
Lightning, 212-215
Liquid expands, 179-180

M

Magnetic energy, 152
Magnetic force:
  conclusion, 203
  demonstrations, 195-203
    "dancing nails," 197
    floating magnet, 203
    heat, 202
    holding power, 197-198
    induction, magnetize by, 200
    invisible lines of force, 195
    invisible mover, 195
    keeper, 199
    like poles repel, 196, 202
    magnetic and nonmagnetic materials, 203
    magnetic field, 196, 202
    magnetic metals, 197
    magnetic radiator, 201-202
    magnetite (magnetic iron ore), 195
    paper clip "bridge," 195
    pendulum stopped by magnet, 198-199
    poles, 195
    principle of electric motor, 202
    test tube magnet, 199-200
    through hand, 197

INDEX
283

Magnetic force (*cont.*)
  unlike poles attract, 196
  weaken magnet, 200, 201
 follow-up exercises, 203-205
 summary, 205
Maritime air mass, 85, 86
Mass, definition, 17
Matter:
 adhesion, 121
 Brownian movement, 129
 capillary action, 126
 cohesion, 120, 121
 conclusion, 131
 definition, 116
 demonstrations, 117-130
 density, definition, 116, 117
 "dry liquid," 121
 elasticity, 129
 follow-up exercises, 131-132
 Hooke's Law, 130
 specific gravity, 118-119
 summary, 132
 surface tension, 122
 tensile strength, 129
Mechanical energy, 152
Metal expands, 180, 184
Meteorite, 58
Meteors, 57, 58
Micrometeors, 58
Moon:
 can't hold air, 59
 inhospitable, 57
 jet-black sky, 58
 lacks gravity, 59
 looking at earth, 59
 meteorite, 58
 meteors, 57, 58
 micrometeors, 58
 never twilight or half-light, 58
 no atmosphere, 57
 no dust or haze, 58
 no "shock absorber" for sunlight, 58
 no sound, 58
 space suit, 58, 59

N

"Negative" acceleration, 140
Newton:
 First Law of Motion, 31, 43
 Second Law of Motion, 43, 44
 Third Law of Motion, 44-46
 Universal Gravitation, Law, 17, 28
Neutral equilibrium, 21

O

Oceanography:
 beginning first class, 96-100
  Archimedes' Principle, 97
  avoiding the bends, 99-100
  body and body fluids, 99
  Boyle's Law, 98
  buoyancy, 97
  diver, 99
  explorers of ocean depths, 98
  gases under pressure, 98, 99
  nitrogen, 99
  pressure is enemy, 98
  pressure on confined liquid, 97
  respiration, 99
  water pressure and depth, 97, 98
 conclusion, 111-112
 demonstrations, 100-111
  apparent loss of weight, 107-108
  Archimedes, 106
  balloon and tire, 111
  buoyancy of balloon, 109-110
  buoyancy of styrofoam, 104-105
  Cartesian diver, 108-109
  cubic foot, 100
  dancing mothballs, 110
  finding volume, 102-103
  hypodermic needle, 111
  judging weight by sinking, 107
  mercury again, 104
  mercury versus water, 101
  metric system, 103-104
  milk carton illustrates pressure, 107
  pipe, 100-101
  pistol for Pascal, 110-111
  push a cubic foot, 103
  sink that boat, 109
  squeeze bottle, 111
  vanishing weight, 102
  volume finder, 106
  water pushes, 101-102
  weigh your hand, 105
  will it weigh more?, 105
 follow-up exercises, 112-113
 summary, 113-114
Ohm's Law, 250
Orbit, how to go into:
 conclusion, 40
 demonstrations, 36-40
  bike wheel gyro, 38-39
  block in jar, 38
  coffee can clothes dryer, 39
  eggbeater, 36

Orbit, how to go into (*cont.*)
    lasso, 39
    mailing tube on bike wheel, 40
    marble in balloon, 37
    marble in glass bowl, 37
    ping-pong slingshot, 36
    pipe and bolt, 37
    rolling marbles, 36
    squashed world, 39-40
    turntable, 36-37
    yo-yo, 37-38
  first class, 30-36
    air resistance, 33
    "center-seeking" force, 33
    centripetal force, 32-33
    earth curves, 34
    earth "falls" towards sun, 35
    equator, 32
    "falling" over horizon, 35
    first second of free fall, 33
    5 miles per second, 35
    horizontal distance, 34
    less or more than 5 miles per second, 35
    "Magic Speed," 35
    Mississippi River, 32
    moon "falls" towards earth, 35
    Newton's First Law of Motion, 31
    orbital velocity, 35
    parabola, 33
    path of bullet, 33
    pitcher's mound, 34
    spinning sphere, 32
    sun, 35-36
  follow-up exercises, 40-41
  physics behind "Space Odyssey," 30
  physics controls daily lives, 30
  summary, 41
Oxidation, 168, 169

P

Pacemaker, 222-224
Pendulum, length, 136
Periscope, 255
"Positive" acceleration, 139
Potential energy, definition, 152
  (*see also* Energy)
"Pulsebeat" of earth, 134

R

Radiation, 175-178
Radio waves, 211-213
Reaction time, 138
Reflection:
  angle, 255
  regular or *diffuse*, 260
Regelation, 180-181
Respiration under water, 99

S

Silver, conductivity, 171-172
Space, travel in:
  beginning first class, 43-46
    action and reaction, 44
    inertia, 43
    jet engine or rocket, 45
    landing jets, 45-46
    Newton's Laws of Motion, 43-46
    recoil principle, 45
    two forces and *two objects*, 44
  conclusion, 52
  demonstrations, 46-52
    basketball versus marble, 48
    car on plank, 47
    catcher's mitt, 48
    cigar box, 47
    clothespins and rubber band, 51-52
    dime-store jet engine, 48
    foam-rubber cushion, 48
    "giveaway" floor, 49
    half-dollar and glass, 46-47
    jet-propelled tin can, 49-50
    jet soda bottle, 50
    leaping basketball, 47
    no-go nail, 50-51
    overcoming inertia, 47
    piano stool and pillow, 52
    plank on pipes, 48
    reaction engine, 49
    rocket on water, 51
    spring scales, 49
    string to block, 46
    toy water wheel, 48-49
    transfer of momentum, 49
    walk-around record player, 49
  follow-up exercises, 52-55
  summary, 55
Specific gravity, 118-119
Stable equilibrium, 20-21
Steel, burn, 167-168
Storm, safety during, 214-215
Sublimation, 181-182
Surface tension, 122

INDEX

T

Tensile strength, 129
Thermal currents, 179
Travel in space, 42-55
   (*see also* Space, travel in)

U

Universal Gravitation, 17, 18, 19, 28
Unstable equilibrium, 19-20

V

Velocity, final, 138

W

Weather:
  beginning your first class, 85-88
    absolute humidity, 87
    air masses, 85-86
    dew point, 88
    relative humidity, 87-88
    saturated air, 87
    ways Nature makes weather, 85
  conclusion, 90-91
  demonstrations, 88-90
    baby-size thermal, 90
    foggy mirror, 89
    ping-pong "rain," 89
    polar breeze, 89-90
    rain in classroom, 88
    "sweaty" glass, 88
  follow-up exercises, 91-94
  summary, 94

Weight, air:
  beginning first class, 70-72
    astronomical observatories, 71
    curvature of earth, 71
    pictures of earth, 70
    thin air, 71
    troposphere, 71
  conclusion, 81
  demonstrations, 72-81
    air pushes, 73-74
    ballerina, 79
    balloon on milk bottle, 72-73
    barometer becomes altimeter, 80
    force on head, 77
    hachet man, 77-78
    holes that don't leak, 75
    hypodermic syringe, 81
    ice pick, 78-79
    measure lung power, 77
    mercury barometer, 76
    pin head, 79
    pop you can't drink, 75-76
    safety razor blade, 78
    snap board, 75
    soda through straw, 80-81
    squashed container, 72
    suction cup, 74
    two suction cups, 74
    upside-down glass, 72
    water in upside-down bottle, 73
  follow-up exercises, 81-83
  summary, 83